ASSET
ROTATION

ASSET ROTATION

The Demise of Modern Portfolio Theory and the Birth of an Investment Renaissance

MATTHEW P. ERICKSON

WILEY

Cover image: © Linda Huber
Cover design: Wiley

Published by John Wiley & Sons, Inc., Hoboken, New Jersey.
Published simultaneously in Canada.

For general information on our other products and services or for technical support, please contact our Customer Care Department within the United States at (800) 762-2974, outside the United States at (317) 572-3993 or fax (317) 572-4002.

Wiley publishes in a variety of print and electronic formats and by print-on-demand. Some material included with standard print versions of this book may not be included in e-books or in print-on-demand. If this book refers to media such as a CD or DVD that is not included in the version you purchased, you may download this material at http://booksupport.wiley.com. For more information about Wiley products, visit www.wiley.com.

Library of Congress Cataloging-in-Publication Data:

ISBN 9781118779194 (Hardcover)
ISBN 9781118779040 (ePDF)
ISBN 9781118779040 (ePub)

Printed in the United States of America
10 9 8 7 6 5 4 3 2 1

*This book is dedicated to anyone who ever saw the world
in a different vein. Who rather than simply follow the path laid
out before them, chose to first look at where that path would lead.
Whose suspicions led them to believe there was a better way,
and who possessed the courage and passion to
pursue their convictions.*

CONTENTS

ACKNOWLEDGMENTS

I'd like to thank a handful of confidants and industry peers who were instrumental sounding boards for me as I was writing this book: Chris Neudecker, Mike Wood, Robert Mitus, Phil Bocketti, Joe Molloy, Robert Roman, Ryan Shubin, Joe Bartell, David Fischer, Jason Nymark, and Brian Pelling.

I'd also like to thank my wife, Jill, for holding down the fort while I locked myself in a room, and my kids, Mackenzie and Jacob, for allowing each other to live—if only for a little while longer.

PROLOGUE

David and Goliath

For 40 days and 40 nights the Philistine champion Goliath stood before the Israelite army, mocking them. He challenged them to send forth one man to face him in a battle to the death. To the victor would go the war.

By biblical accounts, Goliath was a giant, standing just shy of seven feet tall. The mere sound of his thunderous voice made the men of Israel tremble in fear. No one dared to take up arms against him.

David was a young man in his early teens. He was a peasant, sent to the front lines to bring food and carry back news of the battle. When he arrived at camp, David heard Goliath's daily provocation and he was astounded by the Israelites' fear. Without hesitation, wearing no armor and with a sling as his only weapon, David volunteered to fight Goliath; to put an end to the war and preserve the lives of his compatriots.

David charged out to face Goliath, arming his sling with a single rock. As he approached, he hurled the stone at Goliath, striking him square in the forehead and killing him instantly. The Philistine army stood in disbelief as David decapitated the giant and held up his head for all to see. The Philistine army retreated, and the Israelites won the war. Born a peasant, David went on to become the king of Israel.

We are but one small voice, drowned out in a sea of many. In an investment world driven by large-scale institutions and corporate war chests, one might think we are ill-equipped for battle. But like David, the oft unassuming has a way of rising to the occasion.

We are witnessing a *Renaissance*. Conventions are being challenged, and a new way is being forged from the old.

PREFACE

We Stand on the Precipice
of an *Investment Renaissance*

"The Renaissance was a rebirth of man's life on earth. Freed from the shackles of authority, man's mind was viewed as able to understand the universe. Far from being a tortured soul trapped in a deformed bodily prison, man was regarded as rational, beautiful and heroic—worthy of happiness and capable of great achievement. Man, in the Renaissance view, need not bow down in passive resignation, praying for salvation. He can choose to undertake great challenges in the face of seemingly impossible odds; he can actively pursue success, fight for victory—even slay a giant.

"Michelangelo's David is the best expression of this Renaissance sense of life. The sculpture was inspired by the story of the young shepherd boy who chose to fight a far stronger adversary in order to save his people from invasion. Wearing no armor, with a sling as his only weapon, David defeats Goliath using superior skill and courage."

—Lee Sandstead (renowned art historian)

The Renaissance Period spanned from the fourteenth to the seventeenth century and is remembered by historians today as a period of scientific, cultural, and philosophical enlightenment. At the beginning of the Renaissance, it was widely believed that the world was flat and that the Earth was the center of the universe. Throughout this period, widely accepted conventions were challenged that led us to a world of new discoveries and innovations. Without the likes of William of Ockham, Christopher Columbus, Nicolaus Copernicus, Galileo Galilei, Michelangelo, Sir Isaac Newton, and countless others we might well still find ourselves in the Dark Ages.

It was these pioneers of new thought, these architects of originality who dared to think outside of the box that provided the foundation for the world we live in today. But we fear in present times we have strayed too far away from the very principles that led us to such startling revelations.

> *Education rears disciples, imitators, and routinists, not pioneers of new ideas and creative geniuses. The schools are not nurseries of progress and improvement, but conservatories of tradition and unwavering modes of thought.*
> Ludwig von Mises (famed Austrian economist)

The virtues of Modern Portfolio Theory are taught at every business school across the country and to every aspiring individual to enter the financial services industry. During this indoctrination, one is led to believe that these guiding principles provide the bedrock to any sound investment portfolio. And yet on countless occasions, we have seen and personally experienced their failures—if not by the method itself, by the means in which investors fulfill these asset allocations and behave. The financial industry is playing a game, and we fear the vast majority of investors fail to recognize their role as pawns.

Even after experiencing repeated failures and dramatic under-performance, far too often industry professionals and retail investors alike simply maintain the status quo. Yet, taking a "buy, hold, and pray" approach to investing has done little to shield investors from experiencing significant losses in recent years.

As we assess our current economic landscape, these challenges may grow exponentially greater in the very near future, as capital market assumptions (the long view of anticipated returns by asset class) encounter a new paradigm—a paradigm in which what has generally held to be true over the past 40 years, and that which we understood to be safe, is no longer safe anymore.

The reality is that the investment world as we know it is changing. Even what *has* worked in the past may not continue to work in the future. No longer may bonds be viewed as a long-term hold and safe haven asset class. This poses a serious threat to investors aiming to preserve the purchasing power of their capital. Concurrently, the equity markets may present even greater risks, as investors in the United States historically have lost 40 percent or more in their investable assets during the average recession. So where are investors supposed to place their hard-earned savings for preservation of capital and long-term growth?

It is our contention that Modern Portfolio Theory (MPT), like many investment methods, was merely an aberration in time, and not a blueprint for long-term success. When capital market assumptions change, MPT not only becomes fallible, it becomes a serious liability. For all of the financial planners and retail investors projecting retirement cash flow, future investment growth, Monte Carlo analysis, and the like, the realities of tomorrow may be strikingly dissimilar from what one might expect.

In the context of this book, we will present a time-tested approach to investing that has proven to be successful throughout the history of capital markets, in good times and bad. We will present a surprisingly rudimentary approach that may provide a core foundation for true *modern-day* portfolio management, investing in a manner where limiting losses is paramount. What we are referring to specifically is the process of *asset rotation*, and not *asset allocation*.

Rather than attempt to predict the future price of a security, or the future state of our economy (which we firmly believe to be impossible), we will focus our efforts on illustrating a simple price momentum–based approach to investing. This approach does not take into account market headlines, economic forecasts, or emotion. We believe in taking a purely systematic approach, devoid of the very intuitions that often lead investors astray. And, believe it or not, our approach requires that investors assess the state of the markets only once per month and adjust their portfolios accordingly.

In short, we believe in taking a *tactical* approach to investing. Despite what naysayers may proclaim—"it is time in the market, not timing in the market"—this can be done and with far less risk than a more traditional approach. This reminds us of a campaign we once witnessed at a large brokerage firm, trumpeting this message back in the fall 2007, right before the onset of the Great Recession. Surely, many of the investors heeding that advice are still, unfortunately, far from getting back to even. The reality is, whether the masses care to admit it or not, timing is everything.

> *The biggest mistake any investor can make is to buy the wrong thing at the wrong time. While this may seem like an obvious statement, the reality is none of us know when it is the wrong time. Far too often investment decisions are based on fear or greed, frequently selling when things are at their worst and buying when things are expensive. It only seems natural to buy what is working and sell what is not, but it is this very impactful psychological flaw that prevents investors from achieving superior returns. Investing requires discipline. By limiting losses, one can dramatically reduce the impact of buying at the wrong time. Avoiding prolonged declines provides the true engine for the long-term growth of an investment portfolio.*

The process set forth in this text has consistently demonstrated significantly lower risk (beta) than traditional methods, with significantly lower drawdowns from peak to trough, and with low correlations to both equity and bond markets. Most important, this process provides investors with consistently strong risk-adjusted returns.

Throughout the course of this book, we will take a closer look at where we are today, the challenges that lie ahead, and what we as investors can do about it. We hope to do so in a manner that is both educational and enlightening, but, most important, compelling one to step outside of what it is they think they know and to reexamine truths currently held to be self-evident.

To the attentive observer, we are witnessing an exciting time in the investment markets. The paradigm has shifted, and we are standing on the precipice of an *Investment Renaissance*.

CHAPTER 1

TAKING THE 30,000-FOOT VIEW

Where We Are Today

Before we can begin to <u>dissect</u> all of the <u>nuances</u> as to why what has worked in the past may no longer work in the future, we must first start with a "30,000-foot view," putting into perspective both the realities of the individual investor's disposition and historical performance, as well as our current economic landscape. Once we have a general understanding of the challenges at hand, we can examine these issues more intimately and ultimately provide practical solutions as to how investors can more efficiently navigate this tumultuous environment (while inherently reducing the impact of outsized risks).

[handwritten margin note: How do you cut up a nuance?]

THE INDIVIDUAL INVESTOR

It has often been said that when you are in the thick of things, you simply cannot "see the forest for the trees." Because of all of the obstacles that surround us (some real, others imagined), our vision is impaired and it is easy for even the most astute observer to become overwhelmed; so much so that they can no longer see the path which lies ahead, nor the bigger picture at hand.

If we apply this analogy to the investment markets and the daily influx of market-moving headlines, prognostications, and so on, it is easy to see how one might get lost in the myriad of directional noise. After all, CNBC, Bloomberg, and the like need to drive ratings, and there is nothing better than sensationalizing a trivial nonevent for this purpose. For that matter, we must admit we find the circus to be mildly entertaining. In one segment, you'll hear from some expert why the market is going up, and in the next you will hear from another why it is going down. It pains us to think how many people get their investment ideas (particularly stocks) from watching this drama play out.

In the past, we have had the good fortune of sitting in on a handful of small group presentations by renowned economist Dr. Bob Froehlich. While we may not always agree with his message, we can certainly appreciate his enthusiasm and the wildly compelling arguments he makes to support his well-articulated views. Reiterating our previous point, the one thing we heard Dr. Bob say that has stuck with us over the years was, "If you see someone on TV telling you to buy a stock, it is because they own it and they need to get out at a higher price."

The reality is that we live in a world that is dialed into the investment markets 24/7, in the United States and abroad. Whether through TV, radio, the Internet, or a litany of industry-related publications, investors today are flooded with a plethora of information. They are inundated with commentary from very smart people weaving well-crafted messages to convey their views. These experts are backed by industry-related pedigree, impressive educational backgrounds, and fancy initials after their name—all of which leads us to believe they are qualified to know what is coming next, whether for the state of an individual company or the economy at large. But despite all of these superficial pearls of wisdom, more often than not they are wrong. It's not their fault. It is by the conventions we have endeared ourselves to that they are obliged. They are simply purveyors of an ego-driven industry in which individuals believe they can know more than the markets.

A LITANY IS ① a prayer or ② a long chant

PLETHORA = EXCESS & is Redundant

OCKHAM'S RAZOR

"Pluralitas non est ponenda sine necessitate" ("Entities should not be multiplied unnecessarily")

William of Ockham, a fourteenth-century Franciscan monk, born
in the small village of Ockham in Surrey, England

While many of us may not be familiar with the name, historians today regard William as one of the central figures of Renaissance thought, at the epicenter of the major intellectual and political controversies of his time. William is most highly regarded for his contributions to the principles of parsimony. This later came to be known in academic circles as "Ockham's Razor" and centuries later continues to provide one of life's most important guiding principles.

Ockham's Razor essentially states that if one can explain a phenomenon without making unnecessary assumptions, then there is no ground for assuming it, that one should always opt for an explanation in terms of the fewest possible causes, factors, or variables. Today, we know this as the KISS principle—Keep It Simple, Stupid.

When you look out into the landscape of the financial markets, you can see that we certainly don't do a very good job of this. Click on CNBC, pick up your *Wall Street Journal*, or turn on your Bloomberg radio, and this much should be blatantly obvious. There is a whole army of financial wizards trying to decipher the behavior of the investment markets and sharing with us their opinion of what's to come. The irony is that seemingly more often than not, their visions fail to come to fruition. And yet we as investors are encouraged to base our investment decisions on their collective wisdom.

Perhaps this is where William of Ockham comes in. Rather than attempt to predict the future price of a stock or the future state of our economy, encompassing a mountain of data and incalculable variables, rather than attempt the impossible by looking forward, wouldn't it just be easier to "look back"?

The price movement of a security will tell you more than any analyst or economist ever could. In the spirit of Ockham's Razor, price momentum is the one true metric we have that provides clarity to the psychological underpinnings that move the markets. These psychological forces drive both short- and long-term trends.

In the investment world, we like to make things more complex than they need to be. Our industry is famous for as much, and it seems more and more the investment vehicles or methods used today have grown increasingly complex. Whether by virtue of some sort of masochistic, egomaniacal pursuit of proving one can consistently outsmart the markets or the result of simply adhering to the rules that have been laid out before us (attempting the impossible by predicting the future), the results remain the same. Investors have a long history of underperformance.

According to the 2013 Quantitative Analysis of Investor Behavior, conducted by Dalbar, Inc., over the past 20 years (1993–2012) the average rate of return for the retail equity investor in the United States has significantly lagged that of the S&P 500:

- 4.25 percent average annual return for the individual investor in the United States.
- 8.21 percent average annual return for the S&P 500.

Pulling out our financial calculators and computing a few simple time-value-of-money calculations, this would imply that:

- An investor starting with a $100,000 investment, with a 20-year compounded average annual return of 4.25 percent, would have seen their savings grow to $229,890.63 by the end of 2012.
- Conversely, an investor in the S&P 500 Index starting with $100,000, with a 20-year compounded average annual return of 8.21 percent, would have seen their investment savings grow to $484,560.42.

Surely this does not paint the individual investor in the most favorable light. Daily headlines, rumors, and stock market gossip invoke emotive responses out of investors. News that should be regarded as nothing but noise serves as a catalyst for action, either to buy or to sell. Successful investors are wise not to listen.

In one of the great literary works of all time, *The Intelligent Investor*, the father of *value investing* (and mentor to the iconic Warren Buffett),

Benjamin Graham, opined, "Individuals who cannot master their emotions are ill-suited to profit from the investment process." On this point we wholeheartedly agree, as the psyche of the human condition is not wired to endure such gut-wrenching events as watching one's net worth painstakingly decline by more than 50 percent. Suffice it to say this is easier said than done. History has proven as much. Therefore, it would make sense that investors adhere to an investment process devoid of emotion.

Consider the information in Table 1.1 of what it takes for investors to get back to even once they have experienced a significant loss of capital:

TABLE 1.1   It Pays to Lose Less

If you're down this much	You'll need to gain this to break even	Number of Years It Will Take to Break Even at the Following Rates of Return					
		2%	4%	6%	8%	10%	12%
10%	11%	5.3	2.7	1.8	1.4	1.1	0.9
20%	25%	11.3	5.7	3.8	2.9	2.3	2.0
30%	43%	18.0	9.1	6.1	4.6	3.7	3.2
40%	67%	25.8	13.0	8.8	6.6	5.4	4.5
50%	100%	35.0	17.7	11.9	9.0	7.3	6.1
60%	150%	46.3	23.4	15.7	11.9	9.6	8.1
70%	233%	60.8	30.7	20.7	15.6	12.6	10.6
80%	400%	81.3	41.0	27.6	20.9	16.9	14.2
90%	900%	116.3	58.7	39.5	29.9	24.2	20.3

The great Warren Buffett once said, "Unless you can watch your stock holding decline by 50 percent without becoming panic stricken, you should not be in the market." On this point, we may find *some* common ground. We agree that investors simply can't take watching their investments lose significant amounts of money; they fear they will never get it back. They also fear that things will get worse. Such fears begin to consume them and they simply pull the eject lever and get out, potentially locking in a permanent impairment of capital from which they may never recover.

Consider that if an investor is down 50 percent, they will need to go up 100 percent just to get back to even. If you have $100,000 and you lose 50 percent, you are left with $50,000. Even if you go up 50 percent, you still only have $75,000. After losing 50 percent, at a respectable rate of return of 8 percent, it will take nine years to get back to even. Worse yet, if an investor makes the impulsive move into an even more risk-averse security averaging a 4 percent annual rate of return, it will take an astonishing 17.7 years to get back to even.

But who can stomach losing 50 percent?! Who's to say you have not just bought the proverbial "falling knife" (as "value" investing can so often lead one to do)? Does this mean one should not invest? Do all investments bear such risk? We all know stocks do, and we also know that most people can't handle seeing them go down precipitously.

> *It only makes sense that any sound portfolio management process should provide a discipline for reducing participation in prolonged declines in the investment markets.*

Investing based on emotion will never work, but admittedly in a world where we are continually peppered with bombastic news intended to stoke feelings of fear and greed, we are playing in a game we can't win. That is, if you care to listen.

OUR CURRENT ECONOMIC LANDSCAPE

Investors have a strong proclivity to take that which they have experienced in recent years and project that these returns will continue on into the future. Over the course of the past two decades, we have seen this notion play out in dramatic fashion, as the performance of the U.S. equity markets has provided investors with polar extremes from boom to bust. A period that peaked with insatiable greed and consumption morphed into a cataclysm of events that has left investors (and perhaps the U.S. consumer at large) broken and fearful.

During the 1990s, the S&P 500 averaged an astounding annual rate of return of 18.21 percent (see Figure 1.1). It was a decade of tremendous prosperity for Americans. The stock markets were so strong it made nearly anyone look like a market maven. One could throw the proverbial dart and come up a big winner. This created a false sense of confidence and encouraged investors to take on increasingly more risk.

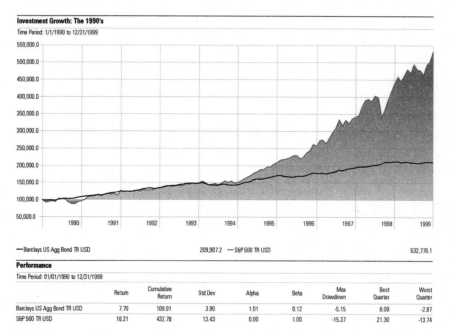

| Investment Growth: The 1990's | | | | | | | | |
| Time Period: 1/1/1990 to 12/31/1999 | | | | | | | | |

| —Barclays US Agg Bond TR USD | | 209,907.2 | —S&P 500 TR USD | | | 532,776.1 | | |

Performance

Time Period: 01/01/1990 to 12/31/1999

	Return	Cumulative Return	Std Dev	Alpha	Beta	Max Drawdown	Best Quarter	Worst Quarter
Barclays US Agg Bond TR USD	7.70	109.91	3.90	1.01	0.12	-5.15	6.09	-2.87
S&P 500 TR USD	18.21	432.78	13.43	0.00	1.00	-15.37	21.30	-13.74

FIGURE 1.1 Historical Performance of the S&P 500, 1990–1999

Source: © 2014 Morningstar, Inc. All Rights Reserved. Reproduced with permission.

At the same time, the Baby Boomer generation was entering their prime earnings cycle, incomes were going up, the unemployment rate was low, real estate was booming, consumption was strong, and so on. In fact, many Americans increased their level of wealth so much over the course of this decade that they began to borrow against existing assets to consume more. Whether taking out a home equity loan to buy their summer cottage, a Winnebago, or a new boat, investors did not seem to consider what might happen if the skyrocketing values of their investments were to fall; they assumed this growth could only continue.

At the time, there were even *New York Times* best-selling books trumpeting why and how this boom may be just the beginning! Take, for example, the *New York Times* Best Seller, *The Roaring 2000s: Building the Wealth and Lifestyle You Desire in the Greatest Boom in History*, in which author Harry Dent forecasted that the Dow Jones Industrial Average would reach as high as 35,000 by the year 2008. As one might expect, investors and consumers alike entered the new millennium with high hopes, assuming what they had experienced in recent years would surely continue.

As we now know all too well, the following decade proved to be the most difficult economic period in the United States since the Great Depression. From the bursting of the tech bubble in the year 2000 to the end of 2009, the S&P 500 generated an average annual rate of return of −0.95 percent; prompting many to refer to this time period as the "Lost Decade" (see Figure 1.2). The Dow Jones Industrial Average once projected to reach 35,000 bottomed in early March 2009, closing at a 12-year low of just 6,547.

The average American lost as much as 50 percent or more of their net worth, as both the stock and real estate markets plummeted. Some of the most well-known and established companies in the United States found themselves bankrupt, as prominent companies such as Lehman Brothers and General Motors failed to escape the depths of the Great Recession of 2008. Unemployment rose to historical highs, and wage growth became nonexistent. In a nation where gross

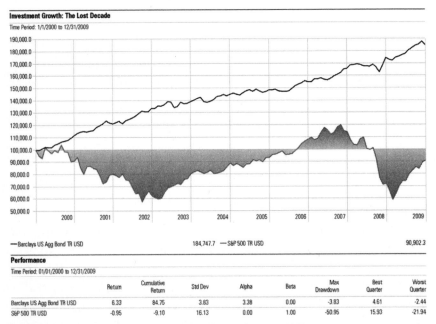

Investment Growth: The Lost Decade
Time Period: 1/1/2000 to 12/31/2009

—Barclays US Agg Bond TR USD   184,747.7 — S&P 500 TR USD   90,902.3

Performance
Time Period: 01/01/2000 to 12/31/2009

	Return	Cumulative Return	Std Dev	Alpha	Beta	Max Drawdown	Best Quarter	Worst Quarter
Barclays US Agg Bond TR USD	6.33	84.75	3.83	3.38	0.00	-3.83	4.61	-2.44
S&P 500 TR USD	-0.95	-9.10	16.13	0.00	1.00	-50.95	15.93	-21.94

FIGURE 1.2 Historical Performance of the S&P 500, 2000–2009

domestic product (GDP) had been so historically reliant on consumer spending for growth, the consumer was badly wounded.

To put these losses into perspective, consider how much the cost of everyday staples have increased in price since the year 1999 (see Table 1.2).

Suffice it to say, when one takes into consideration both the average loss of capital for the U.S. consumer that has taken place since the turn of the millennium, as well as the price increases we have experienced in everyday staples, the past decade has been quite challenging.

Since our most recent market collapse in 2008, in an effort to thwart the perils of what very well could have become another Great Depression (or worse), central banks from around the world have worked in concert to avoid a deepening of the crisis. The Federal Reserve in the United States specifically has taken a litany of accommodative actions, attempting to facilitate growth in the economy and provide relief for consumers.

In an effort to reduce interest rates in the economy and thus increase spending and borrowing, the Fed has undertaken a massive stimulus program, including a large-scale asset repurchasing program. As we know it to date, the total cost of this stimulus is encroaching on $1 trillion. Concurrently, our country's national debt is now nearing a jaw-dropping $17 trillion.

We all know this cannot continue; the government cannot prop up our economy forever. At some point in time, the baton will once again be passed along to the U.S. consumer to provide economic growth.

TABLE 1.2 Historical Cost Comparison (U.S. City Average)

	1999	2012	% Increase
Gasoline, unleaded regular, per gal.	$1.16	$3.64	214%
Ground beef, 100% beef, per lb.	$1.45	$3.03	109%
Flour, white, all-purpose, per lb.	$0.29	$0.52	79%
Potatoes, white, per lb.	$0.39	$0.66	69%
Coffee, 100%, ground roast, all sizes, per lb.	$3.43	$5.68	66%
Sugar, white, all sizes, per lb.	$0.43	$0.69	60%
Apples, Red Delicious, per lb.	$0.90	$1.38	53%
Electricity per KWH	$0.09	$0.13	44%
Chicken, fresh, whole, per lb.	$1.06	$1.42	34%
Milk, fresh, whole, fortified, per gal.	$2.84	$3.49	23%

Source: Bureau of Labor Statistics.

The question is whether U.S. consumers will be ready when the time comes, and what happens if they are not.

Many of the most well-respected and prominent figures in our industry have widely discussed what they believe will be a more difficult investment environment in the United States and abroad in the coming years. PIMCO has referred to this environment as "the new normal," a period of slower, more muted growth, with more frequent recessions. Others have framed the years ahead as "the great deleveraging," as developed countries around the world will be forced to take measures to pay down the massive debts incurred by trying to prevent a global depression during the Great Recession of 2008. This will lead to societal changes unlike that which we have seen in the past, as simultaneously governments and individuals alike aim to reduce debt. In this environment, many believe wage growth will be slow as corporations and small businesses adapt to lower levels of consumption (and potentially higher taxes). Unemployment is also likely to remain above historical norms. With increased uncertainty and businesses operating lean, why hire more employees when the ones you have are just thankful to have a job and are managing a workload previously assigned to two people?

Additionally, in the United States specifically, we are potentially faced with decades of demographic challenges. In the United States, nearly 30 percent of our population is composed of the Baby Boomer generation (those born between 1946 and 1964), and yet this demographic controls more than 40 percent of consumer spending. As these individuals grow older and move on into retirement, they are going to place increased strains on our current social programs (Social Security, etc.). These programs are already under pressure and woefully underfunded; imagine the impact it might have when this entire generation is retired! This generation controls the largest percentage of financial assets in our country; as such, they have incurred the biggest losses over the past decade. How might the spending habits of this generation change in retirement, and what impact will this have on U.S. GDP, 70 percent of which is historically composed of consumer spending? No one can say for sure, but suffice it to say these are valid concerns and questions to which we as of yet have no answers.

The aforementioned challenges will move structural reform to the forefront in the coming years, as political leaders grapple with how to get elected, but at the same time present a framework for "righting the ship." Conventionally, in order to reduce the federal deficit, our government must either reduce spending or increase taxes, or both. Consider what might happen if during a time of economic instability, with the world teetering on the cusp of recession, taxes were increased in the world's wealthiest nation? Common sense will lead you to deduce that consumption would go down. It is a delicate balancing act, and one that must be executed with extreme caution.

So for those investors expecting the next 10 years to look like what they have experienced in recent years, market history cautions us to consider otherwise. Investors today are facing a whole new set of circumstances that have never before been seen in the modern capital markets. This environment will likely wreak havoc on those employing a traditional approach to asset management.

THE BOTTOM LINE

Taking a "30,000-foot view," it is easy to see that we are facing a myriad of challenges ahead. These challenges will collectively make the investment landscape that much more difficult for investors. Timing, execution, and adhering to an investment process devoid of emotion and focused on discipline will provide investors with a margin of safety in these difficult times; it always has. With a process centered on "winning by losing less," investors can better navigate the markets, through all market cycles (good or bad). What we are referring to specifically is employing a *rotational* approach to investing, rather than "buy, hold, and pray."

CHAPTER 2

WHEN THE PARADIGM SHIFTS

Why What Worked in the Past May No Longer
Work in the Future

Christopher Columbus was a fifteenth-century Italian maritime explorer, commissioned by the Spanish crown to set sail in search of a brave *New World*. The fruit of his conquests were to bring new riches to Spain through the establishment of trade routes and colonization, in an attempt to gain an upper hand over rival powers in the contest for the lucrative spice trade with Asia.

In 1492, when Christopher Columbus set sail on his first of what would become four round-trip voyages between Spain and the Americas, many believed he and his crew would surely perish, sailing off the edge of the Earth. At the time, prevailing opinions of common folk were that the world was flat.

In the early years of the Renaissance, people still believed the world was flat because it was all they could conceive; by observation it was all that they had ever known and learned to be true. Today, investors follow similarly contrived notions as to how to mitigate risk and generate positive returns in the investment markets. But as we all know, things are not always as they appear. . . .

According to Dictionary.com, a *paradigm* may be defined as "a framework containing basic assumptions, ways of thinking, and methodology that are commonly accepted by members of a scientific community." In the confines of the financial services industry, the framework and methodology most heavily relied upon with regard to the management of one's overall investable assets is predicated on the basis of Modern Portfolio Theory. But what happens when the rules change and the paradigm shifts? When the assumptions that define this methodology are no longer held to be true? What impact will this have on your investment portfolio, and how can you prepare yourself?

Modern Portfolio Theory (MPT) provides the foundation for the most widely accepted approach to portfolio management practiced in our industry today. It also provides the bedrock for modern-day financial planning. For decades, this diversified approach has afforded investors a modicum of comfort and reassurance that despite what may happen in the investment markets, by spreading out their investable dollars across an array of asset classes, they were mitigating their risks.

With such notable buzzwords as *diversification, buy and hold,* and *asset allocation,* even lay investors can feel well versed in their investment discipline. After all, they have heard it for years. And yet, as highlighted earlier, this approach has done little to shield investors from experiencing significant losses.

Now to be fair, one can certainly argue this has had more to do with the emotional behavior of investors themselves and less to do with MPT, and in some instances, this may very well be true. But the crux of the matter going forward is more about our changing economic landscape and the likely impact this will have on traditional methods of portfolio management in the future.

In order to present a fair and reasonable explanation of the challenges that lie ahead for traditional approaches to portfolio management, we must first begin with a general explanation of Modern Portfolio Theory, and present a brief history. By no means is this intended to be an in-depth analysis of MPT, but rather a primer on the key points. For a more in-depth dissertation, one may be well advised to read Harry Markowitz's seminal work on the subject in the book, *Portfolio Selection: Efficient Diversification of Investments* (first published in 1959).

Once we have highlighted the key concepts of Modern Portfolio Theory, we will take a closer look at historical returns of both U.S.

stocks and the U.S. Treasury bond; in doing so, we aim to exploit long-term trends in motion and draw historical parallels to our present-day environment. And then, finally, we will illustrate the impact of the reversal of long-term trends on the efficient frontier (outlined in MPT) and how this can be expected to impact investors maintaining a traditionally diversified asset allocation.

A PRIMER ON MODERN PORTFOLIO THEORY

In 1952, Harry M. Markowitz (widely regarded as the father of Modern Portfolio Theory) first published his pioneering theories in the *Journal of Finance*, in an article titled "Portfolio Selection." In this article, Mr. Markowitz presents the foundation for his approach to portfolio management, diversification, the reduction of portfolio risk, and, ultimately, how one might create an *optimal portfolio*, given one's specific objectives and individual comfort level regarding portfolio risk.

The basic pretenses for Markowitz's work are based on two very simple objectives (assumptions) common to all investors: (1) they want the highest return possible, and (2) they want this return to be dependable and stable. However, as cited in "Portfolio Selection":

> The portfolio with maximum expected return is not necessarily the one with minimum variance. There is a rate at which the investor can gain expected return by taking on variance, or reduce variance by giving up expected return.

In practical application, financial practitioners often refer to this concept as the "risk/reward" paradigm. In Modern Portfolio Theory, this premise led to the mathematical creation of what Markowitz referred to as the *efficient frontier*, a graphical illustration of the optimal portfolio (and asset mix) given an investor's desired rate of return and their accepted level of variance, as shown in Figure 2.1. At one end is the point of minimum variance (and the lowest return); at the other end is the point of greatest return (and inherently increased variance or volatility).

In order to construct an optimal portfolio, investors are required to diversify their investments among asset classes that are not highly correlated to one another. Historically, this has been most consistently

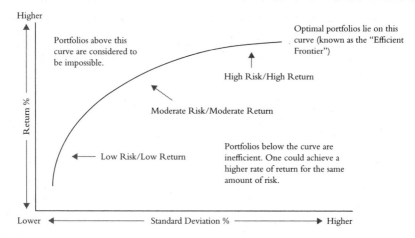

FIGURE 2.1   The Efficient Frontier

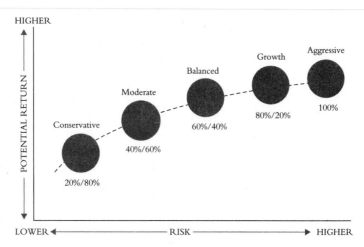

FIGURE 2.2   Portfolio Allocations along the Efficient Frontier

illustrated in the relationship between stocks and bonds. Whereas stocks are considered to provide investors with the greatest long-term return with the greatest variance, bonds have historically provided relatively low rates of return with relative stability. This risk–return relationship, when applied to an overall asset allocation, is depicted in Figure 2.2.

It is imperative to note that the anticipated returns of each respective asset class (i.e., capital market assumptions) are largely based on a broad sampling of historical returns. However, what is not evident in this illustration is how this risk–return scenario may be dramatically impacted when we see a reversion in long-term trends, a shift in the paradigm. Specifically, we are referring to the historical risk-return characteristics of bonds over the past several decades and what one might expect going forward.

The rate of return on a given bond is due to a number of factors: credit quality, maturity date, duration, and so on. But what is most critically important is the interest rate environment our economy is in during the life of the bond. If we find ourselves in a gradually declining interest rate environment, investors can expect the price of their existing bonds to go up. In the early 1980s, it was not uncommon to find corporate bonds with double-digit coupons on investment-grade debt. By the late 2000s, high-quality debt paid only a couple percent. In the early 1980s, inflation was high; now it is relatively low. Additionally, monetary policy enacted by the Federal Reserve has driven interest rates down to all-time lows in recent years. But what does all of this mean for fixed-income investors?

In 2012, we witnessed the yield on the 10-Year U.S. Treasury bond dip below 1.5 percent for the first time in history; at the same time, according to the U.S. Department of Labor, Bureau of Labor Statistics, the Consumer Price Index (widely recognized as the primary gauge for inflation in the United States) registered 2.1 percent. This means that, assuming inflation were to remain at an annualized rate of 2.1 percent over the coming decade, that a conservative investor would actually register a loss on their investment, let alone what might happen when and if interest rates go up.

What does this mean for the long-term viability and risk-reward characteristics for "conservative" fixed-income investors in this environment? If a conservative investor is represented by an asset allocation of 20 percent stocks and 80 percent bonds, are they locking in a guaranteed loss and reduction of purchasing power with 80 percent of their investable assets?

For more than 30 years we have witnessed a gradually declining interest rate environment for bonds. Over this time period the Ibbotson & Associates SBBI Long Term Government Bond Index averaged an annualized total return of 10.77 percent, while the S&P 500 generated an average annual total return of 11.14 percent. During this period, bonds basically generated equity-like returns without providing investors with any significant downside risks.

As you look at the chart in Figure 2.3, illustrating the bull market in bonds, the risk-adjusted returns are astounding. With a beta of 0.04, investors were nearly able match the overall returns of the stock market with essentially 96 percent less risk! Additionally, while stocks incurred a maximum drawdown of greater than 50 percent over this time period, bonds were down less than 15 percent! This period marked a tremendous boom for fixed-income investors, and as such may have created a false sense of expectations. Recall, as noted previously, investors have a tendency to assume that which they have experienced in recent years will continue on into the future.

As recent as May 2013, perhaps the greatest fixed-income investor the world has ever known, the illustrious Bill Gross, CEO of PIMCO, made a brazen call, stating that the 30-year bull market in bonds was over. As the portfolio manager at the helm of the largest bond fund in history, managing more than $267 billion, Mr. Gross was sharing with the masses a stark revelation. In essence, as the world's preeminent fixed-income guru, he was seeking to reset expectations.

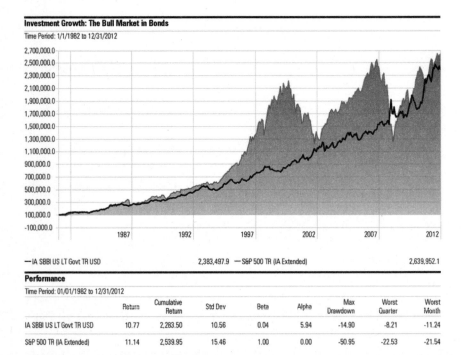

Investment Growth: The Bull Market in Bonds

Time Period: 1/1/1982 to 12/31/2012

— IA SBBI US LT Govt TR USD   2,383,497.9 — S&P 500 TR (IA Extended)   2,639,952.1

Performance

Time Period: 01/01/1982 to 12/31/2012

	Return	Cumulative Return	Std Dev	Beta	Alpha	Max Drawdown	Worst Quarter	Worst Month
IA SBBI US LT Govt TR USD	10.77	2,283.50	10.56	0.04	5.94	-14.90	-8.21	-11.24
S&P 500 TR (IA Extended)	11.14	2,539.95	15.46	1.00	0.00	-50.95	-22.53	-21.54

FIGURE 2.3 The Bull Market in Bonds (1982–2012)

Source: © 2014 Morningstar, Inc. All Rights Reserved. Reproduced with permission.

THE TREASURY RUN

In Figure 2.3, we illustrated the significant run we have seen in bonds over the past 30 years. This run has been even more dramatic during times of peril in the equity markets, and specifically since the bursting of the tech bubble in the year 2000. In the history of the capital markets, we have seen this before, where Treasuries have had such a strong run versus equities, and conservative investors would be wise to take note.

Certainly, some may regard this as a reversion to the mean, but more than that, investors are faced with an interest rate environment that is currently at or near all-time lows. One would be hard pressed to believe they can go any lower. At current rates, inflation eroding any modicum of return should be a concern; should rates rise, and depending on how quickly they do, fixed-income investors could be faced with significant losses on an asset class historically regarded as "safe."

From the beginning of the year 2000 to the end of 2002, the S&P 500 TR Index declined by 37.61 percent, as seen in Figure 2.4. During

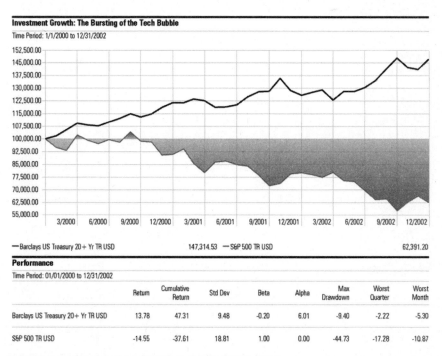

Performance								
Time Period: 01/01/2000 to 12/31/2002								
	Return	Cumulative Return	Std Dev	Beta	Alpha	Max Drawdown	Worst Quarter	Worst Month
Barclays US Treasury 20+ Yr TR USD	13.78	47.31	9.48	-0.20	6.01	-9.40	-2.22	-5.30
S&P 500 TR USD	-14.55	-37.61	18.81	1.00	0.00	-44.73	-17.28	-10.87

FIGURE 2.4 The Bursting of the Tech Bubble (2000–2002)

Source: © 2014 Morningstar, Inc. All Rights Reserved. Reproduced with permission.

this same period, the Barclays U.S. Treasury 20+Year TR Index was up an impressive 47.31 percent! While stocks incurred a maximum drawdown of nearly 45 percent, U.S. Treasury bonds fared far better, posting a maximum drawdown of little more than 9 percent. Collectively, over this three-year period, this return disparity makes for a spread of nearly 85 percent!

During the Great Recession of 2008, investors witnessed an even more dramatic inverse relationship between the returns of U.S. stocks and Treasury bonds as depicted in Figure 2.5. In one year's time, the S&P 500 TR Index dropped by a gut wrenching 37.0 percent. At the same time, the Barclays U.S. Treasury 20+Year TR Index was up 33.72 percent. In a single calendar year, we witnessed a dispersion in returns between risk assets (stocks) and a flight to safety (the U.S. Treasury bond) of greater than 70 percent! And while stocks incurred a maximum drawdown for the period of greater than 37 percent, bonds were down at their worst less than 5 percent.

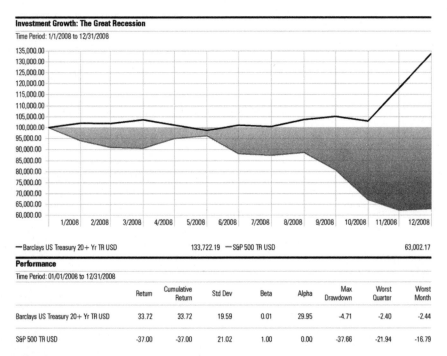

Investment Growth: The Great Recession

Time Period: 1/1/2008 to 12/31/2008

| | — Barclays US Treasury 20+ Yr TR USD | 133,722.19 | — S&P 500 TR USD | 63,002.17 |

Performance

Time Period: 01/01/2008 to 12/31/2008

	Return	Cumulative Return	Std Dev	Beta	Alpha	Max Drawdown	Worst Quarter	Worst Month
Barclays US Treasury 20+ Yr TR USD	33.72	33.72	19.59	0.01	29.95	-4.71	-2.40	-2.44
S&P 500 TR USD	-37.00	-37.00	21.02	1.00	0.00	-37.66	-21.94	-16.79

FIGURE 2.5 The Great Recession (2008)

Source: © 2014 Morningstar, Inc. All Rights Reserved. Reproduced with permission.

Since the year 2000, the outperformance we have witnessed in U.S. Treasury bonds over U.S. stocks has been astounding, as shown in Figure 2.6. Over this period, the Barclays U.S. Treasury 20+ Year Index achieved a cumulative return of +213.77 percent; dwarfing the modest cumulative return on the S&P 500 TR Index of just +23.90 percent. This translates to an average annual rate of return on Treasury bonds of over 9 percent, and only a little more than 1.5 percent on stocks.

During a decade marked with not one but two severe recessions (one taking us to the brink of a depression), Treasuries provided a safe haven for investors. More than that, they posted returns very similar to what one might typically expect out of equities. This aberration marks a time period witnessed only during market extremes. In the history of the U.S. capital markets, we have seen Treasuries go on a run like this once before, during the Great Depression.

It goes without saying that the time period of October 1, 1929, through December 31, 1941, will long be remembered as the worst

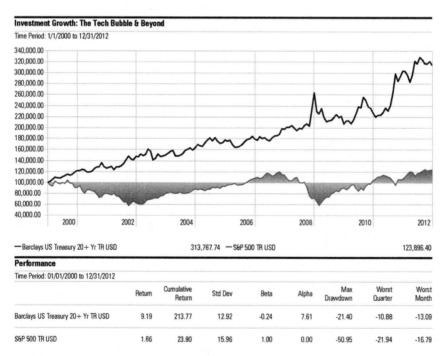

Investment Growth: The Tech Bubble & Beyond

Time Period: 1/1/2000 to 12/31/2012

—Barclays US Treasury 20+ Yr TR USD   313,767.74   —S&P 500 TR USD   123,896.40

Performance

Time Period: 01/01/2000 to 12/31/2012

	Return	Cumulative Return	Std Dev	Beta	Alpha	Max Drawdown	Worst Quarter	Worst Month
Barclays US Treasury 20+ Yr TR USD	9.19	213.77	12.92	-0.24	7.61	-21.40	-10.88	-13.09
S&P 500 TR USD	1.66	23.90	15.96	1.00	0.00	-50.95	-21.94	-16.79

FIGURE 2.6 The Tech Bubble and Beyond (2000–2012)

Source: © 2014 Morningstar, Inc. All Rights Reserved. Reproduced with permission.

and certainly the most volatile period in the history of the U.S. stock market (see Figure 2.7). During this time period, the S&P 500 TR Index incurred a jawboning maximum drawdown of 82.58 percent! While the equity markets proved to be devastatingly perilous, the bond market faced a maximum drawdown of only 8.11 percent, and with a standard deviation of only 5 percent versus nearly 36 percent for stocks.

While certainly not our focus, it is interesting to note that the volatility inherent during this time was unparalleled. In the midst of the Great Depression, in a span of just four months, from March through June 1932, the S&P 500 lost more than 50 percent; then provided investors with returns of 38 percent in back-to-back months (July and August)! And to think we thought 2008 and into 2009 was a wild ride!

Nevertheless, getting back to our point, this period marks the last time (prior to what we have experienced in the markets since the year 2000) that U.S. Treasury bonds have dramatically outperformed U.S.

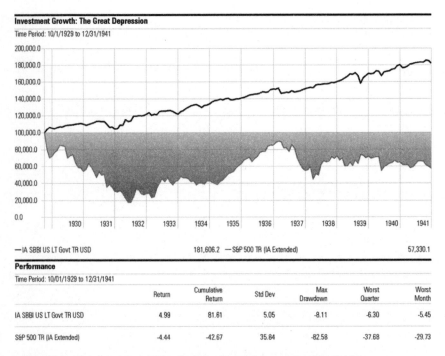

Investment Growth: The Great Depression

Time Period: 10/1/1929 to 12/31/1941

	Return	Cumulative Return	Std Dev	Max Drawdown	Worst Quarter	Worst Month
IA SBBI US LT Govt TR USD	4.99	81.61	5.05	-8.11	-6.30	-5.45
S&P 500 TR (IA Extended)	-4.44	-42.67	35.84	-82.58	-37.68	-29.73

—IA SBBI US LT Govt TR USD   181,606.2   —S&P 500 TR (IA Extended)   57,330.1

Performance

Time Period: 10/01/1929 to 12/31/1941

FIGURE 2.7 The Great Depression (October 1, 1929–December 31, 1941)

stocks. During this period, the S&P 500 TR Index averaged an annual loss of 4.44 percent, while the Ibbotson & Associates SBBI U.S. Long Term Government Bond TR Index averaged an annual gain of 4.99 percent. In other words, the performance spread between stocks and bonds was an average of 9.43 percent per year, not too dissimilar from what we have experienced since the turn of the millennium, when the performance spread was roughly 7.5 percent in favor of bonds. However, what may be of more interest to today's fixed-income investors is what happened after the Great Depression.

What happened after the last time we witnessed U.S. Treasury bonds dramatically outperform stocks for more than a decade was truly amazing. January 1, 1942, marked the beginning of a very long and painful period for conservative investors and savers—a 40-year bear market in bonds (see Figure 2.8).

Over the course of the next four decades, the S&P 500 TR Index would average an impressive annual rate of return of 11.70 percent;

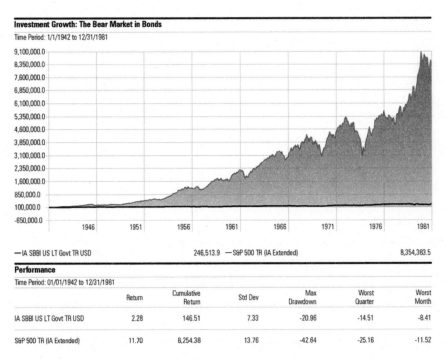

Performance						
Time Period: 01/01/1942 to 12/31/1981						
	Return	Cumulative Return	Std Dev	Max Drawdown	Worst Quarter	Worst Month
IA SBBI US LT Govt TR USD	2.28	146.51	7.33	-20.96	-14.51	-8.41
S&P 500 TR (IA Extended)	11.70	8,254.38	13.76	-42.64	-25.16	-11.52

FIGURE 2.8 The Bear Market in Bonds (1942–1981)

Source: © 2014 Morningstar, Inc. All Rights Reserved. Reproduced with permission.

versus a paltry 2.28 percent over this same period for the Ibbotson & Associates SBBI U.S. Long Term Government Bond TR Index. While on the surface this may not sound wildly dramatic, when one considers the compounding effect on returns over a 40-year time period, the impact is astounding. Over this entire 40-year time frame, the cumulative return on stocks was 8,254.38 percent, versus a cumulative return on bonds of only 146.51 percent. Put another way, had an individual invested $100,000 into the S&P 500, after 40 years their balance would be $8,354,385. The same investor placing $100,000 in the Ibbotson & Associates SBBI U.S. Long Term Government Bond TR Index would have been left with a balance of just $246,513.90—an eye-popping difference of more than $8 million dollars on the same $100,000 investment.

To further illustrate the devastating impact the bear market in bonds had on conservative investors, one must also consider the inflationary environment experienced during this time period. As illustrated in Table 2.1, during the bear market in bonds, the average annual U.S. inflation rate (as measured by the Consumer Price Index) was nearly 5 percent. Therefore, if long-term government bonds averaged a total return of 2.28 percent, and inflation averaged 4.73 percent over this same period, this implies that investors in bonds were locking in an average annual loss of more than 2 percent on their "safe" investment, for over 40 years! Of course, these are averages and certainly not all fixed-income investors shared the exact same experience, but the gist of how difficult this time period was for conservative investors cannot be denied.

We have already discussed the time period that followed this 40-year bear market in bonds: the "30-year bull market in bonds," during which bonds produced equity-like returns with little to no downside risk. Unlike the stock market, which has historically experienced a recession every 4 or 5 years, and secular bull or bear markets every 15 to 20 years, trends in the bond market have a tendency to move much more slowly (and generally with a lot less volatility).

After a 40-year bear market for bonds, we experienced a 30-year bull market, and now—in an environment where interest rates are essentially at or near zero—investors are left to wonder what might come next? When you take the 30,000-foot view, the answer becomes more readily visible; the question now is when and how quickly will

TABLE 2.1 Inflation Rates during the Bear Market in Bonds (1942–1981)

Year	1942	1943	1944	1945	1946	1947	1948	1949	1950	1951
Average inflation rate	10.90%	6.10%	1.70%	2.30%	8.30%	14.40%	8.10%	−1.20%	1.30%	7.90%
Year	**1952**	**1953**	**1954**	**1955**	**1956**	**1957**	**1958**	**1959**	**1960**	**1961**
Average inflation rate	1.90%	0.80%	0.70%	−0.40%	1.50%	3.30%	2.80%	0.70%	1.70%	1.00%
Year	**1962**	**1963**	**1964**	**1965**	**1966**	**1967**	**1968**	**1969**	**1970**	**1971**
Average inflation rate	1.00%	1.30%	1.30%	1.60%	2.90%	3.10%	4.20%	5.50%	5.70%	4.40%
Year	**1972**	**1973**	**1974**	**1975**	**1976**	**1977**	**1978**	**1979**	**1980**	**1981**
Average inflation rate	3.20%	6.20%	11.00%	9.10%	5.80%	6.50%	7.60%	11.30%	13.50%	10.30%

40-Year Average Annual Inflation Rate: 4.73%.
Data provided by the U.S. Department of Labor, Bureau of Labor Statistics.

we see this impact fixed-income investors and ultimately challenge the viability of traditional asset allocation and the efficient frontier outlined in MPT.

After the spectacular run we have seen in U.S. Treasury bonds since the year 2000, in conjunction with the massive stimulus efforts undertaken by the Federal Reserve, at some point our "buyer of last resort" (the U.S. government) is going to have to take a step back from the table, at which point investors are left to question what demand there may be for Treasuries given our current interest rate environment.

Likely, in order to generate demand and attract buyers, the government is going to have to issue bonds with a higher coupon, and this will, of course, have a trickle-down effect on our economy, increasing interest rates. As we have already pointed out, as interest rates rise, the price paid for existing bonds falls. Why buy a 2 percent bond when you can buy one with the same credit quality and maturity paying 5 percent? You wouldn't. Thus, market participants have been waiting

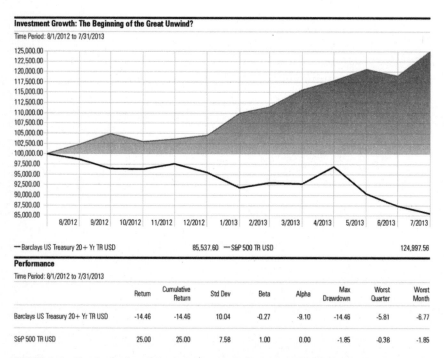

FIGURE 2.9 The Beginning of the Great Unwind? (August 1, 2012–July 31, 2013)

Source: © 2014 Morningstar, Inc. All Rights Reserved. Reproduced with permission.

with bated breath for the slightest inkling that this is beginning to happen. When it does, one can expect an "unwinding" in Treasury prices that up to this point have been largely artificially inflated in recent years. Some have referred to this as the "Great Rotation," as investors will be forced to move investable dollars out of fixed income and into the stock market. While this may very well be the case, we are skeptical that investors are willing to do so at a time when the equity markets are achieving all-time highs (and we are going on five years since our most recent market collapse).

With all of that said, perhaps the "unwinding" from Treasury market highs is already taking place, see Figure 2.9. Since August 2012 we have seen a rather steady decline in Treasury prices. Considering the massive run bonds have had since the turn of the century versus stocks, it is not unreasonable to expect that this might continue. When it does, it will mark the beginning of what may very well prove to be a long and painful period for conservative investors simply aiming to preserve capital (much like the last bear market we experienced in bonds).

However, before we can continue on with our discussion illustrating what investors' might expect from the bond markets in the coming years, we would be remiss if we did not take a moment to pause and highlight a significant inflection point in the stock and bond markets and the corresponding actions taken by investors.

The 1990s will long be remembered by investors as one of the best decades for U.S. stocks in capital markets history (see Figure 2.10). During this decade, the S&P 500 TR Index averaged an astonishing 18.21 percent per year! Simply buying and holding an S&P 500 index fund would have enabled investors to quadruple their money over this time period. With euphoria and hyperbole surrounding the stock market (and the tech sector specifically) investors developed a false sense of expectations. As noted previously, there was even a litany of best-selling books trumpeting that the outlandish returns for stocks would continue on well into the next decade.

At the time, many investors were snubbing the notion that they needed to own fixed income in a diversified portolio; they felt that owning a handful of high-flying companies provided diversification enough. As I have heard the story told on a number of occasions by mutual fund wholesalers, "99 cents out of every dollar was going into equity funds." So when the tech bubble burst in 2000, tragically the

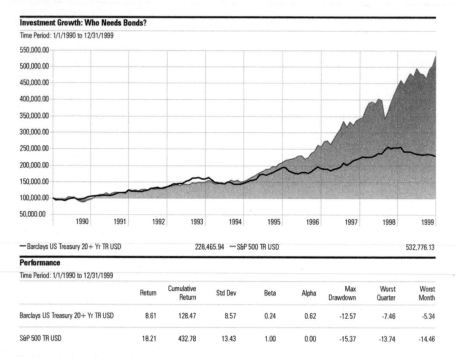

Investment Growth: Who Needs Bonds?

Time Period: 1/1/1990 to 12/31/1999

Barclays US Treasury 20+ Yr TR USD   228,465.94   — S&P 500 TR USD   532,776.13

Performance

Time Period: 1/1/1990 to 12/31/1999

	Return	Cumulative Return	Std Dev	Beta	Alpha	Max Drawdown	Worst Quarter	Worst Month
Barclays US Treasury 20+ Yr TR USD	8.61	128.47	8.57	0.24	0.62	-12.57	-7.46	-5.34
S&P 500 TR USD	18.21	432.78	13.43	1.00	0.00	-15.37	-13.74	-14.46

FIGURE 2.10   Who Needs Bonds? (1990–1999)

Source: © 2014 Morningstar, Inc. All Rights Reserved. Reproduced with permission.

masses did not see it coming. To make matters worse, many refused to believe it, continually buying more of their tech darlings as the prices dropped. But as we now know all too well, this left many investors catching the proverbial falling knife, as many of these companies never recovered; and far too many of these investors incurred a permanent impairment of capital from which they would never recover.

The purpose in rehashing these harsh truths is not to drudge up painful experiences for investors or financial practitioners; it is to highlight a handful of very simple, but impactful truths when it comes to investing in the financial markets. Stating the obvious, as investors we cannot expect what we have experienced in recent years to continue on into the foreseeable future. But perhaps more important, we should take heed of the actions of the herd; they are rarely right. As the great Warren Buffett has famously stated, "Be fearful when others are greedy and greedy when others are fearful."

As we reflect on where we are today, we can't help but notice that since 2008 we have seen a massive outflow out of equity mutual funds and a tremendous inflow into fixed-income mutual funds. So will we see this cycle repeat itself again? You can count on it.

Since the bottom of the equity markets in March 2009, the S&P 500 is up over 150 percent! And during this time, where have the asset flows been going? That's right, fixed income. Once again the herd has missed the mark. Only recently, as bond prices have gradually declined over the past year, have we finally begun to see net inflows into equity funds, although bond funds have continued to drive assets as well.

LOSING MONEY IN BONDS

So here we are. We are coming off of what has been a massive run for Treasury bonds over the past several years; interest rates are at or near zero; the federal deficit is massively unsustainable; the consumer is working hard to deleverage from all that was lost during the "lost decade"; stocks are achieving all-time highs; and the debate wages on about when the Fed is going to back down and allow rates to rise. For the first time in decades, bond investors are fearful. What are they supposed to do? Most are simply looking for modest returns and a minimal amount of "variance" (as it is described in MPT terms). But if and when interest rates do rise, just what will this mean? How much do fixed-income investors stand to lose?

Suffice it to say these are loaded questions. Certainly, much depends on how quickly they may rise; it also depends largely on the quality of the bond, the maturity date, and any number of other factors one might wish to cite. The bottom line is that we need to put this conundrum into perspective so that investors can make informed decisions moving forward.

Before we can begin to explain the problem at hand, we need to first make sure we have covered a few basic principles with respect to investing in bonds. Then we will proceed with illustrating what a bond investor might expect to happen to the price of their bond(s) when and if interest rates rise, as we believe has already begun to take place.

A bond is simply an IOU from an institution (typically government or corporate debt). An investor loans them X amount of money, and after a certain amount of time the investor gets their money back. For their trouble, the borrower pays them an annual interest rate; this is referred to as the *coupon*. This is effectively the cost of borrowing. For the investor, this provides a "known" rate of return and at a historically low risk. This provides the borrower with the flexibility to utilize these invested funds for an agreed-upon period of time, to ultimately achieve a greater rate of return than what they are required to pay out.

While there are many factors that can impact bond prices, the most important one is interest rates. One of the most basic pretenses of bond investing with regard to interest rates is simply that as interest rates rise, bond prices fall, and vice versa. Think of this like a teeter-totter with interest rates at one end and bond prices at the other; when one goes up, the other goes down.

Considering where we are in the interest rate cycle (at historical lows), what investors today should be most concerned about is what will happen when the pendulum swings and interest rates go up, causing prices on existing bonds to fall. The question, of course, is *how much* can an investor lose?

With that said, one should keep in mind that the price movement of a bond from the point of issuance until the maturity date is important only if an investor intends to sell the bond before it comes due. Otherwise, if an investor buys a bond at par (its initial face value) and holds it until maturity, they would receive their initial investment back, as well as all of the interest rate payments made along the way. For example, if we were to purchase $10,000 of a 10-year bond with a 3.5 percent "coupon," regardless of any potential interest rate changes during the life of the bond, if we held it until maturity, we would be paid our $10,000 back; we would have also received $350 in annual coupon payments. Thus, our return is annualized at 3.5 percent. However, when a bond is held until maturity, when it was initially issued and purchased in a low-interest-rate environment, the primary concern for the "buy-and-hold" bond investor is the *real return* on the bond.

Real return may simply be defined as the actual return an investor receives, net of inflation. In other words, if we held our 3.5 percent, 10-year bond until maturity—achieving a 3.5 percent average annual return—but inflation over this same time period averaged 5 percent, then the *real return* on our investment would have actually averaged −1.5 percent per year. In other words, *real return* is simply calculated by taking the return achieved and subtracting out inflation. Ideally, an investor is left with a positive number. This is what is meant when one hears about "preserving the purchasing power of your capital" through investing.

The problem is, today, not only should investors be concerned about getting a negative real return (since the yields on high-quality bonds are so low it would not take much inflation for an investor to end up with a negative rate of return for the life of the bond), they should also be concerned with losing value in the bond when interest rates rise.

In short, there are basically four ways an investor can lose money in bonds:

1. The issuer defaults on the debt. This is rare, but it can happen.
2. Investors begin to question the viability of the issuer to continue to make coupon payments; resulting in a decline in price (but an increase in the yield).
3. The buyer holds the bond until maturity, but achieves a negative *real return* due to an increase in inflation that negates the overall return.
4. The buyer sells the bond prior to maturity, in a rising-interest-rate environment.

Now let's shift our focus to the fourth way an investor can lose money in bonds (cited above), as we believe this presents the greatest risk for conservative investors, both in the near future and over the long term. As cited in a recent Investor Alert issued by the Financial Industry Regulatory Authority (FINRA), "Duration: What an Interest Rate Hike Could Do to Your Bond Portfolio":

If you own bonds or have money in a bond fund, there is a number you should know. It is called duration. Although stated in years, duration is not simply a measure of time. Instead duration signals how much the price of your bond investment is likely to fluctuate when there is an up or down movement in interest rates. The higher the duration number, the more sensitive your bond investment will be to changes in interest rates.

Currently, interest rates are hovering near historic lows. Many economists believe that interest rates are not likely to get much lower and will eventually rise. If that is true, then outstanding bonds, particularly those with a low interest rate and high duration may experience significant price drops as interest rates rise along the way. If you have money in a bond fund that holds primarily long-term bonds, expect the value of that fund to decline, perhaps significantly, when interest rates rise.

Explaining duration risk to those who may not be well versed in the jargon associated with the financial industry can be a very complex discussion. So rather than go further into the weeds than necessary, we will keep our points on this subject both brief and succinct.

According to FINRA, "Duration risk is the name economists give to the risk associated with the sensitivity of a bond's price to a one percent change in interest rates." In order to illustrate this point, let's take the example of a bond (or bond fund) with a duration of 10 years. If interest rates go up just 1 percent, investors can expect this bond (fund) to decline in value by 10 percent. Therefore, if rates were to go up by 2 percent, an investor should then expect a corresponding decrease in the value of the bond (fund) of 20 percent, and so on.

Bonds with a longer-dated maturity will tend to have a greater *duration* and therefore stand to lose even more as interest rates rise. Imagine the decline an investor could see in a long-dated bond fund with a duration of 20. If interest rates were to rise by just 2 percent, an investor could stand to lose as much as 40 percent or more.

Conversely, bonds with shorter maturities tend to have a much lower duration and are therefore less sensitive to interest rate movements. Even still, a short-term bond fund would certainly lose money in a rising-interest-rate environment, just significantly less than a fund with a much higher duration.

For this reason, over the past handful of years we have seen a relatively strong rotation out of longer-dated bonds and into those with a shorter or more intermediate time horizon. This exodus out of the long bond has taken place as investors prepare themselves for a rising interest rate environment, and have begun to reset expectations accordingly, and position their portfolio allocations more defensively.

THE BOTTOM LINE

In 1492, when Christopher Columbus set sail from Spain, he did so with ambitions of bringing greater glory to the crown, but also in pursuit of bettering his own personal riches. Along the way, Columbus achieved both of these conquests, but, more important, he altered the paradigm of how the masses might view the topography of our planet. It seems so simple when we think about it now; of course, the world is not flat, but on the surface the contrary appears to be true.

On the surface, bonds may appear to be safe. They have provided investors with fantastic risk-reward attributes for an exceptionally long period of time. But the educated investor knows better; the paradigm is shifting. For the first time in generations, buy-and-hold fixed-income investors stand to face potentially significant losses. The impact this will likely have on a traditionally allocated, MPT-based asset allocation could be devastating, particularly for more conservative investors locking in negative real returns on the vast majority of their investable assets.

The reality is that the coming years in the capital markets are going to look nothing like what we have experienced over the past 30. While a testimonial from the world-renowned fixed income luminary, Bill Gross, should lend credibility to this claim—it should not require a Mensa-like IQ to disseminate that any long-term change in the trajectory of interest rates is going to have a profound impact on a traditionally managed asset allocation. Rather, we propose that investors should adopt a more disciplined approach than they have employed in the past, with an element of tactical management that will enable them to more adeptly navigate what will assuredly be a more difficult investment landscape for investors in the future.

CHAPTER 3

SHOOTING STARS

The Performance Realities of Mutual Fund Ownership

Until the Copernican Revolution, the Earth was viewed as the stationary center of the universe. Stars were regarded as being embedded in a large outer sphere, rapidly rotating around our planet on a daily basis, while each of the planets, the sun, and the moon were embedded in their own smaller spheres.

After a lifetime of study, in the year of his death, 1543, Nicolaus Copernicus published his theories of "heliocentrism," in his defining work, *De Revolutionibus Orbium Coelestium* (On the Revolutions of the Celestial Spheres). In the context of this book, Copernicus outlined his vision depicting the sun as the center of the universe, around which all other celestial bodies revolve.

The notion of a heliocentric universe debunked prevailing scholarly works and theories, and provided a foundation for future scientific discovery. Copernicus's body of work effectively shot holes in the conventionally accepted theories of the day.

In 1985, Morningstar debuted their now highly regarded "star rating" system. While over the years their process has evolved to account for a broader size and style approach, as well as new measures of assessing risk-adjusted returns, the gist remains the same. According to

Morningstar, "The Morningstar Rating is a quantitative assessment of a fund's past performance—both return and risk—as measured from one to five stars. It uses focused comparison groups to better measure fund manager skill."

Star ratings are determined by a mutual fund's "Morningstar Risk-Adjusted Return," as shown in Figure 3.1. This quantitative risk-adjusted return is calculated on a monthly basis, taking into account the fund's historical returns and volatility. Funds are then compared against their peers and scores are determined using the following scale: the top 10 percent of funds in each category receive a five-star rating, the next 22.5 percent receive four stars, the next 35 percent receive three stars, the next 22.5 percent receive two stars, and the bottom 10 percent receive one star.

Each fund is then given a star rating for the trailing 3-, 5-, and 10-year time periods. The overall rating may be determined by weighting these ratings in one of three ways (depending on the age of the fund):

- *3 to 5 years old:* The overall rating is based on the 3-year rating.
- *5 to 10 years old:* The overall rating is based 60 percent on the 5-year rating and 40 percent on the 3-year rating.
- *10+ years old:* The overall rating is based 50 percent on the 10-year rating, 30 percent on the 5-year rating, and 20 percent on the 3-year rating.

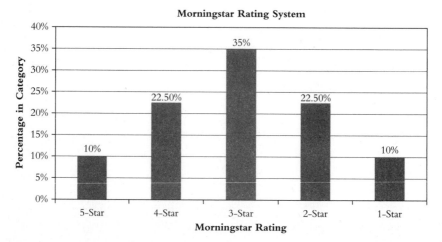

FIGURE 3.1   Morningstar Ratings by Percentile

Morningstar goes on to disclose, "As always, the Morningstar Rating is intended for use as the first step in the fund evaluation process. A high rating alone is not a sufficient basis for investment decisions." The problem is for many investors, the star rating of a mutual fund or fund manager is both their starting and end point; it is also often the foundation upon which many financial practitioners make their investment portfolio recommendations. After all, investors want to see strong historical performance, and an adviser is much more likely to win business and gain acceptance of a proposed allocation recommending all four- and five-star-rated funds; clients are drawn to such gaudy numbers, and the Morningstar "stamp of approval" is widely recognized.

The "industry" knows as much and placates to such tendencies. Whether on commercials or in advertisements in financial publications, one can hardly miss promotions such as "more four- and five-star rated funds than anyone else in our category!" Even on the web sites of mutual fund companies, you will see the performance of their four- and five-star-rated funds highlighted above all others.

In our former life in this industry, we functioned as a financial adviser and partner in a successful wealth management practice, overseeing the management of hundreds of millions of dollars. As such, we have certainly experienced our fair share of mutual fund wholesalers taking us out to lunch or to a ballgame to trumpet the performance of the funds *in their bag.* Without fail, one of the hot-button selling points always comes back to the fund's Morningstar Rating. If *pitches* such as this didn't work, they would not be used. Rather, the approach taken is yet another testament to the power wielded in the industry by these ratings.

Therefore, it should come as no surprise that the vast majority of mutual fund flows are invested predominantly in four- and five-star-rated funds. In the media, on TV, in print, and as promoted by the "boots on the ground"—the message conveyed supports such actions. The problem is, as cited by Morningstar, their rating process should serve only as a "first step" in the fund evaluation process.

Like the Copernican Revolution, the Morningstar Rating system provides a foundation for future discoveries. The notion of recognizing the impact of cost and risk-adjusted returns makes a whole lot of sense and should be variables considered by all investors. However, one should also consider the context of the return, the environment in which these returns were generated, and the tendencies of the human condition (the portfolio manager/driver behind performance) and how these factors might impact performance.

In order to put these points into perspective, in the context of this chapter we will provide insight on the statistical probabilities of continued outperformance by *active* portfolio managers versus their *passive* benchmark, as well as illustrate examples citing *best-in-class* managers. This discussion is intended to provide further illumination on the fallacies inherent in the more commonplace, traditional means of portfolio management widely used throughout our industry today.

In doing so, we will examine the performance of U.S. equity strategies, where by and large the portfolio managers are required to maintain full exposure to equities at nearly all times. Therefore, these managers do not possess the ability to make tactical allocation shifts among inversely related asset classes or cash (which we firmly believe to be necessary to mitigate downside risk).

THE PERSISTENCE OF MANAGER PERFORMANCE

Investors would be wise to look at the long-term performance of highly rated mutual funds, and the sustainability of outperformance versus their peers and benchmarks. Standard & Poor's provides statistical analysis of mutual fund performance for free to both retail and professional investors, via their web site at www.usspindices.com. S&P provides analysis of mutual fund performance in their "S&P Indices Versus Active Funds (SPIVA®) Scorecard," as well as in their "Persistence Scorecard" report.

The most recent Year-End SPIVA Scorecard foreshadows a rather alarming trend of underperformance by active managers in recent years. As shown in Table 3.1, the performance of actively managed funds in 2012 lagged behind the passive benchmark indices for 63.25 percent of large-cap funds, 80.45 percent of mid-cap funds, and 66.5 percent of small-cap funds. These managers fared even worse over three- and five-year time horizons.

Over a three-year period, 86.49 percent of large-cap funds were outperformed by their benchmark, as were 90.22 percent of mid-cap funds, and 82.76 percent of small-cap funds. Over five years, these

TABLE 3.1 SPIVA® Scorecard, Year-End 2012

Percentage of U.S. Equity Funds Outperformed by Benchmarks

Fund Category	Comparison Index	One Year (%)	Three Years (%)	Five Years (%)
All Large-Cap Funds	S&P 500	63.25%	86.49%	75.37%
All Mid-Cap Funds	S&P Mid Cap 400	80.45%	90.22%	90.03%
All Small-Cap Funds	S&P Small Cap 600	66.50%	83.05%	82.76%

TABLE 3.2 S&P Persistence Scorecard, July 2013

Performance Persistence over Three Consecutive 12-Month Periods

Fund Category	Fund Count at Start	Percentage Remaining in Top Quartile	
	March 2011	March 2012	March 2013
All Large-Cap Funds	269	30.11%	3.35%
All Mid-Cap Funds	102	29.41%	0.00%
All Small-Cap Funds	148	30.41%	6.08%

numbers were again very similar: 75.37 percent of large-cap fund managers were outperformed by their benchmark, 90.03 percent of mid-cap funds, and 82.76 percent of small-cap funds.

Additionally, we find it interesting to note that in the tumultuous investment environment we have seen over the past five years, 27 percent of domestic equity funds, 23 percent of international equity funds, and 18 percent of fixed-income funds have merged or been liquidated.

The most recent S&P Persistence Scorecard provides an even more insightful analysis (see Table 3.2). Among all capitalizations of domestic equity (large-mid-small), *best-in-class* portfolio managers experienced an extremely difficult time staying in the top 25 percent of their peer group in performance, over a three-year period. Of those that were in the top 25 percent in the 12 months ending in March 2011, by the 12 months ending in March 2013, nearly all of them failed to maintain any level of superiority: only 3.35 percent of large-cap managers were still in the top 25 percent after three years, 0 percent of mid-cap

TABLE 3.3   Average Fund Statistics for 36 Months Following Morningstar Rating (June 30, 1992–August 31, 2009)

Probability of Outperformance Three Years after the Morningstar Rating

	Five-Star Rating	Four-Star Rating	Three-Star Rating	Two-Star Rating	One-Star Rating
Average probability of positive excess returns	39.00%	37.00%	38.00%	39.00%	46.00%
Average excess returns	−1.32%	−1.26%	−1.00%	−0.67%	−0.04%

managers maintained their standing, and only 6.08 percent of small-cap managers were able to do so.

Taking into account the data provided in both the SPIVA Scorecard and Persistence Scorecard published by Standard & Poor's, it is painfully obvious that even top managers have a difficult time outperforming their benchmark and maintaining superiority among their peers. Our next logical question then should be, given these findings, does a four- or five-star rating by Morningstar make future outperformance any more likely? After all, don't investors typically demonstrate a proclivity toward purchasing those funds currently ranked in the top 25 percent of their peer group (which would typically be composed of four- and five-star funds)?

In a 2010 study conducted by Vanguard, "Mutual Fund Ratings and Future Performance" authors Philips and Kinniry seek to exploit the truth regarding whether or not more highly rated funds outperform lesser rated funds. What they discovered was that "an investor had less than a 50-50 shot of picking a fund that would outperform regardless of its rating at the time of the selection."

From this study it appears that underperformance over a three-year period from the point at which Morningstar provides its rating is likely (see Table 3.3). Further, this study illustrates that over this more than 17-year time period, the more highly rated funds lagged their respective benchmark more than lower rated funds. Additionally, Philips and Kinniry revealed that the ratings persistence of a given fund was unlikely to continue beyond a 12-month time frame, as shown in Figure 3.2.

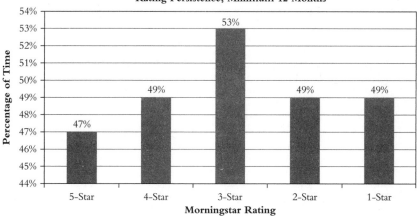

FIGURE 3.2 Morningstar Rating Persistence—Percentage of Time that a Stock Fund Maintained Its Rating for at Least 12 Months
Source: Vanguard.

When one factors all of the statistical analysis cited to this point, by both Standard & Poor's and Vanguard, it's no wonder the average investor has fallen short on their realized returns in the market. It appears to be a game in which the cards are stacked against us. With that said, what about the *guru* investors—those who possess an uncanny ability to outperform the markets? Can't we as investors simply rely on them? How can one argue their track record?

On the surface, this is a very difficult point to contest, but when you submerge yourself into finding the answer, what lies among the murky depths is a harsh reality investors would rather not know, or deny could ever exist. The truth is that even the best of traditionally equipped portfolio managers may experience sharp declines and years of laggard performance, considerably worse than their benchmark. When they do, the question is: what will it take to get back to even and how much risk will they take to make it back?

Recall that the more risk a manager takes relative to the markets (beta), the more they are likely to go up when they are right but the more they are likely to go down when they are wrong. Like a gambler doubling down in an attempt to get even, the losses can compound quickly, even for the *best*. As our industry ever so quietly whispers, "Past performance in not a guarantee of future results."

To illustrate this point, we are going to examine three prominent portfolio managers and mutual funds, who during their best years were thought to be unsinkable (kind of like the *Titanic*): Bill Miller (Legg Mason Value Trust), Ken Heebner (CGM Focus Fund), and Bruce Berkowitz (Fairholme Fund).

Manager: Bill Miller, Legg Mason Value Trust (LMTVX)

Within the mutual fund industry, in his heyday, Bill Miller was a god among men. As illustrated in Figure 3.3, for 15 consecutive years Mr. Miller managed to outperform the S&P 500 (from 1991 to 2005). According to Morningstar, the closest other fund managers have ever come to matching such a streak is 11 years of outperforming the market. Therefore, it should come as no surprise that we have elected to reflect on the stellar career and returns Bill Miller posted as the steward for the Legg Mason Value Trust Fund.

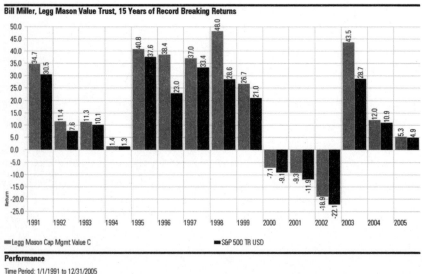

Performance						
Time Period: 1/1/1991 to 12/31/2005						
	Return	Std Dev	Alpha	Beta	Up Capture Ratio	Down Capture Ratio
Legg Mason Cap Mgmt Value C	16.44	17.95	3.57	1.18	124.66	112.24
S&P 500 TR USD	11.52	14.03	0.00	1.00	100.00	100.00

FIGURE 3.3 15 Years of Record-Breaking Returns, Statistical Analysis

Source: © 2014 Morningstar, Inc. All Rights Reserved. Reproduced with permission.

From 1991 to 2005, portfolio manager Bill Miller went on a spectacular run, unlike that which the investment markets have ever seen. For 15 years straight Mr. Miller outperformed the S&P 500, nearly doubling its returns for the period (see Figure 3.4). With an average annual return of 16.44 percent versus a respectable return of 11.52 percent for the S&P 500, a $100,000 investment in the Legg Mason Value Trust grew to nearly $1 million. Long-time investors were ecstatic, and many believed this streak would never end.

In 2006, when for the first time in 15 years the Legg Mason Value Trust failed to outperform the markets, it was regarded as a fluke. In that year the S&P 500 was up nearly 16 percent, while Mr. Miller's fund fell just shy of a 6 percent annual return. The vast majority of investors were confident their captain would right the ship and once again sail them into clear blue seas. But then, in 2007, with the markets up over 5 percent, the Legg Mason Value Trust posted a surprisingly negative return of nearly 7 percent. Investors began to worry, but most held steadfast in

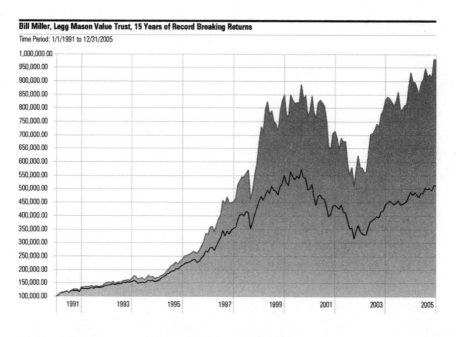

Bill Miller, Legg Mason Value Trust, 15 Years of Record Breaking Returns

Time Period: 1/1/1991 to 12/31/2005

—Legg Mason Cap Mgmt Value C   980,786.67   —S&P 500 TR USD   513,541.94

FIGURE 3.4 15 Years of Record-Breaking Returns, Growth $100,000

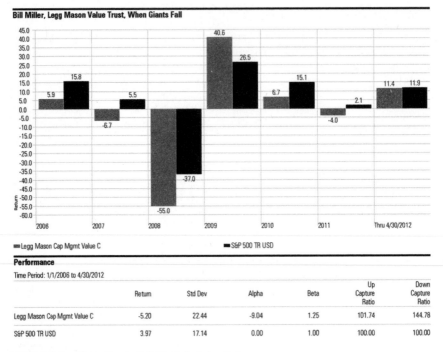

FIGURE 3.5 When Giants Fall, Statistical Analysis

Source: © 2014 Morningstar, Inc. All Rights Reserved. Reproduced with permission.

their convictions. And then it happened—the Great Recession of 2008. With the S&P 500 down a devastating 37 percent in a single calendar year, Bill Miller's flagship might as well have sunk to the bottom of the ocean, posting a stomach-churning decline of 55 percent (see Figure 3.5). From this point on, the Legg Mason Value Trust never recovered, and neither did Bill Miller. In April 2012, Mr. Miller stepped down as the portfolio manager of the Legg Mason Value Trust.

As shown in Figure 3.6, from 2006 until Mr. Miller's departure in April 2012, a $100,000 investment would have been reduced to little more than $71,000, while at the same time a $100,000 investment in the S&P 500 would have grown to nearly $128,000—a disparity of more than $56,000.

While the S&P 500 averaged a modest return of just 3.97 percent, the Legg Mason Value Trust posted average annual declines of 5.20 percent. As one might expect, the fund experienced overwhelming outflows, as investors simply bailed. It was a humbling end to an

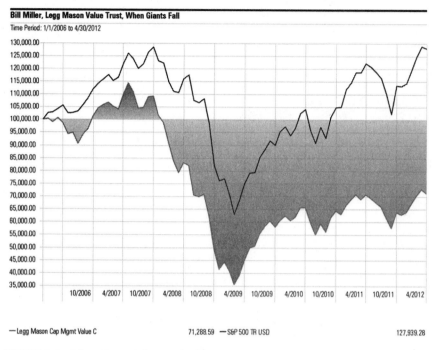

Bill Miller, Legg Mason Value Trust, When Giants Fall

Time Period: 1/1/2006 to 4/30/2012

—Legg Mason Cap Mgmt Value C 71,288.59 —S&P 500 TR USD 127,939.28

FIGURE 3.6 When Giants Fall, Growth of $100,000

Source: © 2014 Morningstar, Inc. All Rights Reserved. Reproduced with permission.

otherwise stellar and remarkable career as one of the greatest mutual fund portfolio managers the world has ever seen.

Manager: Ken Heebner, CGM Focus Fund (CGMFX)

Portfolio manager Ken Heebner founded Capital Growth Management in 1990 and has since experienced tremendous success. Highly regarded for his market savvy and uncanny ability to see what others simply cannot, for much of the past decade Mr. Heebner ranked as America's No. 1 stock picker. Like Warren Buffett, Mr. Heebner prides himself on not buying things that he doesn't understand. While other managers were crushed by the dot-com bubble, the CGM Focus Fund shined, and that was just the beginning of what proved to be a truly legendary run.

As illustrated in Figure 3.7, over an eight-year time span, what Ken Heebner achieved in the investment community was nothing short of miraculous, to the degree we are unsure if a run like this could ever

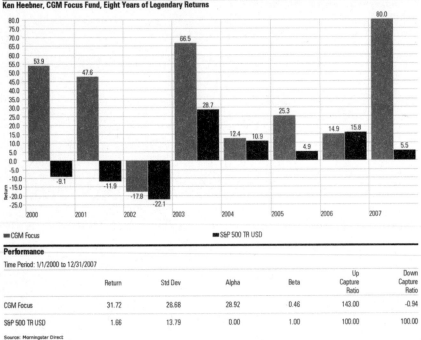

Performance

Time Period: 1/1/2000 to 12/31/2007

	Return	Std Dev	Alpha	Beta	Up Capture Ratio	Down Capture Ratio
CGM Focus	31.72	28.68	28.92	0.46	143.00	-0.94
S&P 500 TR USD	1.66	13.79	0.00	1.00	100.00	100.00

Source: Morningstar Direct

FIGURE 3.7 Eight Years of Legendary Returns, Statistical Analysis

Source: © 2014 Morningstar, Inc. All Rights Reserved. Reproduced with permission.

be equaled or surpassed. From the beginning of the decade through year-end 2007, the CGM Focus Fund averaged an eye-popping 31.72 percent annual rate of return! This level of return is wildly impressive in any environment, but during a period in which the S&P 500 barely managed to squeak out a positive rate of return—a paltry 1.66 percent average annual return—Heebner's performance was unheard of.

Heebner's Midas touch and ability to seemingly walk on water while others fell in lulled investors into blind romance and devotion. Can you blame them? As shown in Figure 3.8, a $100,000 investment at the beginning of the decade in the S&P 500 would have grown into a mere $114,000, while the same amount invested in the CGM Focus Fund would have compounded to nearly $906,000!

Like the immense burst of light and energy radiating from a supernova, at one point in time Heebner's glory shined brighter than the entire galaxy before suddenly, and without warning, his performance began to fade away. According to Charles Stein, in an article entitled

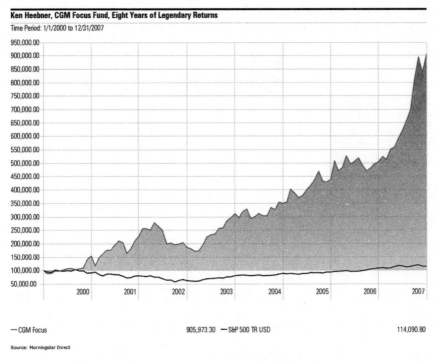

Ken Heebner, CGM Focus Fund, Eight Years of Legendary Returns

Time Period: 1/1/2000 to 12/31/2007

—CGM Focus   905,973.30 —S&P 500 TR USD   114,090.80

Source: Morningstar Direct

FIGURE 3.8 Eight Years of Legendary Returns, Growth of $100,000

Source: © 2014 Morningstar, Inc. All Rights Reserved. Reproduced with permission.

"Heebner at Bottom for Fourth Year in Five Sticks to Bet" published by Bloomberg on June 28, 2012:

> Heebner, whose CGM Focus Fund topped all diversified U.S. stock mutual funds in the decade through 2007, lost an annual average of 6.3 percent in the five years through June 26, trailing 96 percent of the same group, according to data compiled by Bloomberg. CGM Focus has been in the bottom 6 percent of the large-cap growth category every year since 2008, with the exception of 2010, when it beat 66 percent of peers.

After growing an investors capital at the turn of the decade from $100,000 to more than $900,000, after 2008, Heebner had nearly lost half of what he had made, down 48.2 percent on the year. When markets rebounded in 2009, up more than 26 percent, the CGM Focus Fund severely lagged, barely registering a double-digit return—up just 10.4 percent. Investors did not see it coming, nor did they get the

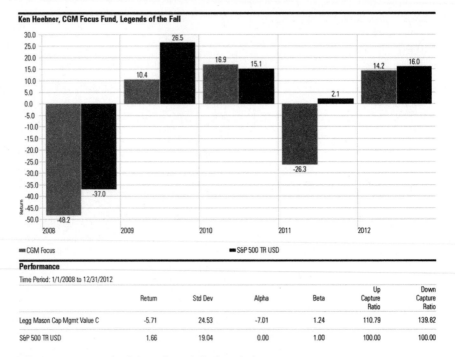

Ken Heebner, CGM Focus Fund, Legends of the Fall

■ CGM Focus   ■ S&P 500 TR USD

Performance

Time Period: 1/1/2008 to 12/31/2012

	Return	Std Dev	Alpha	Beta	Up Capture Ratio	Down Capture Ratio
Legg Mason Cap Mgmt Value C	-5.71	24.53	-7.01	1.24	110.79	139.82
S&P 500 TR USD	1.66	19.04	0.00	1.00	100.00	100.00

FIGURE 3.9   Legends of the Fall, Statistical Analysis

Source: © 2014 Morningstar, Inc. All Rights Reserved. Reproduced with permission.

bounce back they had come to expect. In 2010, Heebner managed to once again outperform the markets, up 16.9 percent versus a return of 15.1 percent for the S&P 500. Those investors who had managed to hang on up to this point began to regain a modicum of faith. And then in 2011, when the market registered a scant return of just 2.1 percent, Heebner was down an astonishing 26.3 percent, after which even the most devout supporters began to lose faith. During a time in which an investment in the S&P 500 managed to generate an average annual return of only 1.66 percent, the CGM Focus Fund averaged a −5.71 percent annual return (see Figure 3.9).

From the onset of 2008 until the end of 2012, a $100,000 investment in the S&P 500 had managed to regain what had been lost during the Great Recession, with a value by year-end 2012 of more than $108,000. A $100,000 investment in the CGM Focus Fund over this same time period was now worth little more than $56,000. In order to just get back to even, the CGM Focus Fund still required a return of 78.6 percent (see Figure 3.10).

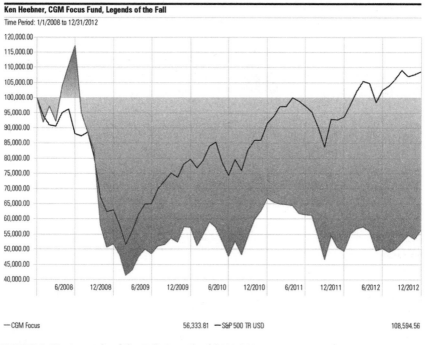

Ken Heebner, CGM Focus Fund, Legends of the Fall

Time Period: 1/1/2008 to 12/31/2012

| —CGM Focus | 56,333.81 —S&P 500 TR USD | 108,594.56 |

FIGURE 3.10   Legends of the Fall, Growth of $100,000

Manager: Bruce Berkowitz, Fairholme Fund (FAIRX)

In 2010, Morningstar named Bruce Berkowitz, portfolio manager for the Fairholme Fund, U.S. Stock Fund Manager of the Decade. Rightfully so, as Mr. Berkowitz managed to steer investors clear of the tech bubble burst, and also held up far better than the markets during the Great Recession. From the turn of the decade through the end of 2009, the S&P 500 produced an average annual return of −0.95 percent, prompting investors to refer to this period as "the lost decade." The lost decade? Not so much for investors in the Fairholme Fund, as they were rewarded with an average annual return of 13.21 percent throughout the period (see Figure 3.11).

Over the course of the decade an investment of $100,000 in the S&P 500 would have been reduced to less than $91,000, while this same investment in the Fairholme fund grew to just shy of $346,000! It was a phenomenal run, to be certain, and one absolutely deserving

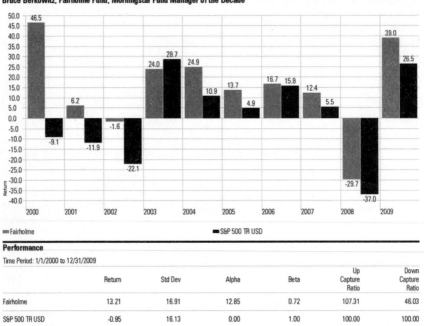

Bruce Berkowitz, Fairholme Fund, Morningstar Fund Manager of the Decade

Fairholme · S&P 500 TR USD

Performance

Time Period: 1/1/2000 to 12/31/2009

	Return	Std Dev	Alpha	Beta	Up Capture Ratio	Down Capture Ratio
Fairholme	13.21	16.91	12.85	0.72	107.31	46.03
S&P 500 TR USD	-0.95	16.13	0.00	1.00	100.00	100.00

FIGURE 3.11 Morningstar Fund Manager of the Decade, Statistical Analysis
Source: © 2014 Morningstar, Inc. All Rights Reserved. Reproduced with permission.

of Fund Manager of the Decade status, but more importantly what we can appreciate most is that during times of peril in the U.S. equity markets, the Fairholme Fund managed to stay afloat, demonstrating the true "win by losing less" mantra in which we so wholeheartedly believe (see Figure 3.12).

With all of the notoriety and acclaim that comes with being named Morningstar U.S. Stock Manager of the Decade, Bruce Berkowitz responded by leading the Fairholme Fund to an impressive gain in 2010. With the S&P 500 up more than 15 percent on the year, the Fairholme Fund easily bested the markets by more than 10 percent, with a highly respectable 25.5 percent gain for investors. And then, as we have seen with so many other highly respected managers, seemingly out of nowhere, the Fairholme Fund experienced its worst year of underperforming the markets in its history (see Figure 3.13).

The year 2011 was difficult for many investors, as the markets provided investors with what may generally be regarded as a rather whipsaw environment (thanks to an S&P downgrade of long-term U.S.

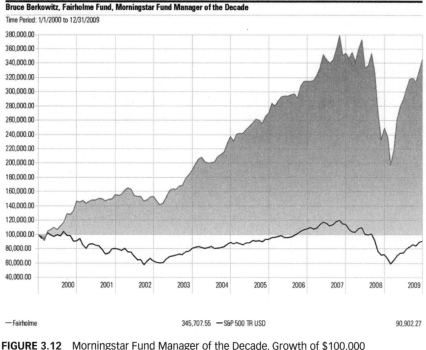

Bruce Berkowitz, Fairholme Fund, Morningstar Fund Manager of the Decade
Time Period: 1/1/2000 to 12/31/2009

—Fairholme   345,707.55 —S&P 500 TR USD   90,902.27

FIGURE 3.12 Morningstar Fund Manager of the Decade, Growth of $100,000
Source: © 2014 Morningstar, Inc. All Rights Reserved. Reproduced with permission.

debt, coupled with fears that the euro might break up). During this time, the markets managed to eke out a positive gain of 2.1 percent, while the Fairholme Fund was down a surprising 32.4 percent!

Since this one-year aberration in performance, the Fairholme Fund and Bruce Berkowitz have rebounded admirably. In nearly every period either before or after 2011, the Fairholme fund has significantly bettered the return of the S&P 500, or at least been very close. However, one year of outsized losses can have a significant impact on the long-term performance achieved by investors. Consider that since being recognized as Morningstar U.S. Stock Manager of the Decade, Berkowitz's Fairholme Fund has averaged a rather ordinary annual return of 8.38 percent, as compared to the considerably stronger return on the S&P 500 of 14.47 percent over the same period (from the beginning of 2010 until the end of the second quarter 2013).

Over this three-and-a-half year measurement period, a $100,000 investment in the S&P 500 would have compounded to slightly more

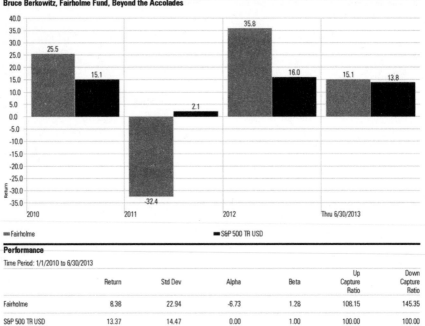

than $155,000. This same investment in the Fairholme Fund would have yielded a cumulative return of a little more than $132,000 (see Figure 3.14). While any positive return for investors should be regarded as a plus, and certainly we are not attempting to imply any sort of impending doom for Bruce Berkowitz and the Fairholme Fund, our point is very simple. Even the best of the best are not always right. Of course, they can't be. But when faced with outsized losses (in comparison to a given benchmark), investors often struggle for years to get back to even—if ever.

In the case of Bill Miller and Ken Heebner, surely investors have incurred a temporary, if not permanent, impairment of capital. When the unthinkable happens, any process that does not provide a discipline to reduce exposure to considerable declines becomes highly fallible; despite the Morningstar Rating of the fund or what the experiences of the portfolio manager may be. Unfortunately, the majority of investors often come in at the tail end of these historic runs, after they have received tremendous acclaim and attention.

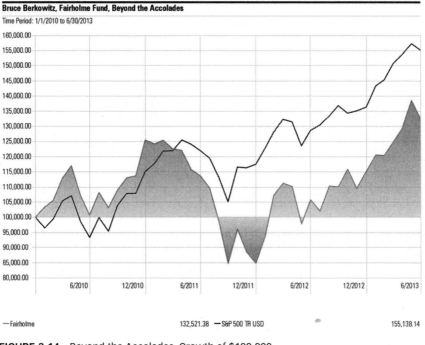

Bruce Berkowitz, Fairholme Fund, Beyond the Accolades

Time Period: 1/1/2010 to 6/30/2013

—Fairholme   132,521.38   — S&P 500 TR USD   155,138.14

FIGURE 3.14   Beyond the Accolades, Growth of $100,000

Source: © 2014 Morningstar, Inc. All Rights Reserved. Reproduced with permission.

THE BOTTOM LINE

The stars simply do not revolve around a stationary earth, nor should we as investors allow our investment decisions to revolve solely around the stars. Over the decades, Dalbar has continued to measure the investment performance of the individual investor versus the S&P 500, and the story never changes. While the overall rates of return may vary to a degree, the disparity by which the individual investor under-achieves does not.

Each of the managers highlighted in this chapter should be held in the highest esteem for what they have achieved in our industry. In many respects, their performances have been unparalleled. Each of these funds were five-star rated by Morningstar, and yet such an endorsement and such stellar track records have not prevented inves-tors from experiencing significant losses (as compared to their bench-mark). Depending on the fund, and dependent on the time in which an investor had money in the fund, investors have endured dramatic underperformance. And this is with the *best of the best!* Imagine how investors have fared with average or poor performing funds.

But that is just it—not only do investors face the outsized odds of purchasing the right fund at the right time, but they are also perennially at war with their emotions. If an investment is down more than others, investors are likely to sell it. Therefore, even if it does bounce back, they will miss it. In turn, they have entered into another investment whose prospects for a positive return may not be any better than the one they sold. Should they elect to move into an investment bearing less risk, they may very well find themselves locking in a permanent impairment of capital from which they will never recover. And around and around it goes.

In our humble opinion, the vast majority of investors are playing a game they don't even realize exists; they are trying to catch *shooting stars.* But if they were to take a step back and reflect on how often their picks or the managers they have picked to guide them on their way have been correct, they would be stunned.

The purpose of this chapter, along with all of the others, is to point out to our readers why the investment markets, and the processes by which the masses manage their investment portfolios, are set up to fail. Do they not see their repeated failures? Is their pride or ego too big to concede? Or do they believe they have some unforeseen and rare talent to predict the future and know how to position themselves accordingly? Haven't we all been wrong on that enough? At this point, investors should take a cold hard look in the mirror and face reality.

Among dedicated asset classes, active managers continually fail to add value with any measure of consistency. So why keep trying to win the game? It is like trying to solve the world's largest and greatest ever Rubik's cube. You can clearly see the colors, and have no discernible problem twisting it all around, occasionally aligning a string of colors; but with all of the variables involved, one simply cannot expect to wrap their head around how they all fit together. Successful investing requires far more discipline.

CHAPTER 4

———

BEYOND THE STARS

Suggestions for Investment Selection Criteria

Born some 20 years after the death of Nicolaus Copernicus, Galileo Galilei devoted a lifetime to championing the Copernican views of a heliocentric universe. Widely regarded as the father of modern astronomy, Galileo was the first to use the telescope to study the heavens. What Copernicus had theorized, Galileo proved, though at the time, these views were not widely accepted. Rather, the notion of a sun-centered universe was wildly controversial, so much so that Galileo later found himself at the center of the Roman Inquisition. He was found guilty of heresy, forced to recant, and spent the remainder of his life under house arrest.

What Galileo observed, through what by today's standards would be viewed as a crude telescope, rocked the very foundations of Aristotle's universe and the theological and philosophical worldview that it supported. Pointing his looking glass to the stars, Galileo discovered craters on the moon, sunspots, the phases of Venus, and the moons of Jupiter. Church officials refused to look through his telescope, believing the devil himself was capable of making anything appear, and surely this was his doing.

The investment world as we know it refuses to look at that which clearly lies in front of them; the *philosophical worldview* of how to navigate the capital markets, mitigate risk, and achieve investment success simply does not work. Time and time again, this has been proven, by manager after manager and fund after fund, and yet it strikes us that no one seems to notice. How can one expect to arrive at a different conclusion, one predicated on achieving strong risk–adjusted returns, if they themselves take the same approach as those whom have repeatedly failed? This is where one needs to step outside of themselves and all that they think they know, and begin anew.

The human condition is not wired for successful investing. We relish our triumphs and yet fail to admit our faults. To recognize our own investment failures is painful. So rather than reflect on them, assess what went wrong, and move forward with a more ironclad battle plan, the majority of investors will simply pretend they never happened.

The most poignant example of such behavior is often on display when the average retail investor delves into purchasing individual stocks. This is where we frequently see highly irrational behavior, akin to the riverboat gambler. After all, who wouldn't like to discover the next Google or Intuitive Surgical (pioneers in robotic surgery), or to have had the foresight to buy Apple (instead of Microsoft) early on after the tech bubble burst for $10, or more recently Ford stock for $1?

With stories of great fortunes made by those placing outsized bets on such speculative stock purchases, the opportunity can be intoxicating. For good measure there appears to be no shortage of analysts, columnists, friends, and neighbors alike, providing us with salient reasons for unbridled enthusiasm. Such arguments often appear sound and highly logical at the time, but unfortunately this often does not increase the likelihood of success. Let us give an example:

In September 2007, when last the markets were encroaching upon all-time highs (just before the markets crashed), *Fortune* magazine's senior editor, Alex Taylor III, published an exceedingly bullish article on General Motors entitled "Is GM a Growth Stock Again?" At the time, shares of GM were trading around $32. In the article, Taylor presented the case for GM to rise to an estimated $57 per share.

Nearly one year later, in June 2008, *Barron's* published a cover story entitled simply "Buy GM," complete with a picture of their new electric car, the Volt. The article was trumpeting GM as *value* stock. With a current price of $17, author Vita Racanelli stated the case for GM to rise to "at least $30 and maybe as much as $45."

About a year after that, in late May 2009, *CNN Money* posted an article on its web site entitled "GM Stock Falls Below $1," documented as part of its "Special Report on Detroit's Downfall." I think we all know where this story ends.

A few days later, on June 8, 2009, General Motors filed for Chapter 11 bankruptcy. GM shares that once traded as high as $93 in April 2000 were now worthless. As shares of the automaker encountered a decade-long slide, devout shareholders added to their positions. GM employees loaded up their 401(k)s with company stock. As the value of the shares continued to drop, articles such as the ones cited here provided a catalyst for new investors to buy in. Little did anyone know at the time that they were catching a falling knife.

We were born, raised in, and continue to call Metropolitan Detroit our home. As such, we have known a great many wonderful people who have made the automotive industry their life's work. The fall of the automotive industry was both gut churning and painfully obvious. The aftermath has forever changed our community.

To our point, living around Metro Detroit and working in the financial industry provided us with a unique perspective on investor behavior at the time. We cannot begin to tell you how many conversations we had with clients, coworkers, and friends regarding whether they should buy GM stock. Not once did we solicit purchasing the shares, but a great many elected to do so of their own accord.

What we so clearly learned during this period is that investors do not have discipline. Investor actions at the time were highly driven by greed. Sensational headlines promising otherworldly returns and the allure of buying a stock that was once worth more than $90 created a pandemic of misfortune.

So when we make reference to investor behavior with respect to risk, we are talking about not only mutual funds, but also investors delving into the foray of individual stocks, where losses can mount far more quickly and we often see investors jump from one stock to another in an attempt to make up their losses, each time placing increasingly more speculative bets. As one might imagine, things can get rather ugly in a very short amount of time.

We recognize that such behavior does not apply to *all* investors, but likely the majority, and certainly the average. Whether we are talking about investors chasing highly rated funds with red-hot performance, or investors in individual stocks, investors at large seem to us to be prone to the temptations of trying to outperform a rising market (or, worse yet, chasing a falling one). There is always someone out there pounding their chest that they are up considerably more than the market—like it is something to brag about at a cocktail party or in intimate conversations with friends. They'll be quick to regale you with their triumphs, and yet fail to share with you their failures.

In an attempt to beat the market, investors often elect to take on exceedingly more risk. If an investor is wrong, they will likely lose more. If you lose too much more, you end up in hole too deep to climb out of. It is a perilous approach and an emotional roller coaster, to say the least. And as we have already expressed, most of us are not wired to hold on when it gets rough. Rather, we pull the eject handle, locking in our losses. But then again, how is an investor supposed to tell the difference between a stock trading at a discounted price and one that is headed to zero?

In the context of this chapter, we will provide some suggestions for investment criteria. Among our suggestions, we will discuss cost, risk, and the overall role the investment environment can play on performance and your decision making. Our focus will be on mutual fund investing and analysis, as mutual funds continue to be the preferred investment vehicle of choice (we will discuss the proliferation of exchange-traded funds in upcoming chapters).

THE COST OF INVESTING

The concept of cost with regard to investing is a rather simple one; the more you pay, the greater the erosion on your returns and the better your investment selection acumen needs to be. High costs plague both mutual fund investors and individual stock investors, although it is not always transparent. Mutual funds embed their costs into what investors see as their net performance (in other words, they don't really see all the fees), whereas investors in individual stocks are likely to pay commissions for trades.

For individual stock investors, there are really only two factors to consider with respect to cost: the frequency of trading and the cost per trade. For those taking a *do-it-yourself* approach, or in any case that pays on a per-trade basis, there are a number of low-cost options. Having traded extensively with Charles Schwab, TD Ameritrade, and Fidelity, we can tell you they all have their strengths and weaknesses. But generally, if an investor is willing to sign up for paperless delivery of proxies, prospectuses, trade confirmations, and the like, the most they should pay per trade is $10. If an investor is not willing to enter the paperless world, costs can be nearly twice as high. However, we should note, for those investors truly employing a do-it-yourself approach, one should do so with extreme caution; like going to the beach, knowing you can't swim, and seeing a sign that says, "Warning, no lifeguard on duty"—you'd better think twice before getting in too deep.

More and more over the years we have seen investors who work with financial advisers enter into *wrap fee* agreements, where regardless of the number or size of the trades, there is a flat fee covering all activity. This fee is generally based on a percentage of assets under management (AUM). For example, a 1 percent fee on a $100,000 account would pay annual commissions of $1,000. Should the account go down in value, the adviser will get paid less; if it goes up, they will get paid more. Depending on the services provided by the financial adviser, these costs could be higher, as these fees often serve as an all-in-one charge incorporating the drafting and monitoring of a personal financial plan, assistance with estate planning, quarterly calls, client meetings, and so on.

For investors working with an adviser, this is a far better structure than simply paying by the trade. Before wrap accounts became commonplace in the industry, investors would pay commissions on a per-trade basis. These fees were often relatively high, and they also provided incentive for the broker to generate activity, whether it was necessary or not. This meant that while investors might suffer significant losses during more difficult times in the market, their broker could actually often make more. When an account is going down, a client wants to feel like there is something being done about it. Therefore, not only are clients driven by fears that their holdings will lose even more, but they are also comforted by moving into something else with supposedly better prospects for growth. That mix can be pretty lucrative for a broker but not such a good deal for the investor.

Beyond the fees paid to a financial adviser for their counsel, or fees paid for trading commissions, certain investment vehicles have additional costs. Some of these costs you might see; others you will not.

The mutual fund industry is notorious for its lack of transparency, with respect to its underlying holdings and also in regards to the visibility of their fees. Even though fees may be disclosed, investors are inundated with so many required shareholder communications that they don't bother to read them; and even if they did, they might need a securities law attorney sitting next to them to explain what the heck it all means.

As cited in our previous chapter, the odds of a mutual fund outperforming its given benchmark over time are very low. It should be common sense that the higher the internal fees are for a specific mutual fund, the greater outperformance has to be in order to overcome these fees, thus decreasing the likelihood of outperformance even further.

In "How Expense Ratios and Star Ratings Predict Success," a 2010 report issued by Morningstar and written by Director of Mutual Fund Research, Russel Kinnel, the industry leader in mutual fund research released some rather humbling findings. In the report, Mr. Kinnel set out to compare the efficacy of both expense ratios of mutual funds and their assigned star rating at the time of purchase, as a predictor of future returns; five-star-rated funds were pitted against one-star funds. While five-star funds generally outperformed their one-star brethren, the primary predictor of future returns was lower internal expense ratios. As Kinnel stated, "How often did it pay to heed expense ratios? Every time. How often did it pay to heed the star rating? Most of the time." Kinnel goes on further to say:

> If there is anything in the whole world of mutual funds that you can take to the bank, it's that expense ratios help you make a better decision. In every single time period and data point tested, low cost funds beat high cost funds.
>
> Expense ratios are strong predictors of performance. In every asset class over every time period, the cheapest quintile produced higher total returns than the most expensive quintile.
>
> Investors should make expense ratios a primary test in fund selection. They are still the most dependable predictor of performance.

Considering the source, we view these to be strong words, particularly highlighting that cost is a much better predictor of future performance than star ratings! It is refreshing to see such objectivity.

Much has been written over the years regarding the high cost of mutual funds. Some have even suggested that investors should utilize only index funds, those tracking specific indices such as the S&P 500, or Barclays Aggregate Bond Index, to which Jack Bogle, the founder of indexing fund giant Vanguard, has long argued that even before costs, mutual funds will collectively deliver the market's average return. Thus, the best way to capture above-average returns is to buy funds with the lowest possible expense ratio. Anything else is essentially luck.

We agree with these points, as our own personal research and experiences have also proved this to be true. At one point in time, we owned both the Janus 40 and Hartford Capital Appreciation mutual funds. We caught them at the tail end of their stellar performance, just in time to experience their fall from grace, as both went on to endure prolonged periods of underperformance.

When you consider cost, the high probability of underperformance, and the additional risks of enduring significantly larger declines than the benchmark, indexing just makes sense. With that said, we would expect that the arguments both for and against active management of mutual funds are sure to continue on into the foreseeable future. Investors just cannot seem to resist falling for the track records of star managers and star ratings; after all, an index fund will never rank higher than average, but it may just provide you with a smoother ride (relatively speaking).

Since we have already made reference to a handful of best-in-class managers, we have provided further analysis on the recent costs incurred by investors in these particular mutual funds. Note the exceptionally lower cost of the Vanguard Total Stock Index versus our trifecta of flagship funds in Table 4.1.

PersonalFund.com provides investors with a great resource to determine the true cost of ownership of a mutual fund. On this web site, investors can register for a free trial, during which they can simply type in the ticker symbols for their favorite funds and discover what is otherwise veiled behind the curtain of our industry.

In addition to evaluating costs, it also interesting to note the performance of these actively managed funds versus a Vanguard passive index fund from 2008 to 2012, as illustrated in Figure 4.1. While this performance comparison may not seem fair, since we now know what a difficult period of time this was for the performance of these flagship funds, the reality is these were all five-star-rated funds at the beginning of the period, and investor confidence in these funds was at or near an all-time high, meaning these funds are likely what investors were buying at the time.

TABLE 4.1   Evaluating Mutual Fund Expenses

Fund	Ticker	Manager	Transaction Costs	Management Fee	Distribution Fee	Total Fund Cost
CGM Focus Fund	CGMFX	Ken Heebner	4.46%	1.33%	0.00%	5.79%
Legg Mason Value Trust	LMVTX	Peters/Yu★	0.50%	0.98%	1.11%	2.59%
Fairholme Fund	FAIRX	Bruce Berkowitz	0.02%	1.18%	0.00%	1.20%
Vanguard Total Stock Market	VITSX	Index	0.04%	0.02%	0.03%	0.08%

*Peters/Yu succeeded Bill Miller as portfolio managers for the Legg Mason Value Trust in April 2012.
The Total Cost of Ownership, as reported by www.personalfund.com, trailing 12 mos. Ending 7/31/2013

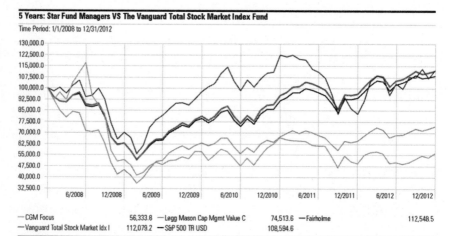

5 Years: Star Fund Managers VS The Vanguard Total Stock Market Index Fund

Time Period: 1/1/2008 to 12/31/2012

—CGM Focus	56,333.8	—Legg Mason Cap Mgmt Value C	74,513.6	—Fairholme	112,548.5
—Vanguard Total Stock Market Idx I	112,079.2	—S&P 500 TR USD	108,594.6		

Performance

Time Period: 01/01/2008 to 12/31/2012

	Return	Std Dev	Alpha	Beta	Up Capture Ratio	Down Capture Ratio
CGM Focus	-10.84	29.74	-11.06	1.25	100.92	151.24
Legg Mason Cap Mgmt Value C	-5.71	24.53	-7.01	1.24	110.79	139.82
Fairholme	2.39	26.53	1.83	1.18	121.11	118.56
Vanguard Total Stock Market Idx I	2.31	19.73	0.66	1.03	105.94	103.59
S&P 500 TR USD	1.66	19.04	0.00	1.00	100.00	100.00

FIGURE 4.1   Active vs. Passive, Growth of $100,000

Source: © 2014 Morningstar, Inc. All Rights Reserved. Reproduced with permission.

Over this five-year period, of the funds selected, only the Fairholme Fund outperformed the Vanguard Total Stock Index. However, it should be noted that it did so only marginally and with more risk, with a standard deviation of 26 percent versus 19 percent, and a beta of 1.18 versus 1.03.

However, if an investor were to have begun their investment in the Fairholme Fund in 2011, one year after portfolio manager Bruce Berkowitz was named Morningstar U.S. Stock Fund Manager of the Decade, their performance would not have been so favorable. After going down considerably less than the S&P 500 in 2008, going up considerably more than the benchmark in 2009, and again besting it by more than 10 percent in 2010, investors were feeling highly confident. But in 2011, with the S&P 500 eking out marginal gains of 2.1 percent, the Fairholme Fund was down 32.4 percent (see Figure 4.2), once again reiterating the outsized risks investors take in selecting even

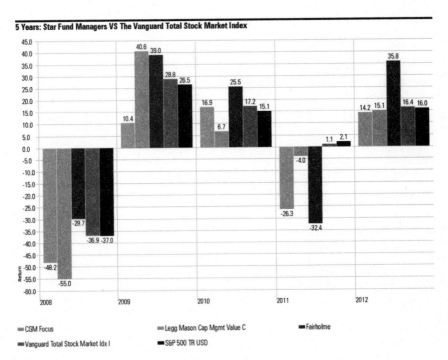

FIGURE 4.2   Active vs. Passive, Calendar-Year Returns

best-in-class managers. When one experiences an unexpected drop, disproportionate to the overall market environment, getting back to even can prove exceedingly difficult at best.

For mutual fund investors seeking to fulfill a traditional asset allocation with conventional buy-and-hold-style box funds, indexing appears to provide the most cost efficient and consistent approach. The additional expenses of actively managed funds in these categories make it far more difficult for an investor to achieve superior returns. The inconsistency of performance and the uncertainty surrounding when a manager will outperform further decrease the likelihood for success. For those employing a traditional Modern Portfolio Theory (MPT) asset allocation approach, indexing is a step in the right direction. However, we don't believe this to be the *most* practical use of indices, but we will elaborate more on that later.

IDENTIFYING RISK

Determining the risks inherent in any investment is exceptionally difficult. It always has been. If not, more people would obviously be successful. But this becomes increasingly more difficult entering a world where fixed income may no longer be viewed as safe. Anyone today using historical metrics calculated by assessing the performance of bonds in recent years is missing what should now be blatantly obvious to us all: the paradigm has shifted.

Unfortunately, there is no clear-cut, singular process for determining the risks borne in a potential investment. Therefore, one needs to take a more holistic approach, incorporating a number of measurables in an attempt to develop a clearer picture. But perhaps the most critical component in determining risk begins with self-reflection.

The concept of first assessing one's individual set of circumstances before engaging in the investment process is nothing new. This is after all the foundation of any sound financial plan. With that said, far too often investors enter into the investment arena as if it were the Wild, Wild West, with just the right mix of bravado and naivety to wind up with a bullet in their head.

When considering any investment, the first question an investor should ask themselves is "what can I afford to lose?" And then follow that up with a rather clinical, "and how do I feel about that?" This may sound elementary, but first and foremost an individual needs to begin by assessing their own personal risks: when do I need the money, what is the purpose, how much can I emotionally stand to watch the return vacillate, and so on.

Once an investor has completed an open and honest self-reflection, they can begin to dive into a litany of quantitative securities analysis. For an elaborate explanation of industry jargon and arcane usage of statistical measures that even savvy industry veterans don't know the meaning of (with words like *kurtosis, Sortino, Treynor, Calmar, calamari, mitosis*, etc.), you may kindly look elsewhere. If you were unable to recognize which of these words were real statistical measures and which were not, the only thing you have to worry about is eating more seafood and the fact that you don't recall anything from high school biology, both of which should not bother you to any large degree (unless you are a marine biologist).

We do not make it our business to overcomplicate the world; rather, we do our best to refine what we are looking for into the simplest possible terms. After all, overanalysis leads to investment paralysis, which leads to greater frustrations, and ultimately less enjoyment and fulfillment of life's riches; we'll leave that to others far smarter than us to calculate, extrapolate, pontificate, and espouse upon.

With that said, and our tongue firmly removed from our cheek, there are a handful of statistical measures that we believe an investor should be familiar with: beta, standard deviation, alpha, drawdown, up capture, down capture, Sharpe ratio, and correlation. It may sound like a mouthful if you are not familiar with these concepts, but rest assured, this will not be too painful.

Rather than provide our readers with a denotative definition of each of these terms, below we have provided a more rudimentary explanation of these metrics, how we feel they should be viewed, and why they are important:

- *Beta.* Beta is a relative measure of risk, comparing one investment to another. The overall market (i.e., the S&P 500) has a beta of 1. Any number lower than 1 indicates that an investment is less risky than the market; any measure greater than 1 may be considered riskier than the market. To put this into perspective, an investment with a beta of 0.6 when compared the market may be said to take 40 percent less risk.

When following a simple buy and hold strategy with an S&P 500 index fund, an investor can expect a beta of almost exactly 1. When an investor selects an investment that is actively managed, or when utilizing an index fund that weights holdings differently than the S&P 500, you will likely get a beta of either more or less than 1. When purchasing a fund with a beta greater than 1 and doing so at the wrong time, an investor will likely lose more money. Conversely, when purchasing a fund with a beta that is lower than 1, an investor is likely to lose less. It should therefore go without saying, noting our affinity for losing less, we very much prefer investments with a beta of lower than 1 (for buy and hold purposes anyway).

- *Standard deviation.* Standard deviation is simply a measure of how volatile an investment is around an average rate of return. For example, if a mutual fund has a five-year average annual rate of return of 10 percent and the fund has a standard deviation of 15, investors over this time period could have expected annual returns to generally fall within a range of −5 percent to +25 percent. Statistically, nearly 70 percent of the time, returns will fall within this range.

  The more volatile an investment is, the greater the chance an investor is going to buy it at the wrong time. Therefore, investors tend to look down on investments with relatively higher standard deviations, categorizing them as more risky. While generally this should be regarded as true, investors need to keep in mind this is all relative to the mean return. If we have an investment with an average annual return of 20 percent that has a standard deviation of 15 (implying a return range from 5 to 35 percent), and another investment with an average annual return of −10 percent and a standard deviation of 10 (implying a return range of 0 to −20 percent), obviously, an investor would prefer the positive rate of return versus the negative. The fact that the standard deviation is lower does not mean that investment bears less risk. In this case, standard deviation does not tell the whole story, but it should be a consideration, and one that investors know how to put into context.

- *Alpha.* Alpha is a measure of risk-adjusted value added by a portfolio manager or by an index fund weighting that is dissimilar from the benchmark. A positive value indicates that the portfolio manager or alternate weighting of the index has provided value. A negative value means they have underperformed and failed to add value.

  Alpha is a good way of simply answering "did this investment do well on a risk-adjusted basis?" In other words, were investors rewarded for the degree of risk taken?
- *Correlation.* Correlation is very simply a measurement of how similarly one investment behaves in relation to another. A correlation of 1 indicates the investments are highly correlated. If a correlation is less than 1, it is said to be less correlated. For example, if a mutual fund had a correlation of 0.9 to the S&P 500, this can basically be interpreted as saying it has a 90 percent correlation to the movements of the market. If an investment has a correlation of only 0.1 to the S&P 500, this would be regarded as having a very low correlation. If there is a rare negative correlation, this implies that the two investments are inversely related, meaning when one goes up, the other can often be expected to go down.

  Great attention should be paid to correlations when constructing an overall portfolio, particularly when constructing a rotational strategy, as will be addressed in the later chapters of this book.
- *Max drawdown.* Max drawdown is a measure of how much a security declined from peak to trough during a given period of time. Typically, when denoted in statistical analysis, these declines are measured on a monthly basis.

  Max drawdown is a very crude measure of risk, but during critical periods of market duress, it is a very blunt way to see how well one investment has held up versus another.
- *Up capture and down capture.* Up capture and down capture is simply a way of statistically illustrating the percentage in which a given investment has participated in both the upside and downside of the investment performance of another. The up capture and down capture of the benchmark is always 100. If an investment has an up capture of 80, it should be regarded as generally participating in 80 percent of the upside of the market over a

given period. Likewise, an investment with a down capture of 50 should then be considered to have participated in approximately only 50 percent of the downside of the market.

Both up capture and down capture can provide useful insight to investors. As stated previously, the most appropriate investments are often those that reasonably participate in rising markets, but more importantly have a strong history of preserving in falling markets. Remember, you don't have to capture all of the upside to win.

- *Sharpe ratio.* The Sharpe ratio is another measure of risk-adjusted performance. Unlike alpha, this performance metric factors in the investment's standard deviation as an element of risk. Ultimately, the Sharpe ratio indicates whether a portfolio's returns are due to good investment decisions or a result of taking on excess risk.

When comparing two investments, the preferred investment should be the one with the higher Sharpe ratio.

Collectively, these statistical measures provide investors with a reasonable gauge to begin to assess the fundamental risks borne by a given investment. As stated in prior chapters, we firmly believe investors to be best served by focusing their investable dollars on investments which present *less* risk on a relative basis, not *more*—to focus on *winning by losing less*. Losing less during periods of market duress provides investors with a more manageable discipline.

As illustrated in Table 1.1, "It Pays to Lose Less" (see Chapter 1), investment losses are compounded such that the further you go down, the more it will take to make it back to even. If an investor is down 10 percent, they need to achieve only an 11 percent rate of return to get back to even. While not painless, certainly in the world of investing this is very doable, whereas an investor losing 50 percent has to go up 100 percent to get back to even. This we do not believe is very doable, as not only will an investor's fears tempt them to sell at the worst possible time, they may also compound losses further by moving into a more speculative investment with supposedly greater return potential (thus taking on perhaps even more downside risk), or sell and go into a more conservative vehicle, essentially locking in their losses.

Seeing as investors are not hard wired for rational investment behavior, constructing a portfolio that is not necessarily focused on capturing all of the upside, but more importantly on dramatically reducing the downside, gives an investors a far better chance of achieving long-term success. This also gives them a discipline their stomach can more easily manage, that is, if they can avoid the temptations of greed and envy that are innate when others are achieving greater returns in rising markets.

Following is an illustration of two lower risk market indices versus the S&P 500, from 2008 to 2012:

> *Morningstar Dividend Yield Focus Index.* This is a proprietary index compiled by Morningstar. According to Morningstar, "The Morningstar Dividend Yield Focus Index offers exposure to high quality U.S. domiciled companies with strong financial health and an ability to sustain above average dividend payouts. The index consists of 75 stocks that are weighted in proportion to the total pool of dividends available to investors." Morningstar began publishing performance of this index in June of 2005. In March 2011, iShares launched an exchange-traded fund (ETF) based on this index: the iShares High Dividend ETF (ticker: HDV).
>
> *S&P High Yield Dividend Aristocrat Index.* According to Standard & Poors, "The S&P High Yield Dividend Aristocrat Index is designed to measure the performance of companies within the S&P Composite 1500 that have followed a managed-dividends policy of consistently increasing dividends every year for at least 20 years." S&P began publishing performance data on this index in December 1999. In November 2005, State Street launched an ETF based on this index: the SPDR S&P Dividend ETF (ticker: SDY).

This five-year period encapsulated both the Great Recession of 2008 and the tremendous bull run in stocks we have seen since the market bottomed in March 2009. As illustrated in Figure 4.3, at different points during this period, both market beta investments (such as the S&P 500 Index) and low beta indices such as the Morningstar Dividend Yield Focus Index and the S&P High Yield Dividend Aristocrat Index experienced periods of outperformance. However, over this full five-year period, our two examples of lower risk investments fared far better. Statistically, both indices exuded the performance characteristics we like to see: with relatively low betas, higher alphas, smaller

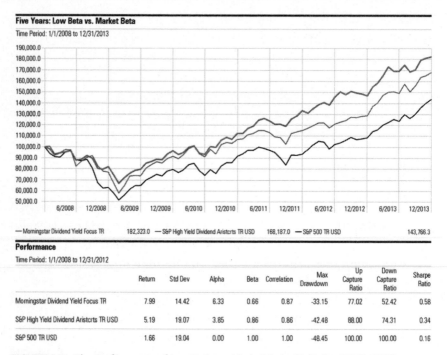

Five Years: Low Beta vs. Market Beta

Time Period: 1/1/2008 to 12/31/2013

| — Morningstar Dividend Yield Focus TR | 182,323.0 | — S&P High Yield Dividend Aristcrts TR USD | 168,187.0 | — S&P 500 TR USD | 143,766.3 |

Performance

Time Period: 1/1/2008 to 12/31/2012

	Return	Std Dev	Alpha	Beta	Correlation	Max Drawdown	Up Capture Ratio	Down Capture Ratio	Sharpe Ratio
Morningstar Dividend Yield Focus TR	7.99	14.42	6.33	0.66	0.87	-33.15	77.02	52.42	0.58
S&P High Yield Dividend Aristcrts TR USD	5.19	19.07	3.85	0.86	0.86	-42.48	88.00	74.31	0.34
S&P 500 TR USD	1.66	19.04	0.00	1.00	1.00	-48.45	100.00	100.00	0.16

FIGURE 4.3   The Performance of Low Beta vs. Market Beta, Statistics (2008–2012)

Source: © 2014 Morningstar, Inc. All Rights Reserved. Reproduced with permission.

max drawdowns, respectable upside participation, but most important, significantly less downside participation.

Beyond any statistical metrics, when you look at the calendar year returns of each of these indices over the period it is easy to see that the lower-beta investments provided a much smoother ride. But, as stated previously, this is where investors require patience and understanding that outperformance is atypical in a strong rising market; this was evident in both 2009 and 2012 (see Figure 4.4).

As shown in Figure 4.5, 2008 was the worst calendar year return in the U.S. equity markets since 1931, with the S&P 500 down 37 percent. During this time, both our lower-beta indices maintained their lower risk profiles: again with low betas, high alphas, smaller max drawdowns, favorable upside participation, but more important, with down capture ratios of less than 60 percent! This enabled these investments to recover far more quickly than investors in the S&P 500.

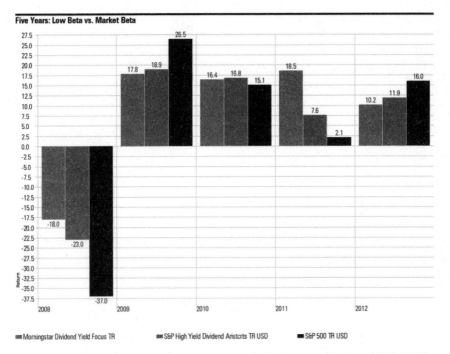

FIGURE 4.4 The Performance of Low Beta vs. Market Beta, Annual Returns (2008–2012)

Source: © 2014 Morningstar, Inc. All Rights Reserved. Reproduced with permission.

The year 2011 was another difficult year for investors. In August, Standard & Poor's announced they were reducing their credit rating of long-term U.S. Treasury bonds. It was a shot across the bow for our federal government, and it rattled the confidence of many investors, as they considered what it might mean for the long-term viability of the United States as the world's leading economy. At the same time, there were widespread concerns and rumors spreading regarding the sustainability of the European Union (EU) and the euro itself as a multination currency.

With the Greek economy spiraling, the EU desperately grasping for solutions, and the United States seemingly running the printing press dry, investor confidence was severely waning, and the two-year-plus rally in equities was in jeopardy. By year-end, nearly all foreign markets posted negative calendar year returns, and yet, surprisingly, the U.S. equity markets managed to barely register a positive return, up 2.11 percent on the year, due in large part to a nearly 11 percent return in

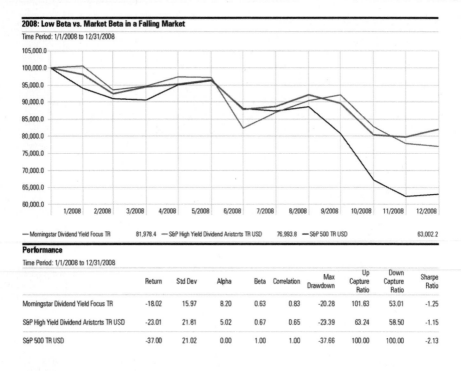

2008: Low Beta vs. Market Beta in a Falling Market

Time Period: 1/1/2008 to 12/31/2008

— Morningstar Dividend Yield Focus TR   81,978.4 — S&P High Yield Dividend Aristocrts TR USD   76,993.8 — S&P 500 TR USD   63,002.2

Performance

Time Period: 1/1/2008 to 12/31/2008

	Return	Std Dev	Alpha	Beta	Correlation	Max Drawdown	Up Capture Ratio	Down Capture Ratio	Sharpe Ratio
Morningstar Dividend Yield Focus TR	-18.02	15.97	8.20	0.63	0.83	-20.28	101.63	53.01	-1.25
S&P High Yield Dividend Aristocrts TR USD	-23.01	21.81	5.02	0.67	0.65	-23.39	63.24	58.50	-1.15
S&P 500 TR USD	-37.00	21.02	0.00	1.00	1.00	-37.66	100.00	100.00	-2.13

FIGURE 4.5   Low Beta vs. Market Beta—The Great Recession (2008)

Source: © 2014 Morningstar, Inc. All Rights Reserved. Reproduced with permission.

the month of October (accounting for the largest one-month return in the U.S. equity markets since December 1991). Not counting dividends, the S&P 500 posted a rather eerie return of 0.00 percent.

While this whipsaw environment wreaked havoc on investor psyche and led to a great number of active managers having terrible years, our low-risk indices once again proved their merit. The Morningstar Dividend Yield Focus Index in particular achieved stellar returns: up more than 18 percent, with a beta of only 0.44, an alpha of 16, a max drawdown of only 5 percent, and a down capture of only 12 percent (see Figure 4.6).

Granted, these are historical measures and therefore, when the *paradigm* shifts, may provide investors with false hope. Neither low cost nor statistical analysis is enough on its own to merit the decision of purchasing an investment. This is where investors need to take things a step further and assess the context of the returns. In what market environment were they generated? Can this environment be expected to continue?

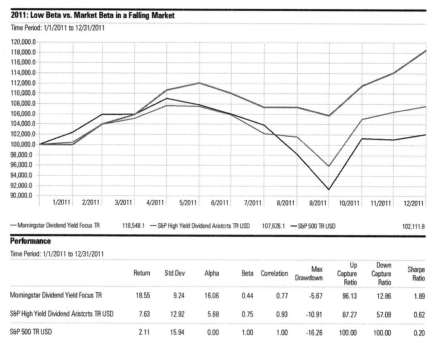

2011: Low Beta vs. Market Beta in a Falling Market

Time Period: 1/1/2011 to 12/31/2011

—Morningstar Dividend Yield Focus TR			118,548.1	—S&P High Yield Dividend Aristcrts TR USD			107,626.1	—S&P 500 TR USD			102,111.8

Performance

Time Period: 1/1/2011 to 12/31/2011

	Return	Std Dev	Alpha	Beta	Correlation	Max Drawdown	Up Capture Ratio	Down Capture Ratio	Sharpe Ratio
Morningstar Dividend Yield Focus TR	18.55	9.24	16.06	0.44	0.77	-5.67	96.13	12.86	1.89
S&P High Yield Dividend Aristcrts TR USD	7.63	12.92	5.68	0.75	0.93	-10.91	87.27	57.09	0.62
S&P 500 TR USD	2.11	15.94	0.00	1.00	1.00	-16.26	100.00	100.00	0.20

FIGURE 4.6 Low Beta vs. Market Beta—The S&P Downgrade (2011)

ASSESSING THE INVESTMENT ENVIRONMENT

For more advanced investors, those with a far keener sense of the industry, the cycles and undercurrents trending beneath the surface of the broader markets, as well as a more elaborate understanding of how available managers or indices might perform in a given environment, another criteria for selection beyond cost and statistical analysis is to assess the current investment environment. In doing so, we caution investors not to get too far ahead of themselves. Stick to the 30,000-foot view and remember it is impossible to predict future prices or the future state of our economy. Even when right, timing is often dramatically off. As William of Ockham so eloquently taught us, we will do our best to Keep It Simple, Stupid (KISS).

This is where investors really seem to get themselves in trouble, taking outsized bets on what they *think* is going to happen. In this vein, we recommend sticking to more general concepts. Go with the obvious and act accordingly, ever mindful of mitigating downside risk.

For example, from the beginning of the Great Recession in October 2007 until the end of 2012, U.S. Treasury bonds went on a miraculous run (see Figure 4.7). During this time, the majority of investors failed to grasp the magnitude of this meteoric rise. In Chapter 2, we made reference to the tremendous run-up in U.S. Treasury prices we have seen over the past decade. From October 2007 until the middle of 2012, this run accelerated at a maddening pace. While the S&P 500 managed only a 0.09 percent average annual rate of return for this period, the Barclays U.S. Treasury 20+ Year Index averaged 12.56 percent! This marked a cumulative return of 77 percent for Treasuries and less than a half percent for U.S. stocks.

Surely, this could not continue. Not only had investor fears driven up Treasury prices to all-time highs, but our government was in the midst of a massive asset repurchasing program, buying up longer-dated

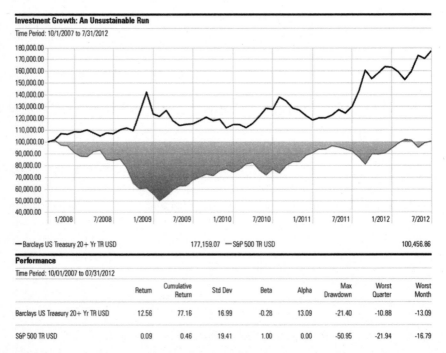

Investment Growth: An Unsustainable Run

Time Period: 10/1/2007 to 7/31/2012

| —Barclays US Treasury 20+ Yr TR USD | 177,159.07 —S&P 500 TR USD | 100,456.86 |

Performance

Time Period: 10/01/2007 to 07/31/2012

	Return	Cumulative Return	Std Dev	Beta	Alpha	Max Drawdown	Worst Quarter	Worst Month
Barclays US Treasury 20+ Yr TR USD	12.56	77.16	16.99	-0.28	13.09	-21.40	-10.88	-13.09
S&P 500 TR USD	0.09	0.46	19.41	1.00	0.00	-50.95	-21.94	-16.79

FIGURE 4.7 Long-Term U.S. Treasury Performance (October 1 2007–July 31, 2012)

Source: © 2014 Morningstar, Inc. All Rights Reserved. Reproduced with permission.

U.S. Treasury bonds with the proceeds of maturing securities. This drove interest rates to all-time lows and stimulated the economy, but for bond buyers this massive run should have served as a warning of what was yet to come. Never before had Treasuries become so overvalued, and surely at some point there would be a reversion to the mean.

We all know the federal government cannot continue repurchasing more than $85 billion in U.S. Treasury bonds on a monthly basis. When they step away ("ease"), there are some serious questions as to who will be left to buy long-dated bonds. And in reference to our earlier discussion on bond characteristics, when rates ultimately begin to rise, bonds and bond funds with a longer duration will be subject to potentially severe declines.

This is where taking the 30,000-foot approach can make sense and where an investor should choose to take action, selling out of longer-dated bond maturities and purchasing bonds or bond funds that will be less susceptible to such interest rate moves. This can be done by simply purchasing bonds or bond funds with lower maturities/durations. However, in doing so, one should also be mindful of how much of a premium price they are paying for these bonds, at which point, if they are too expensive, investors should consider building up some cash in the conservative portion of their investments or further looking into adding monies to stable value funds with a guaranteed rate of return (a staple in most 401(k) plans). While in both instances returns may be negatively influenced by inflation, at least an increase in rates would not erode principle (which should be a primary concern for bond investors today).

Taking things one step further, investors may place additional considerations on whether they are fulfilling their allocations with securities that take more, less, or equal amounts of risk than their benchmark. During good times, often those investments that take greater risks will do better (not always—it's a gamble); in more difficult times, this is less likely. Therefore, if an investor has been utilizing investments posing greater risks, or that otherwise have bested the benchmark by a respectable margin, one might suggest that they lock in these levels of outperformance before they lose them.

This can either be done by simply buying the market (the traditional cap-weighted S&P 500 Index) or by purchasing a broadly diversified index or fund with a lower-than-market beta profile, one that if market conditions reverse has a greater probability of going down less. In this case, an investor would have captured a greater return on the way up and preserved better on the way down. But then again, you don't need to capture more on the way up; you just need to capture less on the way down. That is what is most important.

In theory, this sounds easy, but this is again where things get tricky for investors focused on making these kinds of moves based solely on their opinions or market-driving headlines. Ultimately, any such investment strategy requires significant restraint and a well-articulated and adhered-to buy-and-sell discipline.

THE BOTTOM LINE

Nicolaus Copernicus was the first to propose the theory of a heliocentric universe; Galileo expanded upon these theories and provided the world with measurable proof. The Morningstar Rating system is akin to the foundation established by Copernicus; an analysis of cost and risk-adjusted returns provides a good working foundation. But by peering through the telescope, Galileo was able to see so much more. *Beyond the stars* (as in the Morningstar Ratings) is where an investor truly needs to look; here, they may find some far more meaningful answers.

An investor is best served to begin with an evaluation of cost, a personal reflection on what investment risk means to their own personal situation, and then get a feel for whether statistical measures of risk coincide with where we are in our current environment. Given the gravity of these decisions, it may be best to seek trusted counsel.

Investing in individual stocks involves taking on exponentially more risk, as an investor not only needs to select the right sector at the right time, but also the right company in the sector. There are simply far too many outsized risks for the average investor to bear. While not every individual stock or company is going to turn out like General Motors, Enron, or Lehman Brothers—and certainly there are a handful of uniquely successful investors such as Warren Buffet that have proven stock investing to be successful—the average investor (or analyst, for that matter) has demonstrated little skill in identifying those companies trading at attractive levels versus those going to zero. Further, one cannot be expected to anticipate every earnings miss, an interruption in the supply chain, a disappointing product launch, a change in consumer sentiment, and so on. When buying individual stocks, these are the risks you take. Depending on your concentration in any given holding, losses could be devastating.

Conversely, mutual funds can provide investors with broad diversification, but they can also be very costly and wildly inconsistent with regards to their performance versus a benchmark. Like anything else, cost is only an issue in the absence of value. But when you consider the high probability that a traditionally allocated active manager is going to underperform their benchmark over time (net of fees), if not eventually experience a year of excessive losses (likely at a time when investment confidence is at all-time highs), indexing appears to be the smarter choice.

Coming off of a decade in which investors experienced not one, but two severe market declines in excess of −40 percent, investor appetite for risk is not what it was in the late 1990s. As one might expect, it is quite the opposite. Investors have faced their demons and would rather not go back. But at the same time, our current historically low interest rates are driving investors out of cash, out of bonds, and—gulp—into the equity markets.

Long-time investors who have focused on capital preservation during difficult times have done far better than those chasing market beating returns. While perhaps counterintuitive, and certainly not as exciting, simply adhering to lower risk and lower volatility strategies provides a far more reasonable approach to investing. The investment industry has recognized as much, as over the past few years we have seen a litany of "low-volatility" strategies make their way into the marketplace. We view this as a good thing and encourage investors to consider this approach. With that said, the tools available to investors today have now made possible what was previously impossible; and further, they now have lower-cost and better risk-adjusted performance options available.

CHAPTER 5

THE LANDSCAPE HAS CHANGED

The Proliferation of the ETF

Revered in his lifetime as Il Divino, "the divine one," Michelangelo's hands moved as though by the grace of God, possessing the innate and unparalleled ability to resurrect life from a block of marble, or with the mere stroke of his brush. Producing works of such awe-inspiring grandeur, Michelangelo's legacy embodied the archetypical spirit of the Renaissance.

By now you may be familiar with the story of David and Goliath, but the symbolism behind this biblical account goes far beyond defeating an adversary donning superior strength. Rather, Michelangelo's "David" depicted a mind-set, a willful act of defiance to act upon one's strongest convictions with courage, to break free of the malpractice and injustice of the day and to establish order in an otherwise chaotic world. This much can be seen in David's resilient expression.

Michelangelo's statue of David became a symbol for enlightenment, for courage in the face of oppression, and for the glory and power of the human spirit.

On August 31, 1976, the world's first index mutual fund was launched: the Vanguard S&P 500 (ticker: VFINX). At the time, it was viewed by the majority in the investment community as a slap in the face, proposing that just buying and holding the broad stock market would yield better results than trying to beat it by picking stocks. An indexed approach was dismissed as a recipe for achieving average results. Surely investors could do better by simply eliminating those stocks from the index that would likely underperform and overweighting those likely to outperform. It sounds simple. But as we all know, history has proven this out to be far more difficult than it may appear.

As we have highlighted in previous chapters, the probability of consistent outperformance by a traditional active manager is low, and it is also highly improbable that an investor will select the right fund at the right time. Buying the wrong security at the wrong time can lead to a permanent impairment of capital, particularly when one considers the long history of emotional and rash decisions made by investors. As such, personal investors have long experienced significant underperformance, all of which makes sound arguments for passively investing in indices with a low-cost buy-and-hold approach.

But on January 22, 1993, unbeknownst to the greater investment community at large, in an instant, the investment world changed. On this date, State Street Global Advisors launched the first exchange-traded fund (ETF), also tracking the S&P 500; the SPDR S&P 500 ETF (ticker: SPY). This seemingly insignificant event forever changed the landscape of the investment markets, as though by the grace of God, breathing life into an otherwise lifeless index, and making possible what was previously impossible. This monumental event marked the beginning of the evolution of a new and improved standard for indexing.

Throughout the course of this chapter, we will provide an introduction to the ETF as an investment vehicle, highlighting the inherently unique characteristics of the ETF structure, a brief history, and an overview of how ETFs are generally being utilized in our industry today. In doing so, we aim to provide an educational foundation for what this evolution has now made possible beyond a conventional approach.

THE ETF: WHAT IS IT?

The easiest way to provide an overview of the ETF structure is by comparing it to the more commonly known mutual fund. An ETF is similar to a traditional index mutual fund, in that they are typically not actively managed and both typically seek to mirror the performance of an index. However, the principal difference between an ETF and an indexed mutual fund is that an ETF is traded intraday on an exchange; like the price of a stock, it is constantly changing throughout the day, whereas a mutual fund trades at the closing net asset value (NAV), at the close of the market.

This intraday liquidity provides investors with considerably more control over their investment. Not only can investors in ETFs control when they buy or sell a security, but through the use of various types of orders, they can control the price.

For example, if an ETF were currently trading at $105 and an investor did not wish to pay more than a $100, he could enter a *buy limit* order at their desired price. In this case (assuming the order was also entered as good till canceled [GTC]), should the price of the ETF ever drop to or below the $100 target price in the future, the order would automatically execute. If after purchasing the security this same investor wished to establish a target price to sell the ETF, they could then enter a *sell limit* order to sell all shares at a minimum of $110. Should this target price ever be reached or surpassed, their order would be fulfilled. Additionally, an investor could elect to provide a modicum of capital preservation by entering a *stop-loss* order below the current price of the ETF. In this case, should the investment decline in value to at or below the stop-loss order price (say, for example, $92), the order would trigger to sell the ETF. These additional measures of risk management equip ETF investors with considerably more tools than investors in traditional mutual funds.

In addition to significantly increased liquidity, the ETF structure provides investors with complete transparency. In a traditional mutual fund, holdings are disclosed, but with at least a lag of 30 days and typically one full fiscal quarter. This leads to a host of problems, as investors truly have no way of knowing what they are holding, and we far too often see gamesmanship here practiced by fund managers. Toward the end of the fiscal quarter, mutual fund managers often will buy winning stocks and sell their big losers so that investors will feel reassured when they see their holdings. This all-too-common practice is known as in the industry as *window dressing*. In an ETF, holdings and their complete weightings are published daily by the ETF provider.

ETFs also typically provide investors with a significantly lower cost alternative than mutual funds. Without an active manager to pay management fees to, ETFs are generally based on an index and pay a minimal fee to the index provider (for example, Standard & Poor's, MSCI, or Dow Jones indices). They also tend to have significantly less turnover and therefore incur lower internal transaction costs. ETFs also generally trade on commission (like a stock), and therefore investors do not incur sales loads, minimum holding periods, or required minimum thresholds for investment. Some of the larger custodians such as Charles Schwab, Fidelity, and TD Ameritrade even allow investors to trade select ETFs commission free.

ETFs are also regarded as being much more tax efficient than mutual funds. When there are redemptions in a mutual fund, all shareholders realize capital gains. Whereas ETF shareholders generally incur tax consequences based only on their transactions. Additionally, because ETFs track market indices, turnover is low. Low turnover results in fewer capital gains being distributed and therefore lower taxes.

Beyond dramatically increased liquidity, transparency, lower costs, and better tax efficiency, ETFs also provide investors with access to advanced trading strategies. Such strategies can include the use of options, strategic portfolio rebalancing, and even tactical strategies. Consider that the composition of a portfolio made up by simply a few ETFs can provide investors with a broad diversification of asset classes, and possesses the ability to be dramatically changed with only a handful of trades.

Table 5.1 is a summary of some of the many differences present between mutual funds and ETFs.

TABLE 5.1   Summary: Notable Differences between ETFs and Mutual Funds

	ETF	Mutual Fund
Trading/Liquidity	Trade on exchanges intraday. Various order types provide investors control over the price paid for an ETF and the price at which it can be sold.	Trade at closing price, with access directly through the fund company or a select broker. No control over purchase or sale price.
Transparency	Daily holdings disclosure.	Fund holdings are generally disclosed quarterly.
Costs	Expense ratio plus transactions costs. Internal expenses are generally lower.	Expense ratios (generally higher) in addition to potential sales loads or redemption fees.
Required Minimum Investment	N/A	Most have investment minimums.

	ETF	Mutual Fund
Tax Implications	Transactions generate tax consequences for the shareholder making the transaction only. Must distribute gains to all shareholders, but typically less turnover leads to less frequent capital gains.	Transactions generate tax consequences for all shareholders. Must distribute gains to all shareholders; turnover may be higher or lower depending on the strategy.
Advanced Trading Strategies	Investors can use various order types, options strategies, and employ a tactical portfolio discipline.	N/A

A BRIEF HISTORY

What began with little fanfare in 1993 gradually morphed into a widely accepted and viable investment vehicle by the turn of the millennium. In 1995, State Street Global Advisors introduced the S&P 400 Mid Cap ETF (ticker: MDY), for the first time granting investors access to mid-cap-sized companies through an ETF structure. By the year 2000, investors were not only able to invest in ETFs by capitalization (size of the company), they were also able to invest by style (growth or value), and by even by sector (e.g., energy, financials, health care).

Over the past 10 to 15 years, ETFs have experienced explosive growth, and investors can now gain access to nearly any asset class through this investment vehicle. In early 2000, iShares launched the first real estate investment trust (REIT) ETF (ticker: IYR), for the first time providing investors with access to a tradable real estate index. In 2002, iShares launched the first fixed-income ETF, with the inception of the iShares iBoxx Investment Grade Corporate Bond ETF (ticker: LQD). Over the coming years this lead to the launch of ETFs granting access to the aggregate bond market, U.S. Treasuries, high-yield, emerging-market bonds, International Treasuries, preferred stocks, and so on. In 2004, with the launch of the SPDR Gold Shares ETF (ticker: GLD), State Street set the tone for investor access to individual commodities through the ETF structure. Nowadays, investors can even purchase exchange-traded vehicles as a means of owning exposure to such obscure commodities as coffee, tin, nickel, cocoa, sugar, corn, cotton, and the like.

The proliferation of the ETF market over the past two decades has been truly astounding. Back in 1993 there was only one Exchange Traded Product on the market, with approximately $500 million in assets under management. By the turn of the millennium, these numbers had grown to 81 different offerings with over $65 billion in assets under management (AUM). By March 2013, the number of ETF product offerings had grown to 1,449 different funds, with up to $1.46 trillion in assets! This tremendous growth was illustrated in a recent "Exchanged Traded Asset Update—March 2013" provided by www.alletf.com, as seen in Figure 5.1.

As impressive as the historical growth rates have been in the ETF industry, the penetration of the ETF into the marketplace may only be in its infancy. The majority of retail investors are still not familiar with this investment vehicle or its inherent benefits and superiority over traditional mutual funds. Additionally, ETF usage is only now becoming more prevalent in the practices of professional financial advisers, as the industry continues to transition more and more away from commissionable trades and more toward fee-based asset management platforms. And we have only just recently begun to see ETFs being introduced as investment choices made available to employees

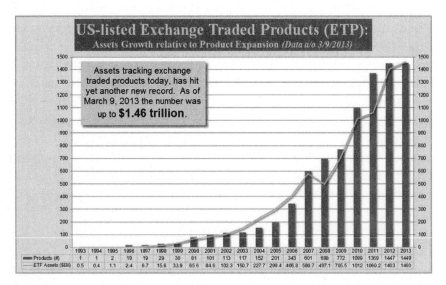

FIGURE 5.1   ETF Industry Growth

Source: http://alletf.com/content/exchanged-traded-assets-update-march-2013.

within employer-sponsored retirement plans. All of these segments of the market will provide a catalyst for the future growth of the ETF industry. In a recent announcement by Blackrock's iShares, the world's largest ETF provider forecast their expectation for total ETF assets to more than double to $3.5 trillion by 2017.

The downside of the rapid growth we are seeing in the ETF marketplace is the relative confusion this has created for the average investor. With the number of ETF choices available to investors growing at an exponential rate, it is becoming increasingly difficult for investors to decide which ETF is right for them, and on what criteria they should base their decision. One useful resource available to investors vetting the ETF landscape is the web site www.alletf.com.

The web site alletf.com is supported by one of the financial industry's leading research providers, Dorsey Wright. This web site provides ETF investors with a wealth of information, including up-to-date industry news, as well as many useful tools for ETF analysis. One of their most useful tools for investors is their ETF Compare function. Utilizing this tool, an investor can enter the tickers for multiple ETFs and compare their costs, weightings of their underlying holdings, and past performance. Additionally, investors can use their ETF Drilldown tool to identify current ETFs trading with their desired sector concentrations. Utilizing their ETF Drilldown tool, investors can easily identify ETFs trading with their desired exposure and avoid those that might otherwise appear to be appropriate.

As one might expect, the tremendous growth we have seen in ETFs in recent years has come at the expense of the mutual fund industry. As highlighted in the "2013 Investment Company Fact Book," published by the Investment Company Institute, by year-end 2012, U.S. domestic equity mutual funds experienced a net outflow of $156 billion. This marked their seventh consecutive year of withdrawals, totaling $613 billion. Conversely, net issuance of broad-based domestic equity ETFs increased to $58 billion in 2012, up from $35 billion in 2011.

With currently still more than $13 trillion in assets, the U.S. mutual fund industry remains the largest in the world, but if recent fund flows and well-defined trends over the past number of years are any indication, investors are catching on; the ETF structure provides investors with a far more efficient investment vehicle, at lower costs, and with increased levels of control. This superior structure, combined with the ability to isolate specific asset classes otherwise inaccessible, provides investors with a world of possibilities. And to think we are currently only on the cusp of what this Investment Renaissance may lead us to.

THE USE OF ETFs IN A PORTFOLIO

Investors today have the opportunity to utilize ETFs in a myriad of different ways within their overall portfolio. Some investors simply use ETFs for a portion of their asset allocation, while others rely solely on ETFs as their preferred investment vehicle. Regardless, there is a place for ETFs in every investor's portfolio. In the remainder of this chapter, we will discuss some of their more common uses.

Core/Satellite

Many investors today utilize ETFs to gain exposure to concentrated sectors of the market or asset classes not covered by a traditional asset allocation. The second-largest ETF in the world, the SPDR Gold Shares ETF (ticker: GLD) is a perfect example of this. Gold is an asset class not typically represented in a standard asset allocation, but for its long-standing history as a hedge against inflation, many investors in recent years have felt the need to diversify a portion of their investable assets into this precious metal. Rather than own physical gold directly, investors today have the opportunity to buy the ETF and benefit from its ease of trade and liquidity.

Investors might also purchase a niche ETF to exploit a trend, personal interest, or even a specific geographic region. There is a litany of ETFs focused on obscure investment opportunities such as solar power, wind, coal, agribusiness, steel, water, and so on. And when it comes to exposure to individual countries, iShares seems to have an ETF for nearly every economy in the world. With more than 100 individual country offerings, iShares has ETFs for both developed and emerging countries.

For Leverage—Long/Short

In 2006, the ETF provider ProShares launched the industry's first leveraged ETFs, providing two times the daily returns of the underlying index. These ETFs can be used by investors to gain either double-long or double-short exposure to the market. This gives investors the opportunity to benefit from either a rising or falling market and to incorporate otherwise sophisticated institutional strategies into a retail portfolio. For example, an investor who is bullish on the stock market but bearish on U.S. Treasury Bonds could purchase the ProShares Ultra S&P 500 ETF (ticker: SSO), and pair it with the ProShares UltraShort 20+Year Treasury ETF (ticker: TBT). Therefore, if the stock market went up, this investor would benefit from their amplified exposure; they would also benefit if the U.S. Treasury market were to fall. The advent of the leveraged ETF has enabled investors to incorporate long/short strategies, as well as benefit from singling out specific sectors of the market for enhanced returns.

Since the inception of the first leveraged ETFs in the marketplace, the investor's appetite for risk has grown, and we have witnessed ETF providers launch a more diverse array of leveraged products. While many investors may lack the intestinal fortitude to own securities providing two times the daily return of the market, by late 2008 the ETF provider Direxion became the first to offer products with daily leverage of 300 percent (or three times the return) of the underlying index; with their launch of the Daily S&P 500 Bull 3x's Shares ETF (ticker: SPXL) and the Daily S&P 500 Bear 3x's Shares ETF (ticker: SPXS). Nowadays, in addition to the availability of both double- and triple-leveraged ETFs on broad-based indices, investors in leveraged ETFs have the ability to invest by sector, style, country, asset class, and even with consideration given for volatility.

The use of leveraged ETFs by and for retail clients has not been without controversy. As one might imagine, if used inappropriately, investors can very quickly incur significant losses. In light of this fact, many of the larger brokerage firms no longer allow their financial advisers to purchase them in discretionary accounts on behalf of their clients. Therefore, much of the use of leveraged ETFs is done by institutional investors, independent firms, and do-it-yourself heroes, the latter of which can be a recipe for disaster. With that in mind, the use of leveraged ETFs can provide tremendous value if used appropriately.

Tax Loss Harvesting

Come tax time, capital gains can have a significant impact on the net gains of an investment portfolio. Because of this, savvy investors often look to sell securities in which they have losses in order to offset the gains they have made in others, thus reducing their tax burden. However, investors wishing to maintain exposure to what has been sold must wait 30 days before repurchasing the security back; otherwise, the "wash sale rule" is enforced and the loss is no longer able to be recognized. In this case, an investor can purchase an ETF offering the same exposure as their losing security. For example, if an investor wished to recognize a loss they have in a large-cap value mutual fund they own, they could sell it and turn around and purchase the iShares Russell 1000 Value ETF (ticker: IWD). Or an individual stock investor who wished to recognize a loss in Exxon Mobil (ticker: XOM) could sell the stock and then purchase the SPDR S&P Energy ETF (ticker: XLE), of which Exxon Mobil is the largest holding.

Traditional Indexing

Perhaps the simplest application of the ETF is in a traditional buy-and-hold asset allocation. Once an investor has determined what percentage of their assets they would like to have in both stocks and bonds, it is very easy to simply fulfill an asset allocation with as few as two ETFs.

- The Vanguard Total Stock Market ETF (Ticker: VTI) provides investors with exposure to the broad U.S. equity market, including large-, mid-, and small-cap equity, and exposure to both growth and value styles. With more than 3,500 holdings, investors capture the broad diversification of nearly the entire U.S. equity markets at an exceptionally low cost, with an expense ratio of only 0.05 percent.
- If an investor wished to add international equity exposure, they could simply utilize the Vanguard Total World Stock ETF (ticker: VT) in place of VTI. Whereas the Vanguard Total Stock Market ETF is made up of 100 percent U.S. domestic equity, the Vanguard Total World Stock ETF is only roughly 50 percent U.S. equity, and the rest is spread out across the remaining developed and emerging international equity markets. With an expense ratio of a mere 0.19 percent, VTI is considerably cheaper than the average global mutual with an internal expense of 1.42 percent, and with nearly 5,000 holdings it is highly diversified.

- For fixed income, an investor could simply utilize the Vanguard Total Bond Market ETF (ticker: BND). Here again, for an exceptionally low cost of 0.10 percent, investors can gain access to a diversified mix of fixed income, including government, corporate, and international dollar-denominated bonds, as well as mortgage-backed and asset-backed securities. The average maturity of the bonds held in BND is between 5 and 10 years.

Strategic Asset Allocations

Moving one step beyond traditional indexing, investors very commonly use ETFs to fulfill a strategic asset allocation. Rather than employ a traditional buy-and-hold approach, strategic allocators attempt to overweight/underweight specific sectors of the markets. While the overall allocation to stocks and bonds may stay the same, the underlying weightings in the assets held may be strategically shifted in an effort to be either opportunistic or defensive.

- In the equity portion of a strategic asset allocation, we commonly see overweighting by style (growth or value), by market cap (large-, mid-, or small-cap equities), or geography (whether overweighting domestic or international).
- Within the fixed-income component of a strategic asset allocation we often see investors overweight by credit quality, class of fixed income, maturity, and geographic location. For example, a strategic asset allocator concerned about the impact of rising rates on the fixed-income portion of their portfolio may strategically shorten the maturities of the bonds held. If they were concerned about a potential fall in the equity markets, they might increase their exposure to U.S. Treasuries.

Tactical Asset Allocations

Tactical asset allocations are highly nimble, in that they typically do not adhere to maintaining a traditional asset allocation whatsoever. A truly tactical portfolio has the autonomy to move either entirely into or out of an asset class or sector of the market. Because of the inherently transitive nature of a tactical portfolio, the ETF structure is critical. In literally a handful of trades, a portfolio's composition can be completely changed.

The proliferation we have seen in ETFs over the course of the past decade has made possible what was previously impossible. Never before could investors so easily employ a tactical mandate. Prior to the past decade, investors in individual stocks and bonds surely did not have the ability to tactically navigate the markets in this vein, and had they tried, they surely would have had a litany of required transactions and paid significant commissions to do so. Even mutual fund investors lacked the control necessary to engage in a tactical discipline, as they would have had to deal with sales loads, required minimum holding periods, limited control over pricing, and the like. Accordingly, as the ETF industry has experienced tremendous growth, so has the tactically managed ETF portfolio segment of the marketplace.

In September 2011, Morningstar announced plans to research and rank ETF managed portfolios. In January 2012, it published its inaugural "ETF Managed Portfolios Landscape Report." In this report, author Andrew Gogerty stated, "ETF Managed Portfolios represent one of the fastest-growing segments of the managed account universe." Gogerty goes on to provide support for this claim by citing the tremendous growth in the ETF industry as a whole, but specifically with respect to the managed ETF portfolio landscape:

- For the one-year ended December 31, 2011, Morningstar estimates that net inflows into ETFs were $121 billion compared with $56 billion for open-end mutual funds.
- At the time of this publication, Morningstar was tracking nearly 370 strategies from approximately 95 firms, with assets under advisement of $27 billion (as of September 2011), a 43 percent growth rate over the prior 12-month period.

In the March 2013 Morningstar publication of the ETF Managed Portfolios Landscape Report (citing data through the end of 2012), this growth story continued. By this time, Morningstar was tracking up to 530 strategies from 125 firms with total assets of $63 billion as of December 2012. Total assets in these strategies had increased by 60 percent in 2012.

By the time the June 2013 Morningstar publication of the ETF Managed Portfolios Landscape Report (citing data through the end of March 31, 2013) was published, it was abundantly clear that this growth trend was firmly in place. Morningstar was now up to tracking 605 strategies from 140 firms with total assets of $73 billion. In the first quarter of 2013 alone, total assets in these strategies increased by 12 percent.

The data collected by Morningstar and its willingness to take notice of this dramatically impactful and growing trend inherent in our industry today is a testament to this shift in investor behavior, to this evolution in how investors could begin to navigate the markets in ways that had never been done before, with the use of ETFs. While certainly not every managed ETF portfolio tracked by Morningstar is "tactical" in nature, they are among the largest and most rapidly growing.

Two of the largest and most notable tactical managed ETF portfolio strategies are the Good Harbor U.S. Tactical Core strategy and the F-Squared AlphaSector Premium Index. Both strategies are highly nimble and have the ability to adapt to current market conditions by going either entirely into equities or fixed income. This flexibility provides both strategies with a discipline to avoid prolonged market declines; rotating out of equities and into securities that will provide a modicum of safety and capital preservation during extended periods of duress in equities. In doing so, investors may live to fight another day and ultimately win by losing less.

Throughout an entire market cycle (including both economic expansion and contraction), this tactical nature has provided investors with superior returns. In Figure 5.2 we have illustrated a five-year time period from October 1, 2008, until September 30, 2013, for both of these tactical managers. While we would have preferred to show returns for all of 2008, to provide further testament of the resiliency these portfolios have historically demonstrated, the F-Squared portfolio's performance data is only available beginning in October. We should note, however, that for the 2008 calendar year the S&P 500 was down 37 percent, while the Good Harbor U.S. Tactical Core portfolio managed a modestly positive return of 1.95 percent—nearly a 40 percent performance spread versus the S&P 500.

During this five year period both Good Harbor and F-Squared handily outperformed the S&P 500, with average annual returns of 23.3 percent and 15.7 percent respectfully, versus a 10 percent return per annum on the S&P 500. As one might imagine, the tactical nature

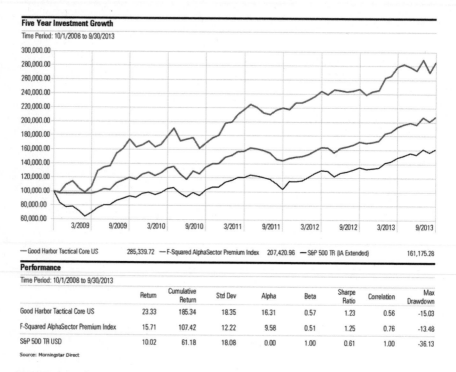

Five Year Investment Growth

Time Period: 10/1/2008 to 9/30/2013

	Return	Cumulative Return	Std Dev	Alpha	Beta	Sharpe Ratio	Correlation	Max Drawdown
— Good Harbor Tactical Core US			285,339.72	— F-Squared AlphaSector Premium Index	207,420.96	— S&P 500 TR (IA Extended)		161,175.28

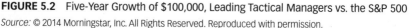

Performance

Time Period: 10/1/2008 to 9/30/2013

	Return	Cumulative Return	Std Dev	Alpha	Beta	Sharpe Ratio	Correlation	Max Drawdown
Good Harbor Tactical Core US	23.33	185.34	18.35	16.31	0.57	1.23	0.56	-15.03
F-Squared AlphaSector Premium Index	15.71	107.42	12.22	9.58	0.51	1.25	0.76	-13.48
S&P 500 TR USD	10.02	61.18	18.08	0.00	1.00	0.61	1.00	-36.13

Source: Morningstar Direct

FIGURE 5.2 Five-Year Growth of $100,000, Leading Tactical Managers vs. the S&P 500
Source: © 2014 Morningstar, Inc. All Rights Reserved. Reproduced with permission.

of these portfolios enabled them to accomplish this feat with considerably less risk, as both registered betas in the 0.5 range. Max drawdowns for the period were also significantly less, at −15 percent for Good Harbor, −13.3 percent for F-Squared, compared to a much more troublesome drawdown of −36.1 percent for the S&P 500.

If you break this down further and look at the returns of these portfolios on a calendar-year basis, you will see that the returns often look quite dissimilar to those of the S&P 500 (see Figure 5.3). This is due, of course, to the rotational nature of both strategies and their inherent ability to tactically move into and out of equities.

During the final quarter of 2008, losses in the U.S. investment markets rapidly increased. By the end of this three month period, the S&P 500 lost nearly 22 percent of its value; conversely Good Harbor's tactical managed ETF portfolio strategy posted an impressive return of better than 14 percent, and F-Squared was down a far more reasonable 3.27 percent. When markets rebounded in 2009, both Good Harbor

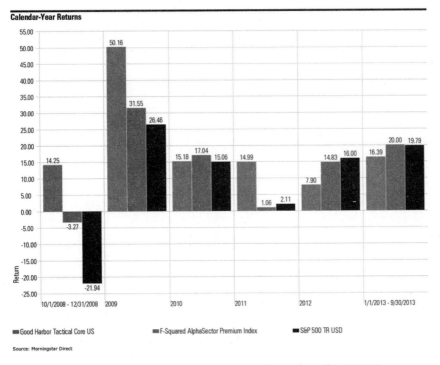

Calendar-Year Returns

Good Harbor Tactical Core US   ■F-Squared AlphaSector Premium Index   ■S&P 500 TR USD

Source: Morningstar Direct

FIGURE 5.3 Calendar-Year Returns, Leading Tactical Managers vs. the S&P 500

and F–Squared outperformed the S&P 500; Good Harbor did so by applying leverage to equities during their strong rise, while F–Squared concentrated holdings in some of the most impactful underlying sectors of the market. Not surprisingly, in stronger years for the S&P 500, both of these strategies posted returns very similar to the benchmark index (2010, 2012, 2013); it is when market extremes take place that we often see the real difference between a tactical manager and an all-equity benchmark.

While the underlying processes may be very different between these two strategies, the overarching tactical and rotational nature of the portfolios is quite similar. Beyond the differences in their vetting processes for determining their holdings, it should be noted that Good Harbor has the ability to utilize leveraged ETFs for both equities and fixed income; specifically, they apply leverage to equities by market cap and also to U.S. Treasuries, whereas F–Squared does not use leverage, and rather than focus their equity exposure by market cap, they employ a more traditional sector rotation strategy, isolating sectors of the equity market in favor and avoiding those under stress.

THE BOTTOM LINE

We believe we are standing on the precipice of an Investment Renaissance, a period of enlightenment that will lead investors to question what they have long held to be true and change the manner in which they invest. No longer must investors succumb to the whim of the markets or suffer its deathly blows. No longer must they remain tortured and trapped by convention and age-old market clichés. Rather, investors are now free to navigate the flow of the markets, to be nimble in ways previously unimaginable. The proliferation of the ETF has led us down this path.

The tremendous growth of the ETF industry over the past two decades has provided investors with a world of opportunities. And while there are certainly many uses for ETFs within the scope of an overall portfolio, we firmly believe that in order to achieve the maximum benefit provided by this unique structure, investors are best served to employ a tactical discipline.

Never before has any previous generation of investors been provided with the tools necessary to implement a truly tactical approach; with the ability to alter the composition of an entire portfolio with simply a handful of trades, to adapt to current market conditions, alternating their posture between "risk-on" and "risk-off."

To the attentive eye, this Renaissance has already begun. And yet the masses have failed to take notice. Despite the vastly superior risk-adjusted returns generated by leading tactical managed ETF strategies, the majority of investors continue to chase shooting stars, to fill in style boxes, and to adhere to time horizon based asset allocations predicated on capital market assumptions that will soon prove to be highly fallible.

The next stage in the evolution of the investment industry is upon us. While we can expect to hear the titans of our industry continue to trumpet "it is time in the market, not timing," enlightened investors know better. Such proclamations are self-serving and provide an excuse for outsized losses. While that may be good for corporate war chests and large-scale institutions, it does little for retail investors mired in the depths of a game they can't even see exists. At the same time, they continue to watch their hard-earned savings evaporate into thin air.

Of course, a historical precedence has been set; investors are notorious for their ill timing in the markets. So despite the tools necessary to do so, how can one expect execute a rotational timing strategy utilizing ETFs? It is far easier than one might imagine.

CHAPTER 6

CHALLENGING CONVENTION

An Introduction to Asset Rotation

Widely regarded as one of the most influential scientists of all time, Sir Isaac Newton's laws of motion and universal gravitation provided the foundation for our modern day understanding of the physical universe we live in. In Newton's groundbreaking work, *The Principia*, first published in 1687, he outlined his three universal laws of motion.

Among these universal laws, Newton's First Law of Motion states, "An object at rest will remain at rest unless acted upon by an unbalanced force. An object in motion continues in motion unless acted upon by an unbalanced force." This law is often called "the law of inertia."

The Newtonian laws of motion provided a final testament as to the validity of a heliocentric model of the universe, first set forth by Nicolaus Copernicus during the 1500s. With curiosity sparked by the Great Comet of 1680, Sir Isaac Newton provided mathematical proof of the existence of gravitational forces and orbital tracts in the cosmos. As a result, this comet later came to be known as Newton's Comet.

As we reflect on the nature of the capital markets, we can't help but draw parallels to Newton's Laws of Motion. If you think about it, the investment markets have a propensity to behave in a very similar manner. Ultimately, more than anything else, it is the underlying psyche of the investment community at large that provides the catalyst for the direction taken by security prices. When investor psyche is positive, the markets have a tendency to move up in price, as increasing confidence invokes more investors to buy. Conversely, when investor psyche is negative, prices will tend to move with a downward trajectory, as fear of loss causes investors to sell. Unless acted upon by an external "unbalanced" force, these trends are likely to continue.

Over the past 13 years, since the turn of the millennium, it seems as though a great many of these "unbalanced" forces have disrupted market returns, and investors have certainly felt the effects. From Y2K, to the bursting of the tech bubble, to the tragedies of 9/11, the Great Recession of 2008, and the government spending-led boom we have seen since, the meddle of even the most ardent investor has been tested.

From 2000 to 2009, the S&P 500 registered an average annual loss of 0.95 percent, prompting many to refer to this period as the *lost decade* (see Figure 6.1). If only it had been that easy. . . . When you look at this time period in terms of average annual returns, it does not appear overwhelmingly painful. While the prospects of losing nearly 1 percent a year over the course of a decade can certainly be frustrating, the reality is that for the average investor this time period was far worse and far more impactful, altering the future livelihoods of many market participants.

At this point, we find it imperative to note, as discussed in Chapter 2, while the performance of stocks was perilous for investors throughout this time period, the U.S. Treasury bond went on quite an extended run. While stocks were down nearly 1 percent per year, the Barclays 20+ U.S. Treasury Index was up nearly 8 percent per annum. Quite an impressive run, to be sure, and as noted previously, this level of outperformance by Treasuries over stocks has been seen only once before, during the Great Depression, right before bonds entered into a 40-year bear market.

Over this 10-year period, investors in the U.S. stock market lost more than 40 percent not once but twice. To make matters worse, during the Great Recession of 2008 and the period that followed,

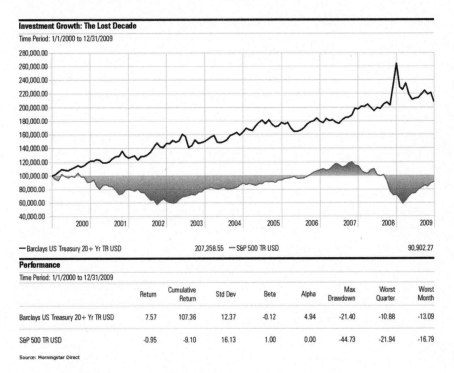

Investment Growth: The Lost Decade

Time Period: 1/1/2000 to 12/31/2009

— Barclays US Treasury 20+ Yr TR USD	207,358.55	··· S&P 500 TR USD	90,902.27

Performance

Time Period: 1/1/2000 to 12/31/2009

	Return	Cumulative Return	Std Dev	Beta	Alpha	Max Drawdown	Worst Quarter	Worst Month
Barclays US Treasury 20+ Yr TR USD	7.57	107.36	12.37	-0.12	4.94	-21.40	-10.88	-13.09
S&P 500 TR USD	-0.95	-9.10	16.13	1.00	0.00	-44.73	-21.94	-16.79

Source: Morningstar Direct

FIGURE 6.1 The Lost Decade (2000–2009)

Source: © 2014 Morningstar, Inc. All Rights Reserved. Reproduced with permission.

many investors also lost as much or more in their real estate holdings. Coming off of the prior decade, where the S&P 500 averaged greater than 18 percent per year and home values seemed to go nowhere but up, no one saw it coming.

As we have now opined throughout the course of this book on several occasions, the human condition is inherently not hardwired for success in the investment markets. In the late 1990s, 99 cents on every dollar was going into stocks and no one wanted bonds. Then for the next decade stocks averaged a negative rate of return and bonds averaged nearly 8 percent. After experiencing the lost decade, the trend reversed and investors were now putting 99 cents out of every dollar into fixed income. Hmmmm? We wonder how that is going to turn out?

It is only natural that investors behave in this manner. After all, we are talking about people's life savings here. Of course, no one wants to see it go down! So, when inundated with "noise" and external forces, fear drives us to sell and greed causes us to buy. Investing requires discipline, both a well articulated buy discipline and a well-defined sell discipline, not our gut instinct.

To put this time period and our points into perspective, let's consider the plight of a 50-year-old investor we will call Tom. After experiencing tremendous growth in his 401(k) and other personal assets during the 1990s, Tom was excited about what his future would hold during retirement; so much so that Tom took out a home equity line on his home to purchase a cottage up north on a lake. Seeing as he was entering his prime earnings years and he had already done so well in stocks, Tom determined that over the next 10 years, between investment and wage growth, he would be able to pay off all of his debts and still retire with a good amount set aside.

During Tom's investment livelihood all he had ever experienced was stocks going up (they had been on quite a run since the early 1980s), so naturally he assumed this trend would continue. In fact, after hearing stories about the seemingly outlandish returns some of his coworkers were achieving buying technology stocks, Tom decided he wanted in on the action. I think we all can see where this is going.

In the year 2000, the S&P 500 was down 9.7 percent, at the same time the technology sector was down a whopping 41.9 percent. As prices continued to decline, Tom continued to add to his positions, excited about getting these once high-flying companies at a significant discount to their previously sky-high prices.

In 2001, the S&P 500 was down 11.8 percent and the tech sector was down another 23.4 percent. Tom began to panic. To make matters worse, for the first time in history, there was an unprovoked terrorist attack on U.S. soil, unlike the world had ever seen. On the morning of September 11, 2001, two planes had crashed into the north and south towers of the World Trade Center. In order to prevent a potentially cataclysmic stock market crash, the New York Stock Exchange and Nasdaq did not open for trading. In fact, the markets remained closed until September 17. This marked the longest shutdown of its kind since 1933. Tom grew increasingly impatient. He had already lost so much! What if there was another attack?

On the first day of trading after 9/11, the U.S. stock markets posted a 7 percent decline. Tom called his broker and told him to sell everything. He liquidated his 401(k) and moved everything into the money market fund. Tom had drawn his line in the sand and he was going to wait out the storm in cash. By week's end the Dow Jones Industrial Average had lost over 14 percent. As one might imagine, during this time airline stocks were among the hardest hit, down roughly 40 percent in little more than a week.

All told, in two years time Tom had seen his investable assets reduced from $1 million to less than $500,000. After a while, Tom just stopped looking at his statements. When his broker called, Tom didn't answer. When the markets began to turn around in 2003, Tom lacked conviction. His confidence had been broken and he was in despair. Tom was still in shock from all that he had lost, it was all he could do to just wake up each morning and go to work. Despite continually moving on up the corporate latter, it seemed to Tom that everything he earned went toward trying to rebuild his savings and at the same time meet the loan payments on his two properties, pay the loan off on his boat, and try to pay college tuition for his children. It was a real struggle.

By 2006 Tom finally began to regain confidence in the markets and moved part of his 401(k) and personal assets back into stocks. He had a decent year of returns and happened to notice in particular how well emerging-market stocks were doing, so he decided to put more of his money into them. After gaining 32 percent in 2006, in 2007 the MSCI Emerging Market Index was up another 39 percent. Conversely, the S&P 500 was only up 15.8 and 5.5 percent, respectively; growth was slowing. It only made sense, the middle class in these emerging economies was growing. As their relative wealth increased, so would consumption. The United States had already had its Industrial Revolution, and therefore growth going forward would be slow. These emerging economies were spring loaded to take off. It seemed like a no brainer, and everyone on CNBC, in the *Wall Street Journal*, or at the water cooler was talking about it.

At the same time, the financial sector of the U.S. markets was down 19 percent in 2007, while six of the other U.S. sectors were up double digits. Tom had been burned before owning the leading sector back during the tech bubble, so he figured this time he was going to employ a contrarian approach. Between the undeniable trends taking place in emerging markets and buying financial stocks on the cheap, Tom was sure he had learned his lesson.

In 2008, whispers began about a burgeoning banking crisis. Tom had told himself he wasn't going to make knee-jerk reactions ever again. This time he was going to ride out the storm and trust in the long-term demographic shift taking place in the emerging markets and the attractive valuations present in financial stocks. Then the unthinkable happened; the proverbial black swan. Financial services giant Lehman Brothers filed for bankruptcy and stock markets the world over headed into a tailspin. By the end of 2008 the S&P 500 was down 37 percent. But emerging market stocks and the U.S. financial sector were down even worse, down 53 and 54 percent, respectively. Tom could not believe it. There hadn't even been time to react!

The year 2009 started off even worse. After being down 37 percent the prior year, the first two months of the new year began down another 19 percent. Tom couldn't take it, and once again he pulled out. In early March of 2009, the S&P 500 reached an eerily strange intraday low of 666. This marked the beginning of one of the strongest stock market recoveries in history, averaging an annualized rate of nearly 25 percent from the lows of 2009 through the end of 2012. Almost quite literally, in short order, investors had been to hell and back.

With Tom having already experienced so much personal trauma over the course of two brutal recessionary declines in such a short period of time, his spirit and confidence were broken. From this point forward, Tom told himself he would just simply stick to CDs, stable value funds, and the money market. Little did Tom realize, not only was he locking in his losses, but with the expected rise in interest rates and likely inflation increases soon to follow, Tom had secured a permanent impairment of capital from which he could never recover.

After 10 years of agony, Tom was not down the average annual decline of 1 percent for the period, he had experienced far worse (as did the majority of investors). After 10 years of pure agony, Tom had nothing to show for it but heavily depreciated assets and mounting debt.

The magnitude of loss and volatility experienced during this time period was unparalleled for today's generation of investors. Only during the Great Depression did market participants incur such outsized losses in the broader markets, let alone what they may have experienced in owning individual stocks. After losing more than 40 percent in the first three years of the decade, the markets averaged a 13 percent average annual return for the next five years, and just as investors were finally coming back into the equity markets we experienced the worst one year decline in the stock markets since 1931 (when the S&P 500 was down 43 percent).

With markets around the world nosediving in concert, central banks from around the globe entered into the most grandiose, stimulative, and accommodative measures and monetary policies the world has ever known. Certainly, from this point forward, the rally we have experienced in stocks has reached epic proportions, at which point we should be asking ourselves why?

In a nation where GDP growth has historically been largely driven by consumer spending, many contend our growth has been artificial; on the back of an ever-expanding and unsustainable national deficit. At some point, governments will have to step back and reduce spending (and likely increase taxes). When they do, the baton will once again be passed on to the consumer to maintain growth. The question is whether or not they will be ready? Or, perhaps more importantly, if the events in recent years have changed the habits of the consumer in the United States (particularly given the wealth distribution and aging demographic in our country)? Suffice it to say we have some challenges ahead of us.

As if these headwinds were not enough for investors to overcome, our environment is made that much more difficult by the society we live in today. We live in the Information Age, where investors have 24/7 access to market news and specifically, sensationalized market moving stimulus. More often than not, this environment routinely leads to irrational behavior by investors, as media pundits and economists alike inundate us with their colorful and well-articulated views of what is about to happen. The irony is, in less than five minutes, viewers of financial television programming are presented with compelling arguments for both why the markets are going to go up and why they are going to go down. How are we supposed to know who to listen to?

Making matters worse, more and more people in this day and age are turning to social media for their news. Whether on Twitter, Facebook, or whatever other social media outlet people may turn to, the reliability of the news can be severely compromised, causing those involved in the investment arena to react to news that may be little more than a false rumor. When you think about it, it's pretty scary to think about how outlets such as these provide a framework for understanding what is going on out there in the world around us.

Earlier in the context of this book we made reference to a fourteenth-century monk by the name of William of Ockham. William is credited with founding what is commonly known today as the "KISS" principle (Keep It Simple, Stupid). We believe this ideology is absolutely vital to the long-term success of any investor. Why overcomplicate things and try and predict the impossible? Absent the ability to travel forward in time, it is impossible for anyone to know with any degree of certainty what the future state of our economy will look like, or the future price of a stock, let alone when. There are just simply too many variables to calculate, and even if one could, there is always the outside risk of some external event dramatically altering potential outcomes. Who knew two planes would fly directly into the World Trade Center, or that Lehman Brothers would file bankruptcy, or that there would be a massive tsunami in the world's third-largest economy (Japan) disrupting the global supply chain?

One never knows. It is impossible. And yet investors are continuously led to believe they should be taking actions based on little more than what amounts to a personal opinion. Over and over, this approach has failed us, and yet the masses continue on like sheep to the slaughter.

The irony is that what is most critically important is right before our eyes, and it may also be the most obvious. Simply put, price movement will tell you more about our economy or an individual security than any economist or analyst ever could, no matter their qualifications. It's simple. If the price of a security is going up, investors like it; if it is going down, investors don't. Like Newton's First Law, this momentum has a tendency to stay in place until acted upon by an external force. In other words, the Law of Inertia, as applied to the investment markets, equals price momentum.

What we are referring to in its most rudimentary form is the notion of *trend following*. A great many books have been written on this very topic (though we are biased to recommend author Michael Covel's book appropriately titled *Trend Following*) and there are a litany of wildly successful, if not lesser known investors employing such techniques. Why? Because it works.

Price movement is often contrary to prevailing economic forecasts. In this regard, the stock markets are regarded as a leading indicator. So, effectively, one can deduce that something as simple as being aware of what is going up in price and what is going down can lead to greater success in the investment markets. We know this may come off as shockingly elementary to some, but price momentum has long served as a critical component to many successful investment strategies used throughout the decades; rather than try and guess what is going to go up, in its simplest application, you simply buy what already is.

In James O'Shaughnessy's acclaimed book, *What Works on Wall Street*, he set out to critically analyze some of the most influential and successful approaches to investing utilized by market participants over the course of the past several decades, in order to determine what works best. While the context of the book generally focuses on individual stocks, one of O'Shaughnessy's findings was that *relative strength* was the only growth variable that consistently beats the market. However, it should be noted that when applied to individual stocks price momentum based strategies can take on high levels of risk.

Relative strength–based individual stock strategies focus on buying those companies whose stock prices are outperforming the broader markets. Suffice it to say that anytime you are dealing with individual stocks you take on increasing amounts of asymmetrical risk. When momentum turns in an individual stock, the downside can be swift and painful. However, when using price momentum in an asset rotation–based portfolio, that risk is mitigated by using far more broadly diversified exchange-traded funds (ETFs).

So just what is "asset rotation"? Asset rotation is very simply a price momentum based methodology for portfolio management where investors focus their holdings on the respective asset class that is in favor, while avoiding another that is not. So rather than maintain a broadly diversified traditional asset allocation with dedicated weightings in each respective asset class, an asset rotation–based portfolio seeks to exploit the pendulum as it swings.

The proliferation of the ETF in recent years provides investors with the opportunity to manage an investment portfolio in a manner that was previously unthinkable—to be nimble and tactically navigate the markets with reduced exposure to downside risks. Ten to 20 years ago, managing a portfolio in this manner would have been impossible, but now with the inherent liquidity and broad diversification provided by ETFs, an investor can alter the entire construct of their portfolio in just a handful of trades.

A TIME-TESTED APPROACH

When evaluating the long-term efficacy of any investment strategy, just as O'Shaughnessy did in *What Works on Wall Street*, it is critically important to understand how that strategy has performed throughout all market cycles. In doing so an investor can not only build more comfort and confidence in what they are doing, they can establish reasonable expectations. Ideally, an investor should utilize strategies that have proven their merits in a myriad of different economic environments and avoid those that rather benefited from unique conditions present in the time period measured.

We are seeing this today with Modern Portfolio Theory (MPT)-based asset allocations. If executed properly, this diversified approach to investing has rewarded investors in recent decades with respectable risk-adjusted returns. However, as discussed previously, we have some very serious concerns about how these traditional allocations will perform in a rising interest rate environment that will surely wreak havoc on the fixed-income portion of these portfolios, creating losses where previously investors could count on steady returns. The paradigm has shifted.

While decades ago investors did not have ETFs available, and therefore could not have truly managed a tactical asset rotation portfolio, since many of the largest ETFs out there are based on major indices it is very easy to determine how these portfolios would have performed in the past.

First and foremost, for any asset rotation–based portfolio to be effective, the underlying eligible assets need to possess a low correlation to each other. This significantly increases the likelihood of one doing considerably better than the other at all times. The objective is to own the one that is doing well and not the one that is doing poorly. When this trend changes, you simply sell what is no longer working and buy what is.

A low correlation, and often an inverse relationship, has been evident throughout the course of history in the long-term relationship between U.S. stock prices and U.S. Treasury bonds. During times of economic peril, when equity prices have fallen, the U.S. Treasury bond has always provided investors with a modicum of capital preservation, whether during the prolonged bull market we have experienced in bonds since 1982, or during the 40-year bear market in bonds we experienced prior to that, the efficacy of this relationship has persevered.

To illustrate this point, going as far back as the Great Depression, investors in the United States have experienced 24 calendar years of negative equity market returns. In 19 out of these 24 instances the U.S. Treasury bond actually generated a positive rate of return on the year. During *all* periods, the U.S. Treasury bond protected investors from incurring a permanent impairment of capital and served as a flight to safety (holding up far better than stocks). See Figure 6.2.

The fundamental premise of asset rotation, like any trend following strategy, is not to catch the first move up, but to participate in the trend once it becomes evident. We participate in these trends until they end. At which point we move on and into something else that is doing better. Inherent in this process, we are not likely to capture all of the upside versus a more risk-oriented benchmark (i.e., the S&P 500). More specifically, this methodology wins by avoiding the sharp declines that can take place in the equity markets.

In order to illustrate these points we will spend the remainder of this chapter illustrating and discussing a very rudimentary two-asset-class

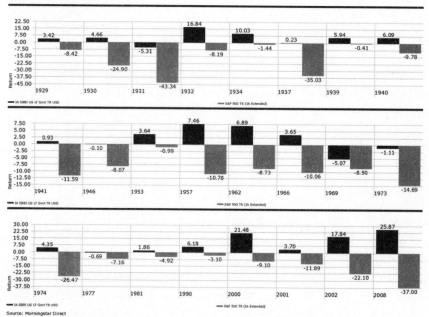

FIGURE 6.2 Historical Equity vs. U.S. Treasury Bond Returns (1929–2012)

Source: © 2014 Morningstar, Inc. All Rights Reserved. Reproduced with permission.

rotation. In this case, we will use the S&P 500 Index and the Ibbotson & Associates SBBI U.S. Long Term Government Bond Index. While many investors may be more familiar with the Barclays bond indices more commonly used today, their performance history does not go back as far and to better illustrate efficacy over longer periods, we felt it was important to trace our roots as far back as the Great Depression; when markets were at their worst and most volatile.

In this rudimentary illustration, our process for determining holdings throughout all periods is based on one single factor—buying the index that was up the most the previous month. So if the S&P 500 was up more than the Long Term Government Bond Index during the prior month, then for the current month we would simply own the S&P 500, and if the Government Bond Index was up more the prior month, then that would be what we own for the current month.

The purpose of this illustration is *not* that this extremely elementary method should actually be used by investors, but rather that the efficacy of even this very simple price momentum based asset rotation strategy establishes a foundation from which to build. In order to do this, we will look at the performance of this basic strategy throughout every decade going back to the Great Depression. This case study covers eight different measurement periods and more than 80 years of market history, or in other words the good, the bad, and the ugly for both stocks and bonds. Since recent years are more likely to be remembered by investors, we will make our way back in reverse, starting with the period that began with the lost decade.

THE 2000S

The performance of the stock markets from the year 2000 through the end of 2012 marked an extremely volatile time for investors. As previously chronicled, while the overall returns by the end of this period were minimally positive, the average investor fared far worse. With that said, after 13 years the S&P 500 had averaged a total return of 1.66 percent per year. At the same time, our very simple two-asset-class rotation portfolio would have averaged nearly 8 percent.

While surely neither rate of return may sound overly impressive, when you consider the cumulative returns we are talking about a

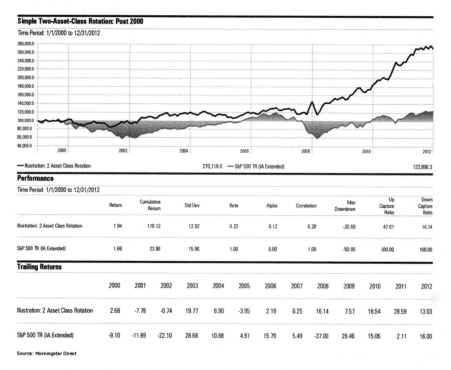

Simple Two-Asset-Class Rotation: Post 2000									

Time Period: 1/1/2000 to 12/31/2012

— Illustration: 2 Asset Class Rotation   270,119.0   — S&P 500 TR (IA Extended)   123,896.3

Performance

Time Period: 1/1/2000 to 12/31/2012

	Return	Cumulative Return	Std Dev	Beta	Alpha	Correlation	Max Drawdown	Up Capture Ratio	Down Capture Ratio
Illustration: 2 Asset Class Rotation	7.94	170.12	12.92	0.23	6.12	0.28	-20.69	47.01	14.14
S&P 500 TR (IA Extended)	1.66	23.90	15.96	1.00	0.00	1.00	-50.95	100.00	100.00

Trailing Returns

	2000	2001	2002	2003	2004	2005	2006	2007	2008	2009	2010	2011	2012
Illustration: 2 Asset Class Rotation	2.68	-7.78	-0.74	19.77	6.90	-3.95	2.19	6.25	16.14	7.57	18.54	28.59	13.03
S&P 500 TR (IA Extended)	-9.10	-11.89	-22.10	28.68	10.88	4.91	15.79	5.49	-37.00	26.46	15.06	2.11	16.00

Source: Morningstar Direct

FIGURE 6.3   A Simple Two-Asset-Class Rotation (2000–2012)

difference of almost 150 percent, in favor of the two–asset-class rotation. From a calendar year perspective, when equities struggled the most (2000, 2001, 2002, and 2008) our two-asset-class rotation held up far better, actually preserving capital when the stock markets were perilous. Consider that in 2008, while the S&P 500 was down 37 percent, our two-asset-class rotation would have actually registered a positive 16 percent; a performance spread of greater than 50 percent.

The risks of the two-asset-class rotation portfolio were considerably less than the S&P 500 throughout the period. With a standard deviation of 12.9 versus 15.9, investors achieved a more consistent return. More important, with a beta of only 0.23, the two-asset-class rotation was basically 77 percent less risky than the S&P 500.

Beyond providing investors with a superior rate of return with considerably less risk, the two-asset-class rotation also only demonstrated a correlation of 28 percent. In other words, when taking into account the entire period, the two-asset-class rotation provided investors with performance that at times moved very incongruent to the equity markets. In most instances, this was a good thing; avoiding sharp declines. However, it should also be noted in years like 2005, when advances in either asset class were less consistent, this single factor price momentum strategy lagged. With its low correlation and pension for avoiding sharp declines, our two-asset-class rotation would have provided a true diversifier to an overall portfolio (e.g., in combination with a traditional MPT allocation during the period). See Figure 6.3.

THE 1990S

Wouldn't we all just love to go back to the 1990s! This decade provided the second-strongest decade of equity returns since the Great Depression, with the S&P 500 averaging an impressive 18.2 percent per year. Other than 1990, when the U.S. equity markets were down a mere 3.1 percent, stock market returns were very strong. In fact, five calendar years generated returns of over 20 percent, and three of those five were greater than 30 percent!

In an environment such as this, many investors would not have recognized the need for a risk-adjusted investment approach. Not only because this prolonged bull run had started to build unrealistic expectations and irrational exuberance, but also because most risk-adjusted strategies demonstrate a severe lag when markets go on an extended run. This often significant performance lag leads many investors to abandon such strategies, often leaving themselves exposed to significant downside risks when suddenly out of nowhere the bull run ends.

Given the nature of this environment, investors should expect our two-asset-class rotation portfolio would lag the returns of the S&P 500 for the period. Often, when rotating into fixed income (due to the negative one-month return in the S&P 500 for the prior month), the stock markets would quickly bounce back. At which point, by spending the month in bonds, an investor in the two-asset-class rotation portfolio would have missed out on this gain. For basically the entire decade, amazingly there was no downward trend established for stocks.

As the S&P 500 averaged more than 18 percent per year, our two-asset-class rotation still managed to average a very respectable 14.5

percent return per annum. So as noted previously, while an asset rotation portfolio should generally not be expected to capture all of the upside of a risk-oriented benchmark, it should demonstrate respectable participation, as was the case over this time period.

Despite this modest lag in performance experienced throughout the decade, investors should realize that the primary purpose of any asset rotation portfolio is on significantly reducing investment risk, and in this respect the risk-adjusted performance was outstanding. Again, the two-asset-class rotation portfolio demonstrated a much lower standard deviation of 10.2 versus 13.4 for the S&P 500. The beta was also exceptionally lower at 0.54 (meaning the two-asset-class portfolio was 46 percent less risky than the S&P 500). Here, too, the correlation to the S&P 500 was relatively low, at 71 percent. From a risk-adjusted standpoint, again our two-asset-class rotation portfolio was a resounding success (see Figure 6.4).

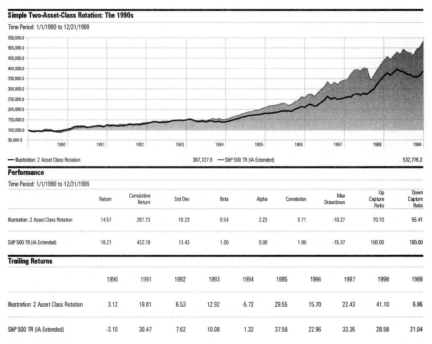

Simple Two-Asset-Class Rotation: The 1990s

Time Period: 1/1/1990 to 12/31/1999

— Illustration: 2 Asset Class Rotation 387,727.8   — S&P 500 TR (IA Extended) 532,776.2

Performance

Time Period: 1/1/1990 to 12/31/1999

	Return	Cumulative Return	Std Dev	Beta	Alpha	Correlation	Max Drawdown	Up Capture Ratio	Down Capture Ratio
Illustration: 2 Asset Class Rotation	14.51	287.73	10.23	0.54	2.23	0.71	-10.27	70.10	55.41
S&P 500 TR (IA Extended)	18.21	432.78	13.43	1.00	0.00	1.00	-15.37	100.00	100.00

Trailing Returns

	1990	1991	1992	1993	1994	1995	1996	1997	1998	1999
Illustration: 2 Asset Class Rotation	3.12	19.81	6.53	12.92	-5.72	29.55	15.70	22.43	41.10	6.86
S&P 500 TR (IA Extended)	-3.10	30.47	7.62	10.08	1.32	37.58	22.96	33.36	28.58	21.04

Source: Morningstar Direct

FIGURE 6.4 A Simple Two-Asset-Class Rotation (1990–1999)

Source: © 2014 Morningstar, Inc. All Rights Reserved. Reproduced with permission.

THE 1980S

Apparently hairstyles, popped collars, Bermuda shorts, and pastel colors were not the only thing cool about the 1980s. Very similar to the 1990s, the 1980s were also an outstanding decade for stock investors. The beginning of the 1980s are actually regarded as the beginning of the strongest and longest equity bull market in the history of the U.S. capital markets. For the decade, U.S. stocks averaged an annual return of more than 17 percent and just like the 1990s, there were five calendar-year returns of greater than 20 percent, and three with greater than 30 percent! Certainly, this was a great time for building wealth and long-term savings. From this decade through the 1990s is when the majority of today's Baby Boomers amassed their wealth (how could they not?).

Given the context of this economic backdrop, one should expect our two-asset-class rotation portfolio to have performed very similarly to how it would have performed in the 1990s. In fact, the performance was

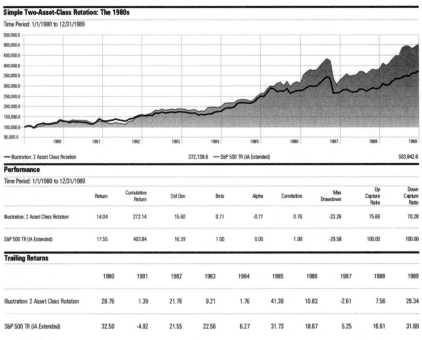

Simple Two-Asset-Class Rotation: The 1980s

Time Period: 1/1/1980 to 12/31/1989

| | Illustration: 2 Asset Class Rotation | 372,139.8 | S&P 500 TR (IA Extended) | 503,842.6 |

Performance

Time Period: 1/1/1980 to 12/31/1989

	Return	Cumulative Return	Std Dev	Beta	Alpha	Correlation	Max Drawdown	Up Capture Ratio	Down Capture Ratio
Illustration: 2 Asset Class Rotation	14.04	272.14	15.60	0.71	-0.77	0.76	-23.26	75.68	70.28
S&P 500 TR (IA Extended)	17.55	403.84	16.39	1.00	0.00	1.00	-29.58	100.00	100.00

Trailing Returns

	1980	1981	1982	1983	1984	1985	1986	1987	1988	1989
Illustration: 2 Asset Class Rotation	28.75	1.39	21.76	9.21	1.76	41.39	10.83	-2.61	7.56	28.34
S&P 500 TR (IA Extended)	32.50	-4.92	21.55	22.56	6.27	31.73	18.67	5.25	16.61	31.69

Source: Morningstar Direct

FIGURE 6.5   A Simple Two-Asset-Class Rotation (1980–1989)

almost identical. During the 1980s this very simple two–asset–class rotation portfolio would have posted an average annual return of 14 percent.

It should also come as no surprise then that the risk-adjusted returns of the two–asset–class rotation portfolio were also very respectable. While the standard deviation was only slightly lower than the S&P 500 (15.6 versus 16.4), as has been the case during all measurement periods, the beta was significantly lower at 0.76. Again, this essentially reflects that the asset rotation portfolio presented investors with 24 percent less risk than the S&P 500. The 1980s, just like the 1990s and 2000s, again would have provided investors in our simple two–asset–class rotation portfolio with very strong overall performance (see Figure 6.5).

THE 1970S

The 1970s were a more typical investment environment for stock investors than the 1980s and 1990s were. While there were certainly some outstanding calendar-year returns to be had, there were also three years of declines. From 1973 to 1974 specifically, investors in the S&P 500 would have lost more than 40 percent. Conversely, investors in our two-asset-class rotation portfolio would have been down roughly 15 percent, certainly a much more manageable loss from which to recover.

During this entire time period, our simple two-asset-class rotation portfolio not only would have generated strong risk-adjusted returns, but superior overall returns as well. For the period, the S&P 500 averaged a modest return of 5.9 percent per year, while the two-asset-class rotation portfolio would have average slightly better at 6.5 percent per annum. More important, the standard deviation on the two-asset-class was significantly lower, at 11.1 versus 16 for the S&P 500 and the beta was only 0.48! Collectively this indicates our simple two-asset-class rotation portfolio generated higher returns, with greater consistency, and with considerably less risk.

Further, it should also be noted that in each of the three years of negative calendar returns, the two-asset-class rotation portfolio held up far better, particularly in 1974, when the S&P 500 was down more than 26 percent and the two-asset-class rotation portfolio would have only been down little more than 3 percent. Ideally, this ability to rotate into inversely related asset classes during periods of prolonged equity

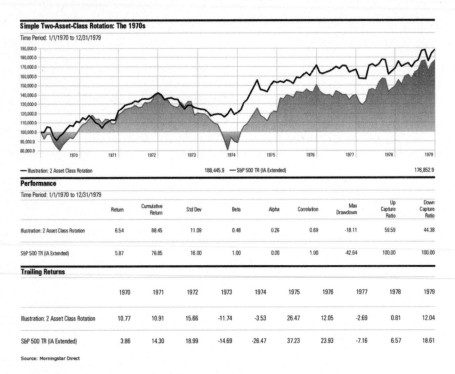

FIGURE 6.6 A Simple Two-Asset-Class Rotation Portfolio (1970–1979)

Source: © 2014 Morningstar, Inc. All Rights Reserved. Reproduced with permission.

market declines provides the engine for the sustainable growth of an asset rotation–based investment portfolio (see Figure 6.6).

THE 1960S

During the 1960s, our simple two-asset-class rotation portfolio would have again posted very respectable risk-adjusted returns. For the decade the S&P 500 managed an average annual return of 7.8 percent, while the two-asset-class rotation portfolio would have averaged roughly 4.8 percent. As we have seen in previously discussed decades, the two-asset-class rotation based portfolio achieved these returns with both a lower standard deviation and lower beta than the S&P 500. The standard deviation was 9.4 versus 12.2, and the beta was only 0.54.

While perhaps not the best decade of returns for our two-asset-class rotation portfolio, with a lower return variance, less overall risk,

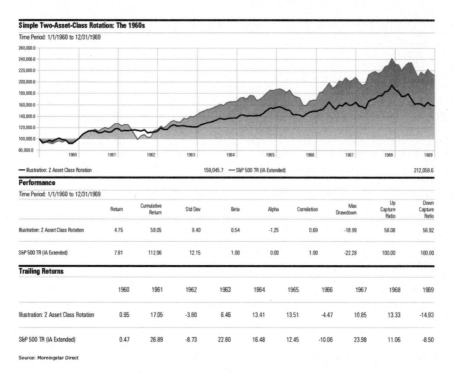

| Simple Two-Asset-Class Rotation: The 1960s | | | | | | | | | |
| Time Period: 1/1/1960 to 12/31/1969 | | | | | | | | | |

— Illustration: 2 Asset Class Rotation   159,045.7 — S&P 500 TR (IA Extended)   212,058.6

Performance

Time Period: 1/1/1960 to 12/31/1969

	Return	Cumulative Return	Std Dev	Beta	Alpha	Correlation	Max Drawdown	Up Capture Ratio	Down Capture Ratio
Illustration: 2 Asset Class Rotation	4.75	59.05	9.40	0.54	-1.25	0.69	-18.99	58.08	56.92
S&P 500 TR (IA Extended)	7.81	112.06	12.15	1.00	0.00	1.00	-22.28	100.00	100.00

Trailing Returns

	1960	1961	1962	1963	1964	1965	1966	1967	1968	1969
Illustration: 2 Asset Class Rotation	0.95	17.05	-3.80	6.46	13.41	13.51	-4.47	10.85	13.33	-14.93
S&P 500 TR (IA Extended)	0.47	26.89	-8.73	22.80	16.48	12.45	-10.06	23.98	11.06	-8.50

Source: Morningstar Direct

FIGURE 6.7   A Simple Two-Asset-Class Rotation Portfolio (1960–1969)

and a relatively low correlation of 69 percent to the S&P 500—this very elementary strategy still continued to demonstrate a high degree of efficacy and present investors with a complementary approach to their overall portfolio (see Figure 6.7).

THE 1950S

While surely many investors may not remember this period in stock market history, surprisingly the 1950s has proven to be the best decade to date for U.S. stocks since the Great Depression! The average annual return on the S&P 500 in the 1950s was an impressive 19.3 percent. Perhaps even more impressive was the fact that during this decade there were four calendar years of greater than a 30 percent rate of return (two of which were even greater than 40 percent)!

As we have seen during previously highlighted decades where stocks have been on such a tear, a risk-adjusted approach to investing should not be expected to keep up; after all, the focus is first and foremost on downside protection and not on beating a rising market. Over time, this approach leads investors to ultimately win by losing less, and therefore enable investors to stay the course when others might throw in the towel (potentially locking in losses).

While the S&P 500 was able to deliver returns of greater than 19 percent per year, our simple two-asset-class rotation portfolio would have still managed to average a very respectable annual return of 12.2 percent. As we should now be accustomed to, the asset rotation portfolio was able to do so at a considerably lower level of risk. The standard deviation of the two-asset-class rotation portfolio was 9.4, while the variance of returns on the S&P 500 was 11.8, the beta of the two-asset-class rotation portfolio was only 0.49, and the portfolio only had a correlation of 62 percent to the market (see Figure 6.8).

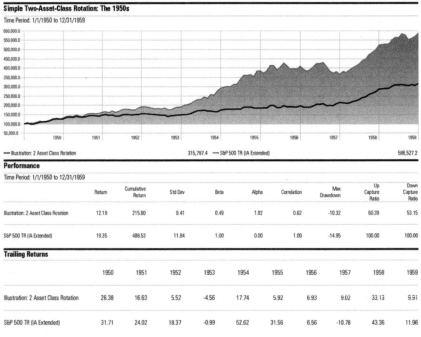

FIGURE 6.8   A Simple Two-Asset-Class Rotation Portfolio (1950–1959)

THE 1940S

The 1940s marked the beginning of a 40-year bear market in bonds. As such one might expect, our simple two-asset-class rotation would have struggled, and yet this did not happen? Why, because as we pointed out earlier in Figure 6.2, whether in a bull or bear market in bonds, during times of increased uncertainty in the equity markets, bonds have always served as a relative safe haven, and the ability to rotate between asset classes with a low correlation to each other will always maintain a high degree of efficacy.

During the 1940s the S&P 500 averaged a respectable average annual return of 9.2 percent per year. Over this same time period, our simple two-asset-class rotation portfolio would have averaged 7.5 percent. As it has during all measurement periods, this return was achieved with lower levels of risk. This was evident with a standard deviation of 12.2 versus 15.9 on the S&P 500, and also by the fact that the down capture ratio was only 53.7 percent (see Figure 6.9).

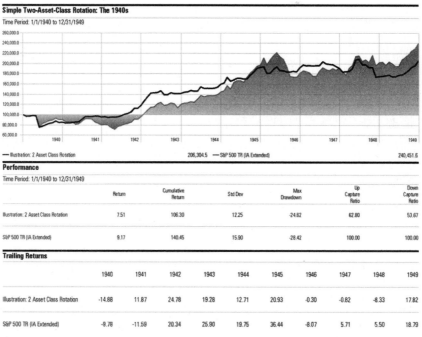

Simple Two-Asset-Class Rotation: The 1940s

Time Period: 1/1/1940 to 12/31/1949

— Illustration: 2 Asset Class Rotation 206,304.5 — S&P 500 TR (IA Extended) 240,451.6

Performance

Time Period: 1/1/1940 to 12/31/1949

	Return	Cumulative Return	Std Dev	Max Drawdown	Up Capture Ratio	Down Capture Ratio
Illustration: 2 Asset Class Rotation	7.51	106.30	12.25	-24.62	62.80	53.67
S&P 500 TR (IA Extended)	9.17	140.45	15.90	-28.42	100.00	100.00

Trailing Returns

	1940	1941	1942	1943	1944	1945	1946	1947	1948	1949
Illustration: 2 Asset Class Rotation	-14.88	11.87	24.78	19.28	12.71	20.93	-0.30	-0.82	-8.33	17.82
S&P 500 TR (IA Extended)	-9.78	-11.59	20.34	25.90	19.75	36.44	-8.07	5.71	5.50	18.79

Source: Morningstar Direct

FIGURE 6.9 A Simple Two-Asset-Class Rotation Portfolio (1940–1949)

THE GREAT DEPRESSION

In October of 1929, equity markets in the United States began what would prove to be the most difficult investment environment the world has ever seen. While today's generation of investors may think they have seen it all, having now been through the bursting of the tech bubble and the Great Recession of 2008, the volatility and risk experienced was nothing like it was back in the 1930s.

To put this into perspective imagine investing in a decade where the maximum drawdown in the S&P 500 was over 82 percent, the variance in returns (standard deviation) was 38.1, and calendar-year returns ranged from down 43 percent to up 53 percent! During this period the S&P 500 did not gradually move in any one direction, even the monthly returns were tremendously volatile, double-digit percentage moves from month to month in either direction were not uncommon. In both July and August 1932 the S&P 500 was up over 38 percent, after having been down 11, 20, and 22 percent in March, April, and May. For the year the S&P 500 managed to be down only a little more than 8 percent, but as we can only imagine, with this kind of whipsawing environment the average investor was likely down exponentially more.

Given this tremendously volatile landscape, we cannot imagine worse conditions for an asset rotation portfolio; as simply being in the wrong asset class for a single month could prove to be perilous. With that said, despite the outrageous volatility present in this time period, our two-asset-class rotation portfolio still managed to handily outperform the S&P 500. Over this greater than 10-year time frame the S&P 500 managed an average annual return of −3.2 percent, while our simple two-asset-class rotation portfolio would have actually achieved a positive average annual rate of return of 4.6 percent.

With that said, it certainly would not have been a smooth ride. While the standard deviation for the S&P 500 over this period was alarmingly high at over 38, the variance on our two-asset-class rotation was still over 27. Certainly, that measure too should be regarded as exceptionally high, but as it is anytime you make a portfolio comparison, it is all relative. So even though the two-asset-class rotation portfolio would have experienced a maximum drawdown of greater

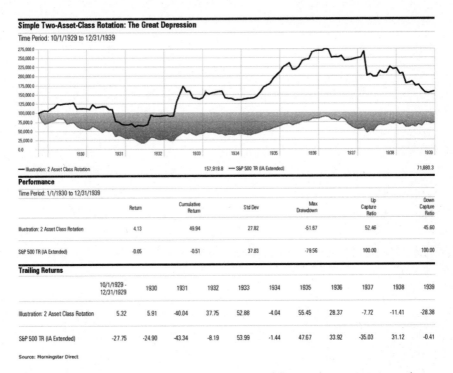

Simple Two-Asset-Class Rotation: The Great Depression

Time Period: 10/1/1929 to 12/31/1939

| | Illustration: 2 Asset Class Rotation | 157,919.8 | S&P 500 TR (IA Extended) | 71,880.3 |

Performance

Time Period: 1/1/1930 to 12/31/1939

	Return	Cumulative Return	Std Dev	Max Drawdown	Up Capture Ratio	Down Capture Ratio
Illustration: 2 Asset Class Rotation	4.13	49.94	27.82	-51.67	52.46	45.60
S&P 500 TR (IA Extended)	-0.05	-0.51	37.83	-78.56	100.00	100.00

Trailing Returns

	10/1/1929 - 12/31/1929	1930	1931	1932	1933	1934	1935	1936	1937	1938	1939
Illustration: 2 Asset Class Rotation	5.32	5.91	-40.04	37.75	52.88	-4.04	55.45	28.37	-7.72	-11.41	-28.38
S&P 500 TR (IA Extended)	-27.75	-24.90	-43.34	-8.19	53.99	-1.44	47.67	33.92	-35.03	31.12	-0.41

Source: Morningstar Direct

FIGURE 6.10 A Simple Two-Asset-Class Rotation Portfolio (October 1, 1929–December 31, 1939)

Source: © 2014 Morningstar, Inc. All Rights Reserved. Reproduced with permission.

than 50 percent, it is surely better than the greater than 80 percent drawdown investors experienced in the S&P 500 (see Figure 6.10).

Should we ever again experience a market environment like that of the 1930s, one can expect a great deal of investment strategies to fail. With that said, despite the increased volatility, even in the midst of this catastrophic market landscape, an investor adhering to even a very simple, single-factor (one-month price return), two-asset-class rotation portfolio would have achieved positive rates of return!

FROM THE GREAT DEPRESSION TO TODAY

Surprisingly, if we take a look at all of these measurement periods collectively, you will see that from the onset of the Great Depression in October 1929 until the end of 2012, the overall average annual

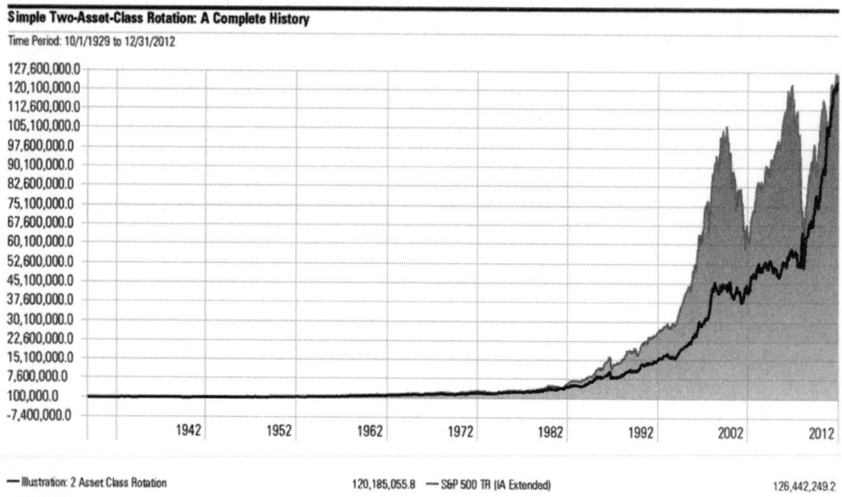

Simple Two-Asset-Class Rotation: A Complete History

Time Period: 10/1/1929 to 12/31/2012

	Return	Cumulative Return	Std Dev	Max Drawdown	Up Capture Ratio	Down Capture Ratio
Illustration: 2 Asset Class Rotation	8.89	120,085.06	14.64	-66.64	60.21	43.90
S&P 500 TR (IA Extended)	8.96	126,342.25	19.20	-82.58	100.00	100.00

Source: Morningstar Direct

FIGURE 6.11   A Simple Two-Asset-Class Rotation Portfolio (October 1, 1929–December 31, 2012)

Source: © 2014 Morningstar, Inc. All Rights Reserved. Reproduced with permission.

return of the S&P 500 and the two-asset-class rotation portfolio are nearly identical; the average annual rate of return on the S&P 500 was 8.96 percent versus 8.89 percent on the simple two-asset-class rotation portfolio. However, as has been proven throughout each and every one of our measurement periods, the asset rotation–based portfolio took on considerably less risk in order to achieve these returns (see Figure 6.11).

Since the Great Depression, equity investors in the United States have faced not one but two lost decades; from 2000 to 2009 when the S&P 500 averaged an annual return of −0.95 percent, and previously when it averaged −0.05 percent from 1930 to 1939. Over more than 80 years of market history, the worst decade of returns for our simple two-asset-class rotation portfolio took place in the 1930s, when it still would have averaged a respectable 4.13 percent per year (see Table 6.1).

TABLE 6.1 Average Annual Returns by the Decade

	S&P 500	Two-Asset-Class Rotation
1930s	−0.05%	4.13%
1940s	9.17%	7.51%
1950s	19.35%	12.19%
1960s	7.81%	4.75%
1970s	5.87%	6.54%
1980s	17.55%	14.04%
1990s	18.21%	14.51%
2000s	−0.95%	4.60%
2010–2012	10.87%	19.88%

THE BOTTOM LINE

Investors today have resources and tools available to navigate the markets in ways prior generations could only imagine. The ability to tactically manage a portfolio, alternating between risk assets and those that will provide a margin of safety, provides investors for the first time with a risk-adjusted approach that has a history of generating positive returns in all market cycles.

This is particularly impactful when you consider where the markets stand today. If bonds as an asset class now possess the potential for loss, and stocks lose an average of 40 percent during the average recession, and headwinds are increasing in our economy, where is an investor supposed to put their hard earned savings for capital preservation and long-term growth? Surely, investors cannot endure another lost decade or succumb yet again to the emotional pitfalls of buying the wrong thing at the wrong time?

When the paradigm shifts, how can an investor make money? How can one employ a reasonable investment discipline in a world where there is no safe asset class? The purpose of any investor should at least be to maintain the purchasing power of their investments over time. That has now become increasingly harder to do.

What if rather than maintain a traditional asset allocation of stocks and bonds, based on capital market assumptions the majority of us can likely agree will prove to be highly fallible, there were another way? A simple, rules-based process that would lead you to participate in rising markets, but more importantly preserve during times of peril.

MPT has largely benefited from a long-term decline in interest rates (resulting in a long-term increase in bond prices), but what can we expect out of this portfolio construct going forward? Should a conservative investor still be 70 to 80 percent in bonds?

Despite what our industry might lead you to believe, managing a tactical portfolio isn't just possible—it's already being done and is one of the fastest-growing segments of the investment markets today. Why? Because not only does it work, but even individual investors have the tools available at their disposal to orchestrate such a strategy with a high degree of efficiency.

As the paradigm shifts, we simply need to rethink what it is we think we know and allow ourselves to see what is already there; what has already been proven, and is measurable in a meaningful way. A simple two-asset-class rotation based on only one single factor—one-month price return—provides a foundation for further discussion.

Trends exist in the market place. They always have and they always will. Like Newton's Law of Inertia, these trends are likely to stay intact until met by an *unbalanced* force. In recent years, this "unbalanced" force has been the stimulative actions taken by governments around the world to inject liquidity and effectively prop up the global economy and our stock markets. While we don't believe we are the first to refer to government forces as "unbalanced," we do believe investors need to be paying attention to what the long-term ramifications of these actions may be on asset prices in the future. In such an environment, investors will benefit from taking a more risk-adjusted approach, one that is not married to either stocks or bonds, but rather simply invests in each when they are in favor and avoids them when they are not.

The human condition causes investors to trade on fear and greed, not on rational behavior. As headlines get worse, fear grows, and markets go lower. As headlines get better, greed increases, and markets rise. In the spirit of William of Ockham, we really believe it is that "simple." Unless the inherent psychology of market participants can somehow change, trends are here to stay. But that would be like asking the masses to stop being human. The masses won't read this book or care to understand anything any different than what they have always done and held to be true. Their irrationality creates an arbitrage opportunity for the rest of us to financially gain from their naivety.

CHAPTER 7

BUILDING A BETTER MOUSETRAP

Advanced Asset Rotation

Edmond Halley was a seventeenth-century English astronomer, perhaps most well-known today for deciphering the orbit of the eponymous Halley's Comet. During his time, the prevailing astronomical opinion was that comets traveled the universe in a straight line, passing by the Earth on only a single occasion.

Sir Isaac Newton believed that comets could travel in an orbit, but he never fully developed this theory. It was Edmond Halley who used Newton's laws of motion to calculate the effect the gravitational fields of Saturn and Jupiter would have on comets. Utilizing Newton's theorems, Halley was able to determine that a comet observed in 1682 followed the same path as one observed in 1607, and another in 1531. Halley postulated that each of these three observations was in fact the same comet and he predicted it would return in 76 years. Seventy-six years later Halley's Comet returned and continues to this day to pass by the Earth every 75 to 76 years.

Newton's laws of motion provided the foundation for future discoveries; for Edmond Halley to ultimately determine not only that comets traveled in an elliptical path around the universe, but, more important, that by studying their path, their return could be predicted.

In, Chapter 6, we provided a rather lengthy and elaborate illustration of a very elementary two-asset-class rotational investment discipline, based on only a single catalyst—one-month price return—and drew correlations between price momentum in the investment markets and Newton's First Law of Motion, citing that "an object in motion continues in motion unless acted upon by an unbalanced force."

We believe the investment markets behave in a very similar manner and that underlying trends exist until acted upon by an external "unbalanced" force. When met by this external force, trends reverse course and another asset class rotates into a position of leadership.

Just like Newton's laws of motion provided the foundation for Edmond Halley to prove and ultimately predict the elliptical orbit of comets around our solar system, our two-asset-class rotation case study serves as a cornerstone for future discoveries. The two-asset-class rotation is not a means to an end, but a beginning as to how investors can more effectively navigate the markets and mitigate risk.

While the overall risk-adjusted returns of our two-asset-class rotation portfolio may be outstanding in their own right, by our humble assessment to actually manage a portfolio around this seemingly elementary approach would be rather extreme. The simple two-asset-class rotation may be regarded as an all-or-nothing discipline; you are either 100 percent in or 100 percent out of the market. This rather drastic trend following approach is more susceptible to lag in volatile markets. What makes more sense is if the allocation could move incrementally between stocks and bonds and, more important, be able to take advantage of underlying trends in the stock market.

BUILDING A BETTER MOUSETRAP

The constituents of the S&P 500 can be broken down into nine major sectors: consumer discretionary, consumer staples, energy, financials, health care, industrials, materials, technology, and utilities. During various points in our economic cycle, one can expect certain sectors to lag and others to outperform. For example, more cyclical sectors like consumer discretionary, materials, industrials, and energy can be expected to lead during expansionary cycles, whereas during a contraction more defensive sectors such as health care, consumer staples, and utilities will often rotate into positions of leadership.

What we are referring to specifically is sector rotation. It only makes sense that an investor would want to participate in those sectors experiencing positive price momentum and avoid those under extensive pressure; in doing so, they could achieve market-beating returns. While the performance of the S&P 500 as a whole often serves as a benchmark for stock market performance, the sectors that make up this index often have returns that are very dissimilar from it, and often very different from each other.

In order to illustrate this point, we will make reference to what we have experienced in the U.S. stock market since 1999 (see Figure 7.1). Back in 1999, the technology sector was still on quite a tear. While the S&P 500 that year was up over 21 percent, the tech sector was up over 65 percent! This after already posting consecutive years of massive outperformance.

In the year 2000, when the tech bubble burst, the technology sector lost nearly 42 percent, while the S&P 500 itself was only down 10 percent. This period is remembered by the vast majority of investors as one that was extremely painful, but what most people fail to recognize is that despite losses in the broader market and certainly in tech, there were actually five sectors of the market that posted a positive rate of return on the year. In fact, four of them were up over 20 percent! (It may come as no surprise that these were the four worst-performing sectors during the prior year.)

In 2001, losses in the U.S. stock market continued to pick up steam. The S&P 500 was down almost another 12 percent, and the tech sector was down another 23 percent, but there were still two sectors of the equity markets with a positive rate of return.

In 2002, after already experiencing two consecutive years of losses, the equity markets began to capitulate. The S&P 500 registered its worst calendar year return of the period, down over 21 percent. The technology sector that had already been decimated lost another 38 percent. Investors were devastated, and none of the nine sectors of the S&P 500 were able to generate a positive rate of return.

In years like 2002 and 2008, when all equity sectors are experiencing prolonged declines, there has always been a flight to safety: the U.S.

U.S. Sector Periodic Table of Returns
Measured by the Select Sector SPDR ETFs & the SPDR S&P 500 ETF

1999	2000	2001	2002	2003	2004	2005	2006	2007	2008	2009	2010	2011	2012
Information Technology	25.87% Financials	12.75% Consumer Discretionary	-1.57% Health Care	38.11% Information Technology	33.26% Energy	40.52% Energy	20.48% Utilities	36.40% Energy	-14.79% Consumer Staples	51.32% Information Technology	27.82% Industrials	19.62% Utilities	28.42% Financials
23.20% Materials	25.55% Consumer Staples	2.21% Materials	-5.34% Materials	37.59% Materials	23.99% Utilities	16.12% Utilities	18.81% Financials	22.07% Materials	-23.09% Health Care	48.17% Materials	27.46% Consumer Discretionary	14.08% Consumer Staples	23.60% Consumer Discretionary
22.22% Industrials	24.41% Energy	-0.82% Health Care	-16.11% Energy	37.20% Consumer Discretionary	18.05% Industrials	6.47% Health Care	18.51% Consumer Discretionary	18.99% Utilities	-29.14% Utilities	40.57% Consumer Discretionary	21.78% Energy	12.39% Health Care	17.37% Health Care
20.39% S&P 500	22.50% Utilities	-9.42% Financials	-15.25% Financials	31.61% Industrials	13.28% Materials	6.19% Financials	18.30% Energy	15.32% Information Technology	-33.22% Consumer Discretionary	26.37% S&P 500	20.55% Materials	5.99% Consumer Discretionary	15.99% S&P 500
19.52% Consumer Discretionary	6.73% Industrials	-9.91% Consumer Staples	-18.67% Consumer Discretionary	31.53% Financials	12.98% Consumer Discretionary	4.83% S&P 500	18.29% Materials	13.22% Industrials	-36.81% S&P 500	21.75% Industrials	15.06% S&P 500	2.84% Energy	15.30% Information Technology
19.51% Health Care	-9.73% S&P 500	-10.19% Industrials	-20.90% Consumer Staples	28.26% Energy	10.70% Financials	4.08% Materials	15.85% S&P 500	12.36% Consumer Staples	-38.46% Industrials	21.62% Energy	13.79% Consumer Staples	2.61% Information Technology	14.92% Industrials
17.95% Energy	-11.60% Health Care	-11.75% S&P 500	-21.59% S&P 500	28.18% S&P 500	10.70% S&P 500	2.88% Consumer Staples	14.44% Consumer Staples	6.85% Health Care	-38.78% Energy	19.51% Health Care	11.91% Financials	1.89% S&P 500	14.70% Materials
2.67% Financials	-15.74% Materials	-12.99% Utilities	-24.61% Industrials	26.39% Utilities	7.89% Consumer Staples	2.87% Industrials	13.36% Industrials	5.14% S&P 500	-41.43% Information Technology	16.68% Financials	11.39% Information Technology	-1.11% Industrials	10.74% Consumer Staples
-3.79% Utilities	-16.87% Consumer Discretionary	-18.14% Energy	-28.77% Utilities	15.88% Health Care	5.34% Information Technology	-0.12% Information Technology	12.00% Information Technology	-13.40% Consumer Discretionary	-44.01% Materials	14.28% Consumer Staples	5.39% Utilities	-10.93% Materials	5.20% Energy
-14.27% Consumer Staples	-41.89% Information Technology	-23.35% Information Technology	-37.79% Information Technology	12.03% Consumer Staples	1.32% Health Care	-6.68% Consumer Discretionary	6.95% Health Care	-19.05% Financials	-54.68% Financials	11.71% Utilities	3.30% Health Care	-17.15% Financials	1.04% Utilities

Data Source: Morningstar

FIGURE 7.1 14 Years of Sector Returns (1999–2012)

Treasury bond. As we have highlighted previously, going all the way back to 1929, whenever the stock market has experienced negative returns, the U.S. Treasury bond has always held up significantly better, and in most cases actually achieved positive rates of return. For this reason, this asset class should be represented in any asset rotation–based portfolio.

When constructing an asset rotation portfolio, there must be two types of assets among the eligible securities to invest in: risk assets and those that will provide a margin of safety. The correlation between these two types of assets should be low, so that there is a greater chance that one is doing well when the other is not; ideally, there should be a negative correlation, indicative of an inverse relationship. If this is the case, then we always have a positive trend to participate in.

It is also important that there are multiple risk assets within the eligibility list, and that these eligible securities also possess a relatively low correlation to each other. The nine sectors of the S&P 500 are a perfect example of this.

As you can see in line 11 on the correlation matrix in Table 7.1, the nine sectors of the S&P 500 have a correlation to the broader market ranging from as low as 48 percent, to as high as 89 percent. The long-term government bond index previously cited in our two-asset-class rotation illustration actually possesses a negative correlation.

The efficacy of an asset rotation–based portfolio is enhanced as you increase the number of eligible risk assets, provided the risk assets selected are subject to trends that will lead them either into positions of market leadership or into periods in which they will lag (during which it is likely we will not hold them). It doesn't work if all of the eligible risk assets move at the same time, even if they do demonstrate varying degrees of magnitude. With that said, we would caution investors to not get carried away creating a lengthy eligibility list; stick with what makes sense, securities with relatively low correlations to each other, and a propensity for long-term outperformance.

In order to elaborate further on these points, we have created a follow-up to our original two-asset-class rotation portfolio illustrated in the previous chapter. In this case, rather than simply alternate between the S&P 500 and a Treasury index, we will replace the S&P 500 as an eligible asset with the underlying nine sectors of the S&P 500 so that we can participate in underlying trends in the stock market.

We are still using only a single factor to determine our monthly holdings, simply buying what was up the most during the previous month.

TABLE 7.1 Correlation and Performance Attributes, Sectors, and Treasury Bonds (1999–2012)

Correlation Matrix

Time Period: 1/1/1999 to 12/31/2012

	1	2	3	4	5	6	7	8	9	10	11
1 Consumer Discret Select Sector SPDR	1.00										
2 Consumer Staples Select Sector SPDR	0.49	1.00									
3 Energy Select Sector SPDR	0.45	0.37	1.00								
4 Financial Select Sector SPDR	0.77	0.57	0.48	1.00							
5 Health Care Select Sector SPDR	0.68	0.48	0.41	0.63	1.00						
6 Industrial Select Sector SPDR	0.81	0.52	0.62	0.77	0.70	1.00					
7 Materials Select Sector SPDR	0.76	0.45	0.66	0.70	0.62	0.86	1.00				
8 Technology Select Sector SPDR	0.68	0.24	0.39	0.49	0.63	0.66	0.54	1.00			
9 Utilities Select Sector SPDR	0.37	0.51	0.50	0.41	0.43	0.48	0.44	0.22	1.00		
10 IA SBBI U.S. LT Govt TR USD	−0.21	−0.06	−0.23	−0.20	−0.16	−0.26	−0.30	−0.24	0.04	1.00	
11 S&P 500 TR USD	0.86	0.57	0.63	0.82	0.79	0.89	0.80	0.85	0.48	−0.26	1.00

Performance

Time Period: 1/1/1999 to 12/31/2012

	Return	Cumulative Return	Std Dev	Beta	Alpha	Sharpe Ratio	Up Capture Ratio	Down Capture Ratio	Max Drawdown
Consumer Discret Select Sector SPDR	5.48	111.09	19.57	1.07	2.98	0.25	114.63	104.09	−54.85
Consumer Staples Select Sector SPDR	3.91	71.09	12.15	0.44	1.42	0.18	48.30	36.96	−32.67
Energy Select Sector SPDR	10.12	285.35	22.35	0.89	8.21	0.44	109.74	77.40	−53.15
Financial Select Sector SPDR	−0.49	−6.65	23.64	1.22	−2.19	0.00	106.14	123.36	−78.72
Health Care Select Sector SPDR	4.50	85.27	14.40	0.72	1.79	0.21	79.62	69.79	−35.56
Industrial Select Sector SPDR	5.03	98.73	19.82	1.12	2.53	0.23	110.37	101.53	−56.84
Materials Select Sector SPDR	6.58	143.95	22.89	1.16	4.55	0.29	122.58	107.71	−55.50
Technology Select Sector SPDR	0.04	0.50	26.30	1.41	−1.34	0.04	134.45	151.39	−80.35
Utilities Select Sector SPDR	4.80	92.88	15.18	0.46	2.67	0.23	54.91	40.24	−43.39
IA SBBI U.S. LT Govt TR USD	7.60	178.70	11.11	−0.18	5.87	0.50	−0.14	−38.05	−14.90
S&P 500 TR USD	2.94	49.97	15.79	1.00	0.00	0.11	100.00	100.00	−50.95

Each month we will hold the top five best-performing sectors of the market. When less than five of the nine sectors of the market have a positive rate of return, the portfolio will rotate incrementally into fixed income (assuming fixed income has a positive rate of return). Therefore, our portfolio can assume any of the following overall allocations on a monthly basis:

- 100 percent stocks
- 80 percent stocks/20 percent bonds
- 60 percent stocks/40 percent bonds
- 40 percent stocks/60 percent bonds
- 20 percent stocks/80 percent bonds
- 100 percent bonds

This monthly ranking is purely based on the top five best relative performers, even if their returns are negative. So as not to mislead our readers or inject other variables that might otherwise impact performance beyond anything more than simply using the S&P sectors in place of the S&P 500 and having the ability to move incrementally versus the all-or-nothing simple two-asset-class rotation, we have not made any other changes with regard to the eligible safe asset. As it was in our rudimentary two-asset-class rotation, it is simply the Ibbotson & Associates SBBI U.S. Long Term Government Bond TR Index. Thus, Table 7.2 makes up our list of eligible securities:

TABLE 7.2 Asset Class Sector Rotation Portfolio Eligibility

ETF/Index	Ticker
Consumer Discretionary Select Sector SPDR	XLY
Consumer Staples Select Sector SPDR	XLP
Energy Select Sector SPDR	XLE
Financial Select Sector SPDR	XLF
Health Care Select Sector SPDR	XLV
Industrial Select Sector SPDR	XLI
Materials Select Sector SPDR	XLB
Technology Select Sector SPDR	XLK
Utilities Select Sector SPDR	XLU
IA SBBI U.S. Long Term Government Bond TR Index	n/a
IA SBBI U.S. Long Term Government Bond TR Index	n/a
IA SBBI U.S. Long Term Government Bond TR Index	n/a
IA SBBI U.S. Long Term Government Bond TR Index	n/a
IA SBBI U.S. Long Term Government Bond TR Index	n/a

As you may recall, the data on this Ibbotson & Associates SBBI U.S. Long Term Government Bond TR Index goes back as far as the 1920s, and therefore we needed to use it in our more lengthy two-asset-class rotation illustration. So that we do not compromise performance of our flight to safety asset in this more elaborate illustration (versus our prior case study), we will continue to use this index. It should be noted that this index does not have an exchange-traded fund (ETF) tracking it. However, the performance of the iShares Barclays 20+ Year U.S. Treasury ETF (ticker: TLT) is highly comparable.

We recognize it may seem redundant to list the bond index five times, but the purpose is to illustrate it needs to take up five spaces in the ranking so that by simply entering the monthly returns of each eligible security and then ordering them from best to worst, it is obvious what if any percent goes into bonds. In order to get a better feel for this process, let's take a look at April and May 2010, shown in Table 7.3.

In May 2010, market participants experienced the *flash crash*. In a matter of minutes, the Dow Jones Industrial Average lost nearly 1,000 points, down roughly 9 percent. This marked the biggest one-day point decline in the history of the Dow. As you might imagine, many investors began to panic. Inexplicably, no one knew why it had happened. Rumors of a rogue trader or large error ran rampant. By the end of the trading session, markets had recovered most of their losses, but this event set the tone for a more than 13 percent loss in the S&P 500 over the next two months.

In April, the S&P 500 had been up 1.58 percent. Among the eligible securities in our two-asset-class sector rotation portfolio, there were a number of securities up more than this. Specifically, the consumer discretionary, industrials, and energy sectors of the equity markets were the top performers, followed closely by the Ibbotson & Associates SBBI Long Term Government Bond Index. Simply highlighting the top five performing assets from the month of April led us to a weighting of 60 percent equities and 40 percent bonds for May.

This rotation paid off, as in lieu of the market shock caused by the flash crash, the S&P 500 turned negative; posting a decline of -7.99 percent on the month. Conversely, with widespread uncertainty on

TABLE 7.3 Sample Monthly Ranking (April–May 2010)

	Ticker	April	May
Consumer Discretionary Select Sector SPDR	XLY	6.03%	−7.04%
Industrial Select Sector SPDR	XLI	4.26%	−9.12%
Energy Select Sector SPDR	XLE	4.16%	−11.45%
IA SBBI U.S. Long Term Government Bond TR Index	n/a	3.04%	4.37%
IA SBBI U.S. Long Term Government Bond TR Index	n/a	3.04%	4.37%
IA SBBI U.S. Long Term Government Bond TR Index	n/a	3.04%	4.37%
IA SBBI U.S. Long Term Government Bond TR Index	n/a	3.04%	4.37%
IA SBBI U.S. Long Term Government Bond TR Index	n/a	3.04%	4.37%
Utilities Select Sector SPDR	XLU	2.63%	−5.52%
Financial Select Sector SPDR	XLF	1.31%	−9.15%
Technology Select Sector SPDR	XLK	1.25%	−7.48%
Materials Select Sector SPDR	XLB	0.21%	−9.53%
Consumer Staples Select Sector SPDR	XLP	−1.07%	−4.63%
Health Care Select Sector SPDR	XLV	−3.89%	−6.51%
			−3.77% Return for the month of May

the rise, the level of fear increased in the stock market, and long term government bonds experienced a relatively sharp increase in price; up nearly 4.4 percent during the month of May. With the Ibbotson & Associates SBBI Long Term Government Bond Index making up 40 percent of our allocation on the month, this significantly cushioned the blow for investors, as our two-asset-class sector rotation portfolio would have been down a much more palatable 3.77 percent.

Incidentally, this downward trend in the stock markets continued on into June, with the S&P 500 down another 5.2 percent. Due to the strong rotation out of equities that took place during May, our two-asset-class sector rotation portfolio rotated entirely into bonds for the month of June and went on to post a monthly return of 4.46 percent, almost 10 percent better than the S&P 500.

While this is certainly a very short time period, from which investors should generally draw very few conclusions, in this case the relative price movement of the securities in our eligibility list led us to first reduce equity exposure and then ultimately to get out of them altogether. This rotation in such a short period of time provides a strong illustration of how a tactical portfolio can much more effectively mitigate downside risks versus a traditionally managed portfolio. When and if this downward trend in equities were to persist, a tactical asset rotation–based portfolio has the opportunity to preserve capital; pulling into a safe harbor until the storm passes by, and then resuming the course in calmer seas.

To get a better appreciation for how a sector rotation overlay on top of our basic two-asset-class rotation discipline impacts performance, it is important to examine the effectiveness of this process over longer time periods, just as we did with our initial illustration. In doing so, we will compare our returns not only to the S&P 500, but also to the Ibbotson & Associates SBBI Long Term Government Bond Index and our original simple two-asset-class rotation. The purpose of this exercise is to demonstrate how by going beyond the broad index we can better exploit underlying trends, and how navigating the markets incrementally between stock and bond allocations can help us avoid whipsawing market environments that can wreak havoc on an asset rotation portfolio.

Before we begin this illustration, it is important to note that the monthly performance returns used for the individual sectors of the market in our analysis were derived from both reported index data and actual ETFs. In December 1998, State Street launched the first ETFs actively tracking the S&P select sector indices. Therefore, any performance data from 1999 onward is based on the actual net returns of these securities. Performance data on the sectors prior to this point are based on the S&P select sector indices themselves. Since data on the select sector indices is available going back only to December 1989, our illustration will focus on the time period from 1990 to 2012.

While we would certainly prefer to go back further, we are comforted to know that this time period encapsulates more than two decades that in and of themselves reflect both the best and worst of times in the equity markets. Collectively, when coupled with our more than 80-year study of a simple two-asset-class rotation, we feel this provides us with more than a large enough sample size to measure the utility of the root process, and may be further used to create reasonable expectations as to how this portfolio might perform in any given environment.

THE 1990s

As we have previously documented, the 1990s were a fantastic time to be an investor in U.S. equities. The S&P 500 averaged an annual return of more than 18 percent. During this time, long-term government bonds also averaged a very respectable 8.8 percent, but with stocks performing like they had been since the early 1980s, it seemed like nobody was really paying much attention to bonds. This does, however, provide support for just how conducive this environment was for a Modern Portfolio Theory (MPT)-based asset allocation.

As we have now highlighted on numerous occasions, one should never expect a risk-adjusted asset rotation–based portfolio to outperform on the upside. While this can happen on occasion, it is certainly not the norm. With the primary objective on reducing downside risk, an asset rotation–based portfolio in an environment such as the 1990s, when stocks seemingly went nowhere but up and often in large moves, should be expected to provide investors with a high degree of participation.

In this case, our simple two-asset-class rotation portfolio averaged 14.5 percent throughout the period. Our more refined two-asset-class sector rotation portfolio averaged slightly more than 2 percent better, at 16.6 percent per annum (roughly 1.5 percent lower than our pure risk-oriented benchmark, the S&P 500). Over a 10-year measurement period, an investment of $100,000 would have grown to nearly $464,000, more than quadrupling in value. By the end of 1999, investing in our sector rotation portfolio would have generated $76,000 more than our basic two-asset-class rotation model.

While the average annual return of 16.6 percent for the sector rotation portfolio slightly trailed the average annual return of 18.2 percent for the S&P 500, as was the case in our previous illustration, it did so with significantly less risk, with a standard deviation of 11 versus 13.4 for the S&P, and a beta of 0.70. It should also be noted that the Sharpe ratio was higher for the sector rotation portfolio than it was for any other. As you may recall from Chapter 4, the Sharpe ratio is a measure of risk-adjusted returns. Effectively, this statistical measure indicates whether the portfolio's returns were due to good investment decisions or the result of taking on excess risk. The higher the Sharpe ratio, the better.

All things considered, our two-asset-class sector rotation portfolio would have performed outstandingly in the 1990s, providing investors with nearly the entire upside of the equity markets with a lot less risk (see Figure 7.2). When a portfolio has less risk, this also decreases the likelihood of buying it at the wrong time (as investors so often have a tendency to do). As one might expect, the nature and overall superior returns of this more elaborate asset rotation portfolio also outdistanced our simple two-asset-class rotation model by a fairly significant margin.

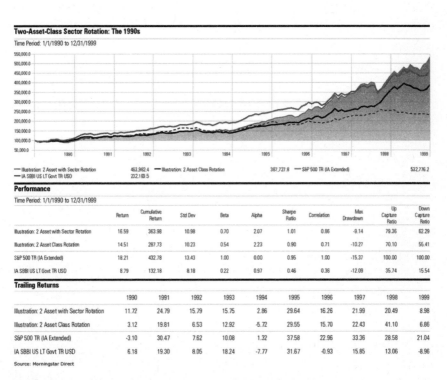

Two-Asset-Class Sector Rotation: The 1990s

Time Period: 1/1/1990 to 12/31/1999

	Return	Cumulative Return	Std Dev	Beta	Alpha	Sharpe Ratio	Correlation	Max Drawdown	Up Capture Ratio	Down Capture Ratio
Illustration: 2 Asset with Sector Rotation	16.59	363.98	10.98	0.70	2.07	1.01	0.86	-9.14	79.36	62.29
Illustration: 2 Asset Class Rotation	14.51	287.73	10.23	0.54	2.23	0.90	0.71	-10.27	70.10	55.41
S&P 500 TR (IA Extended)	18.21	432.78	13.43	1.00	0.00	0.95	1.00	-15.37	100.00	100.00
IA SBBI US LT Govt TR USD	8.79	132.18	8.18	0.22	0.97	0.46	0.36	-12.09	35.74	15.54

Performance

Time Period: 1/1/1990 to 12/31/1999

Trailing Returns

	1990	1991	1992	1993	1994	1995	1996	1997	1998	1999
Illustration: 2 Asset with Sector Rotation	11.72	24.79	15.79	15.75	2.86	29.64	16.26	21.99	20.49	8.98
Illustration: 2 Asset Class Rotation	3.12	19.81	6.53	12.92	-5.72	29.55	15.70	22.43	41.10	6.86
S&P 500 TR (IA Extended)	-3.10	30.47	7.62	10.08	1.32	37.58	22.96	33.36	28.58	21.04
IA SBBI US LT Govt TR USD	6.18	19.30	8.05	18.24	-7.77	31.67	-0.93	15.85	13.06	-8.96

Source: Morningstar Direct

FIGURE 7.2 Two-Asset-Class Sector Rotation Portfolio Returns (1990–1999)

THE 2000s

As we all know by now, the 2000s were absolutely terrible for equity investors in the United States, but they were fantastic for U.S. Treasuries. Recall from 2000 to 2009 the S&P averaged an annual return of –0.95 percent, while long-term government bonds averaged 7.69 percent. Given this environment, it should come as no surprise that our basic two-asset-class rotation averaged a respectable 4.6 percent per year. What may be surprising to some, however, is just how much more impactful the ability to participate in underlying trends in the equity markets was on performance, as our two-asset-class sector rotation portfolio averaged a much more impressive annual return of 9.27 percent throughout the period, more than double the return of our basic two-asset-class rotation illustration (see Figure 7.3).

To put this into perspective, during what might otherwise be referred to as the lost decade, $100,000 invested in our sector rotation portfolio would have grown to over $242,000 by the end of 2009. Conversely, this same $100,000 investment in the S&P 500 would have been reduced to less than $91,000, and that's if investors had the stomach to hang on throughout a gut-churning roller-coaster ride of a decade.

From 2000 to 2002, the cumulative return on the S&P 500 was –37.6 percent. During this same time the cumulative return on our sector rotation portfolio would have been an impressive 11.3 percent; outdistancing the S&P by nearly 49 percent in little more than three years, but more importantly preserving capital for investors when it mattered most.

In 2008, when the S&P 500 was down 37 percent, once again our two-asset-class sector rotation portfolio provided investors with a positive rate of return—up nearly 13 percent. Again, this marked a performance disparity of nearly 50 percent versus the S&P 500, but this time in only one year!

Of course, there were years like 2003 and 2006 when the S&P 500 handily outperformed our two-asset-class sector rotation port- folio, but this is where we need to remind investors that the premise of this portfolio construct is very candidly, to win by losing less over time. Investors absolutely need to understand this point. By avoiding the declines investors experienced in 2000, 2001, 2002, and 2008— you don't have to capture all of the upside. With a correlation of little

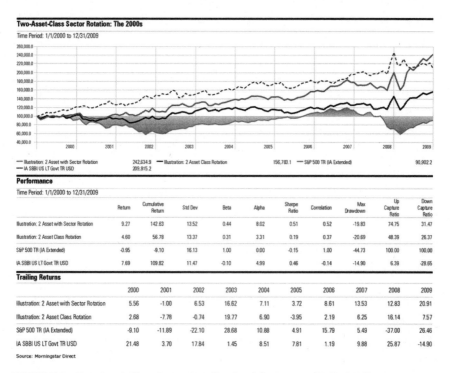

Two-Asset-Class Sector Rotation: The 2000s

Time Period: 1/1/2000 to 12/31/2009

	Return	Cumulative Return	Std Dev	Beta	Alpha	Sharpe Ratio	Correlation	Max Drawdown	Up Capture Ratio	Down Capture Ratio
Illustration: 2 Asset with Sector Rotation	9.27	142.63	13.52	0.44	8.02	0.51	0.52	-19.83	74.75	31.47
Illustration: 2 Asset Class Rotation	4.60	56.78	13.37	0.31	3.31	0.19	0.37	-20.69	48.39	26.37
S&P 500 TR (IA Extended)	-0.95	-9.10	16.13	1.00	0.00	-0.15	1.00	-44.73	100.00	100.00
IA SBBI US LT Govt TR USD	7.69	109.82	11.47	-0.10	4.99	0.46	-0.14	-14.90	6.39	-28.65

Trailing Returns

	2000	2001	2002	2003	2004	2005	2006	2007	2008	2009
Illustration: 2 Asset with Sector Rotation	5.56	-1.00	6.53	16.62	7.11	3.72	8.61	13.53	12.83	20.91
Illustration: 2 Asset Class Rotation	2.68	-7.78	-0.74	19.77	6.90	-3.95	2.19	6.25	16.14	7.57
S&P 500 TR (IA Extended)	-9.10	-11.89	-22.10	28.68	10.88	4.91	15.79	5.49	-37.00	26.46
IA SBBI US LT Govt TR USD	21.48	3.70	17.84	1.45	8.51	7.81	1.19	9.88	25.87	-14.90

Source: Morningstar Direct

FIGURE 7.3 Two-Asset-Class Sector Rotation Portfolio Returns (2000–2009)

Source: © 2014 Morningstar, Inc. All Rights Reserved. Reproduced with permission.

more than 50 percent to the S&P 500 over this time period, an inves-tor should not expect our risk-adjusted methodology to look like the markets at all times. If you don't expect it to look like the markets when markets fall, then you can't always expect it to look like the mar-ket when equities rise. This is largely due to the uneven performance of equities versus Treasuries and among the sectors at various inflec-tion points in the market, as longer-term trends are in question and rotational leadership is being challenged.

We should also highlight some of the key risk-adjusted return met-rics demonstrated by our sector rotation portfolio during this decade. As if beating the S&P 500 by more than an average of 10 percent per year were not enough, this feat was accomplished with dramatically reduced risks. With a standard deviation of 13.5 versus 16.1, our vari-ance in returns was significantly lower. Our beta of 0.44 illustrates that we achieved our massive outperformance while inherently taking on 56 percent less risk than the market. This was evident in our max drawdown of 19.8 percent versus 44.7 percent for the S&P 500. And again, as was the case in the 1990s, our sector rotation portfolio registered the highest Sharpe ratio.

After now highlighting the returns of an asset rotation–based sector rotation methodology over one of the best and one of the worst investment climates investors in the United States have ever seen, the superiority and efficacy of this process should be supremely evident. But before we can begin to touch on the absolutely amazing results of compounding these risk-adjusted returns over the entire period, we first need to complete our analysis by examining the first three years of the new decade.

FROM 2010 TO 2012

We always caution investors not to draw too many conclusions from very short measurement periods. The overall utility of any investment strategy can be distorted when only capturing a fragment of an economic cycle and encourage investors to be mistakenly short sighted (not something the average investor needs any encouragement to do, by the way).

With that disclaimer now having been said, it's not like our asset rotation strategies didn't fare well over the past three years. Rather, it would have been the opposite, with such dramatic extremes the risk-adjusted metrics would not be sustainable over a longer time horizon. This was due not only to the fact that we have been in a rising market, but frankly also because 2011 in particular highlighted the perfect environment for our trend-following asset rotation–based portfolios.

After getting off to a strong start in 2011, by midyear whispers began to surface regarding a breakup of the euro. This started a gradual five-month-long slide for broad-based equity indices. As fears of contagion increased, Treasuries rallied. When Standard & Poor's came out and did the once seemingly unthinkable by downgrading their credit rating of long-term U.S. debt, the markets cascaded downward another 12 percent in August and September.

This well-established trend was fantastic for our asset rotation–based strategies; they caught a big chunk of the upside to start the year, then continued to achieve strong returns when equities went on a multimonth downward path, and when equities rebounded to end the year, we got back in. By year-end, the S&P was only up 2.11 percent (not including dividends the actual return was *zero*, the first time in history that has ever happened), but our sector rotation portfolio was up nearly 22 percent, and surprisingly our very basic two-asset-class rotation illustration was up even closer to 29 percent (see Figure 7.4).

Collectively, over this three-year period, our two-asset-class sector rotation portfolio would have averaged 16.7 percent per year, while the S&P 500 averaged a very respectable 10.9 percent. While our outperformance of nearly 6 percent is what may catch everyone's eye, what is most shocking is the extremely limited degree of risk taken to achieve these results. In short, our standard deviation was 11.8 versus 15.3, our beta was only a ridiculous 0.04, our alpha was 15.68, the Sharpe ratio was 1.36 versus 0.75, and our correlation to the S&P 500 was only 5 percent—all of this with a max drawdown of only 4.96 percent!

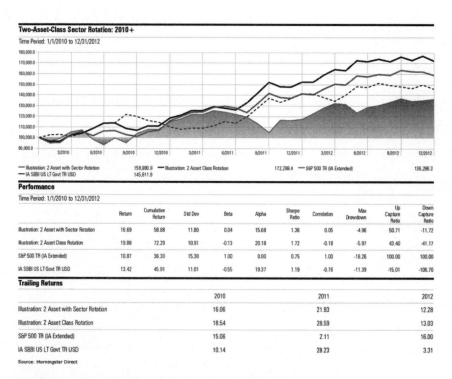

FIGURE 7.4 Two-Asset-Class Sector Rotation Portfolio Returns (2010–2012)

Source: © 2014 Morningstar, Inc. All Rights Reserved. Reproduced with permission.

Let's call it like it is. These results over this admittedly too short measurement period are downright cartoonish and borderline unbelievable. As we have now traced the effectiveness of asset rotation back more than 80 years, we are not surprised by these results whatsoever. However, we recognize over longer time periods our risk-adjusted metrics are much more likely to fall in line with what they were in the 1990s and 2000s.

23 YEARS: 1999–2012

As I intimated earlier, what is *truly* impressive is the long-term compounded results of our two-asset-class sector rotation portfolio over this entire 23-year time period. From January 1, 1990, to December 31, 2012, this sector rotation portfolio would have averaged an annual return of 13.36 percent (see Figure 7.5). Over this same period, the S&P

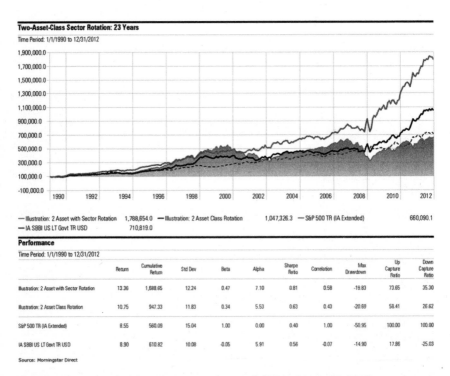

Two-Asset-Class Sector Rotation: 23 Years

Time Period: 1/1/1990 to 12/31/2012

| — Illustration: 2 Asset with Sector Rotation | 1,788,654.0 | — Illustration: 2 Asset Class Rotation | 1,047,326.3 | — S&P 500 TR (IA Extended) | 660,090.1 |
| — IA SBBI US LT Govt TR USD | 710,819.0 | | | | |

Performance

Time Period: 1/1/1990 to 12/31/2012

	Return	Cumulative Return	Std Dev	Beta	Alpha	Sharpe Ratio	Correlation	Max Drawdown	Up Capture Ratio	Down Capture Ratio
Illustration: 2 Asset with Sector Rotation	13.36	1,688.65	12.24	0.47	7.10	0.81	0.58	-19.83	73.65	35.30
Illustration: 2 Asset Class Rotation	10.75	947.33	11.83	0.34	5.53	0.63	0.43	-20.69	58.41	26.62
S&P 500 TR (IA Extended)	8.55	560.09	15.04	1.00	0.00	0.40	1.00	-50.95	100.00	100.00
IA SBBI US LT Govt TR USD	8.90	610.82	10.08	-0.05	5.91	0.56	-0.07	-14.90	17.86	-25.03

Source: Morningstar Direct

FIGURE 7.5 Two-Asset-Class Sector Rotation Portfolio Returns (1990–2012)

Source: © 2014 Morningstar, Inc. All Rights Reserved. Reproduced with permission.

500 averaged only 8.55 percent and the Ibbotson & Associates SBBI Long Term Government Bond Index averaged a modest 8.90 percent.

While to some an outperformance difference of nearly 5 percent may not sound remarkable (it is!), when compounded over 23 years the results are nothing less than incredible. A $100,000 investment in our sector rotation portfolio would have grown to nearly $1.8 million. This is almost three times as much as what an investment in the S&P 500 would have yielded (approximately $660,000).

As should be expected by now, this was achieved with far less risk. The long-term standard deviation was 12.2 versus 15.0, our beta was 0.47, the alpha was 7.10, our sharpe ratio was 0.81 versus 0.40, the correlation was only 58 percent, and the max drawdown was 20 percent compared to 51 percent. Do we really need to say any more?

GOING TOE TO TOE WITH THE BEST

In Chapter 5, we made mention of two of the largest and most successful tactical, managed ETF portfolio managers: Good Harbor and F-Squared. Both of these firms employ an iteration of an asset rotation–based portfolio. These portfolios are not only tactical in nature, but they are nimble and possess the ability to exit the equity markets altogether (very much like the methods we have just finished explaining).

Each of these portfolio managers utilize a very different process to navigate the investment markets; relying on a number of varied catalysts and market signals to warrant allocation changes in the portfolio. Good Harbor, for example, uses broad capitalization–based ETFs to make up their eligibility list (like the S&P 500 or S&P Mid Cap 400). For fixed income, they use Treasury ETFs. They can also use leveraged versions of these ETFs to increase their exposure. F-Squared, however, uses the sectors of the S&P 500 as their eligible risk assets, and utilizes Treasuries for safety.

Since for whatever reason many of the actual portfolios we run are most often compared to Good Harbor's U.S. Tactical Core portfolio, it would make sense that we offer a comparison between the simple two-asset-class sector rotation portfolio outlined in this chapter versus their historical performance post 2004. Keep in mind, whereas Good Harbor may employ leverage (enhancing portfolio returns when their timing is right and increasing portfolio risk when timing is wrong), our portfolio in this illustration does not.

Before taking a closer look, we should mention that the long-standing performance of Good Harbor's U.S. Tactical Core portfolio has been extremely competitive. As such, they have seen their assets under management grow from less than $100 million a little more than a few short years ago, to the point where now they are encroaching on $10 billion. This is a testament to both their unmitigated performance successes and the exponential growth we are now seeing in the tactical managed ETF portfolio marketplace.

More and more investors are learning that these portfolios actually exist and the fact that returns like those we have presented in this chapter are really possible, even by using a simple single-factor, one-month price momentum model.

From 2004 to 2012, both the Good Harbor U.S. Tactical Core portfolio and our two-asset-class sector rotation portfolio outdistanced the returns of the S&P 500 by a wide margin. In this case, the S&P 500 averaged an annual return of 4.94 percent, Good Harbor averaged 12.46 percent, and our sector rotation portfolio averaged slightly better at 12.85 percent per annum.

While Good Harbor certainly posted returns far superior to the S&P 500, it should be noted that the standard deviation was higher for the period, at 17.14 versus 15.03 for the S&P 500. Our sector rotation portfolio illustrated in this chapter, however, managed to achieve both the highest rate of return and also the lowest standard deviation of the group, at 13.48.

The betas of the portfolios over this measurement period were to be expected. Since both of the tactical portfolios employ a rotational discipline predicated on avoiding large declines in the equity markets, it should come as no surprise that both had a beta lower than 1. It should also be expected that due to the leveraged component in the Good Harbor portfolio that their beta would be higher than that of our sector rotation portfolio, at 0.69 versus only 0.39.

In short, one should also take note of the following key metrics: the alpha for Good Harbor was a very respectable 8.53, while the alpha for our sector rotation portfolio was even slightly higher at 9.61. The Sharpe ratio for the S&P 500 was 0.28, it was 0.66 for Good Harbor, and best for our sector rotation portfolio, at 0.83. Good Harbor demonstrated a

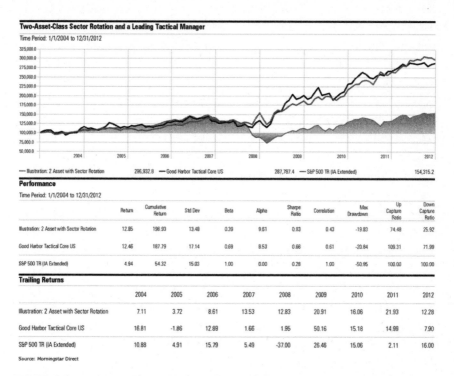

Two-Asset-Class Sector Rotation and a Leading Tactical Manager

Time Period: 1/1/2004 to 12/31/2012

	Return	Cumulative Return	Std Dev	Beta	Alpha	Sharpe Ratio	Correlation	Max Drawdown	Up Capture Ratio	Down Capture Ratio
Illustration: 2 Asset with Sector Rotation	12.85	196.93	13.48	0.39	9.61	0.83	0.43	-19.83	74.48	25.92
Good Harbor Tactical Core US	12.46	187.79	17.14	0.69	8.53	0.66	0.61	-20.84	109.31	71.99
S&P 500 TR (IA Extended)	4.94	54.32	15.03	1.00	0.00	0.28	1.00	-50.95	100.00	100.00

Legend: — Illustration: 2 Asset with Sector Rotation 296,932.8 — Good Harbor Tactical Core US 287,787.4 — S&P 500 TR (IA Extended) 154,315.2

Performance

Time Period: 1/1/2004 to 12/31/2012

Trailing Returns

	2004	2005	2006	2007	2008	2009	2010	2011	2012
Illustration: 2 Asset with Sector Rotation	7.11	3.72	8.61	13.53	12.83	20.91	16.06	21.93	12.28
Good Harbor Tactical Core US	16.81	-1.86	12.89	1.66	1.95	50.16	15.18	14.99	7.90
S&P 500 TR (IA Extended)	10.88	4.91	15.79	5.49	-37.00	26.46	15.06	2.11	16.00

Source: Morningstar Direct

FIGURE 7.6 Two-Asset-Class Sector Rotation Portfolio vs. Good Harbor (2004–2012)

Source: © 2014 Morningstar, Inc. All Rights Reserved. Reproduced with permission.

61 percent correlation to the S&P 500, while our sector rotation portfolio only had a 43 percent correlation to the broader equity markets.

All in all, both the Good Harbor U.S. Tactical Core portfolio and our two-asset-class sector rotation portfolio would have provided investors with far superior risk-adjusted performance (see Figure 7.6). Upon further statistical analysis, while the overall returns were similar, investors in our sector rotation model would have taken significantly less risk to achieve their return.

THE BOTTOM LINE

When you think about it, it all seems really silly. For decades, investors have clamored about markets being great or markets being terrible, about rockstar managers, blowups, and lagging mutual fund returns. Time and time again, they have allowed their emotions to get the best of them; they have chased returns, and they have allowed what they have personally experienced in the markets to formulate false long-term expectations. Over and over, we have heard the tired mantra of buy and hold and the virtues of Modern Portfolio Theory shouted from the rooftops. Heck, the entire financial planning community continues to offer investment advice based on the archaic outputs generated by false capital market assumptions. None of it makes any sense to us.

Just this morning, as we were working on this chapter, we I had CNBC tuned in on the television in the background. The time was 9 A.M. EST and across the screen they had highlighted "INVESTOR ALERT: Markets poised to open sharply lower!" What the hell is that? Sharply lower? The futures were down less than 1 percent? A 1 percent down open is mundane; it is commonplace. A move up or down 1 percent happens on an almost daily basis. What was the point of this sensationalized headline? Are they really doing anyone any favors?

As flippant as this may sound, investors would be best served to simply unplug, enjoy their time on this planet, and stick to an investment discipline that is measurable, proven throughout all market cycles, has a high degree of efficacy, presents lower downside risks, and, in the spirit of William of Ockham, is simple. Why is it that human nature will often lead us down the path of trying to solve a problem with the most complicated answer? It's as if we can somehow justify our answer's value and validity by showing all the work we did. The more variables we incorporate, the more unknowns, the less likely we are to actually come up with the right answer; and yet our brethren nod in approval of our efforts, as if welcoming us to the club.

We know in this day and age tuning out the world is obviously easier said than done, but you should take a step back for a moment, remove yourself from all of the commotion, and honestly ask yourself a few questions:

- Does all of this actually make any sense?
- These people telling me what is going to happen in the markets, how often are they right?
- Is it reasonable we should expect them to know the future?
- If not, and the end result does not justify the means, why keep banging your head against the wall and waste all that energy for returns that ultimately are likely to be less than average?

For those that have endured the excruciating pain doled out by the investment markets in recent years, it's like there is great big fraternity ready to welcome you with open arms, like a support group for those that have suffered abuse. After a while, the pain wrought in the investment markets can cause you to go numb, to become listless, at which point it becomes very easy to just buy into the notion that this is just the way things are. Just hold on through thick and thin and you will eventually be all right. Don't listen to those fools out there telling you that the market can be timed (you have already tried and failed)—remember, it's time in the market, not timing in the market. Try telling that to a client in the year 2000. More than a decade later, many of their financial plans have surely changed.

For decades, generations of investors have gotten it all wrong, and yet the answer was right in front of us the whole time. It's just that we weren't looking, and in fairness even had we known, up until recent years when the vehicles necessary to more adeptly navigate the investment markets became available, there wasn't much we could do about it. That is no longer the case. We are standing on the precipice of an Investment Renaissance, a period of enlightenment where a single epiphany has the potential to open up a whole new world of understanding, to provide a cornerstone upon which future discoveries can be made.

The proliferation of the ETF as an investment alternative has provided astute investors with the ability to manage a portfolio in ways that were previously unimaginable. This is already being done, and the precedent has been set. While this may be the fastest-growing segment of the asset management marketplace, and for good reason, the vast majority of investors still don't even have a clue it exists.

While some may continue to argue that Modern Portfolio Theory has worked, we can concede that over the past 30 years, if executed appropriately (that's a big *if*), it likely has. But given the changing paradigms present in today's investment landscape, we believe this approach may present a liability moving forward. What makes the most sense is to follow an investment discipline that has worked in all market cycles, and not simply had the benefit of an extended period of declining interest rates. An asset rotation–based portfolio not only provides a solution for the future landscape of our markets, but one that has provided far superior risk-adjusted returns in the past.

One of the fundamental pretenses of Harry Markowitz's seminal work on Modern Portfolio Theory was that it was impossible for a portfolio to exist above the efficient frontier, that a portfolio could not exist that demonstrated both superior returns and a lower standard deviation. Not only do we believe our work has dispelled this widely regarded investment tenet as nothing more than a myth, the existence and performance of leading tactical managed ETF portfolio managers over the past several years proves it.

For those who might doubt our findings, we have done the unthinkable, and published exactly, step by step, how to manage a simple two-asset-class sector rotation portfolio based on only a single factor (just buy what was up the most the prior month). Therefore, anyone simply with access to the monthly returns of the securities cited in our eligibility list should be able to recreate the entire performance history outlined in this chapter.

Our world is not driven by those that are asleep at the wheel. It is driven by those unafraid to pick up a rock and throw it—by those who, rather than simply follow the road before them, choose to first look at a map to see where that road might lead, whose suspicions lead them to believe there is a better way, and who possess the courage and passion to pursue their convictions.

CHAPTER 8

CHOOSE YOUR OWN ADVENTURE

Building Your Own Asset Rotation Portfolio

"Je pense, donc je suis"—translated into English, "I think, therefore I am." Perhaps most often remembered today for what on the surface may appear to be a rather elementary act of deduction, seventeenth-century French philosopher René Descartes has long been regarded as the Father of Modern Philosophy.

This famous quote, found in part IV of his 1637 publication, *Discourse on the Method of Rightly Conducting One's Reason and of Seeking Truth in the Sciences*, set the tone for what would become one of the most influential works in the history of modern philosophy and in the development of scientific reasoning. In this literary treatise, Descartes laid out his philosophical approach for the evolution of natural sciences and established a process by which knowledge could be attained.

Descartes began his line of reasoning by first rejecting everything currently held to be true, so that one could assess the world from a fresh perspective, devoid of any preconceived notions that might otherwise impair one's perceptions. Descartes was mindful to reject his senses, believing them to be inconclusive and unreliable. Rather, he attempted to arrive at a fundamental set of principles that one can know to be true without a doubt, based solely on deduction. "I think, therefore I am" was his rudimentary illustration of this philosophy, which according to Descartes, served as the only appropriate method for acquiring knowledge.

"I think, therefore I am.". . . If indeed you are no longer asleep behind the wheel, you have very likely developed a higher level of consciousness and can now see with eyes wide open the greater investment landscape taking shape all around us; there is a brave new world to explore.

Our previous chapters have led us up to this point, where we can now have an intelligible discussion on how one might actually *manage and customize* an asset rotation–based portfolio. The possibilities are nearly limitless, but there are certainly some potholes in the road investors would be wise to steer clear of, and some generally established ground rules for practical navigation.

With that said, we will not pretend to have all of the answers. There are quite frankly too many possibilities to consider and so many variables that could be incorporated, that at this point the optimal asset rotation portfolio construct is likely still in its infancy.

Throughout the remainder of this chapter, we will present additional vetting factors to be considered beyond the simple two-asset-class sector rotation, single-factor approach highlighted in our previous chapter. Just as Copernicus first proposed the concept of a sun-centered universe, and over the course of the Renaissance Period the likes of Galileo, Newton, and Halley expanded further on this concept, making new discoveries and forever changing the way we view the world around us, we aim to provide the greater investment community with the knowledge base and tools necessary to be successful in what will surely be a more difficult investment environment going forward.

CHOOSE YOUR OWN ADVENTURE

As a child, we enjoyed a series of books entitled "Choose Your Own Adventure." In each book, you reached various inflection points in which you were presented with a choice to be made. If you made one decision, you were directed to a particular page in the book, and your adventure would continue. If you made the other decision, you were directed elsewhere. If you made the wrong decision, your adventure often abruptly came to an end and your story was over.

Back then, if you made the wrong decision and you were inclined to keep reading, you simply went back to the page where you had been presented with the initial choice and followed the alternate decision. Books can be very forgiving in this manner; the investment markets, however, can be an entirely different story altogether.

At this point, it is appropriate that we caution investors that the following factors and suggestions for further refinement of an asset rotation–based, tactical, trend-following process are very likely best left to a professional in the financial industry—not a jack of all trades but a true asset manager. The fundamental premise of any asset rotation portfolio should first and foremost be on generating strong risk-adjusted returns. If not constructed and managed appropriately, an investor could end up with just the opposite. Therefore, the contents outlined in this chapter should be considered *bonus* material, and not suitable for all investors.

ADDITIONAL FACTORS TO CONSIDER: ELIGIBLE RISK ASSETS

In Chapter 7, the rotational discipline was based on only a single catalyst, simply buying the best-performing exchange-traded funds (ETFs) on our eligibility list from the prior month. While it may sound too good to be true and outrageously simple, more than 80 years of market history has proven the virtues of this rudimentary approach. Throughout all decades, this all-too-simple approach has worked, providing investors with respectable participation in the upside of equity markets, but, more important, with a discipline to avoid prolonged declines. If nothing else, we know using this elementary process with cap-weighted sector-based ETFs and Treasury ETFs will provide investors with extremely competitive risk-adjusted returns over time—as good as the best of the best with currently published track records in the tactical managed ETF segment of the market.

Therefore, as one might expect, adding additional factors may either increase or decrease the efficiency of the portfolio. One needs to be mindful of the impact of each potential vetting factor added and not simply throw a bunch of them against the wall to see what sticks.

As we have previously mentioned, any asset rotation portfolio should be composed of at least two asset classes—one representative of risk assets and another that has a propensity to act as a flight to safety or for capital preservation. Within each asset class, there can be any number of ETFs on your eligibility list, but ideally those assets should not be highly correlated to each other. Due to the economic sensitivity of sector based ETFs at various stages in the market cycle, whether our economy is currently expanding or contracting, these ETFs often have lower correlations to each other than a number of other equity-based ETFs and therefore provide investors with the opportunity to exploit underlying trends in the investment markets.

Chapter 7 highlighted the use of capitalization-weighted sector ETFs made available by State Street. These were the first sector ETFs to come to market in the late 1990s and track underlying indices with extensive data prior to the inception of the ETF. They are also the most liquid of all of the sector-based ETFs and by far have the highest average daily trading volume. For these reasons, it made the most sense to provide a sector-based two-asset-class rotation utilizing these ETFs in our illustration. However, it should be noted there are a growing number of ways investors today can play sector rotation through alternatively weighted ETFs, as summarized in Table 8.1.

As far as the best way to utilize sector-based ETFs in an asset rotation–based portfolio, it depends entirely on your objective. If, for example, the objective is on a lower-beta, lower-cost sector rotation approach, then each of the three largest ETF providers (iShares, State Street, and Vanguard) all provide investors with exceptional options. If an investor is willing to pay a slightly higher cost for the ETF and incur a slightly higher beta, then, for example, the equally weighted sector ETFs provided by Guggenheim can certainly add value; they generally have greater up-capture ratios than the capitalization-weighted ETFs.

It should be noted that when equity securities possess a higher beta in an asset rotation–based portfolio, it is not necessarily a bad thing. Higher-beta securities have a tendency to go up more in rising markets and fall more in market declines, but in an asset rotation–based portfolio, you likely will not be holding the higher–beta equity sector ETF for very long should the downward trajectory of the markets continue.

TABLE 8.1 The Various Types of Sector ETFs Available

Sector Focus	ETF Provider (s)	Commentary
Capitalization-Weighted Sector ETFs	State Street, iShares, Vanguard	The staple of the group. Most commonly used. The only drawback is in certain sectors there can be an exceptionally high concentration in only a handful of companies. It should be noted, due to the mega cap nature of these ETFs, betas tend to be lower than all of the other sector-based ETFs.
Equally Weighted Sector ETFs	Guggenheim	A truly diversified approach to playing the sectors and, in our opinion, a more pure representation of what is going on in the sector itself. It is surprising to us that these ETFs have not garnered more attention.
Small-Cap Sector ETFs	Powershares	Since over longer periods small-cap stocks have a tendency to outperform large-cap stocks, it makes sense that a sector rotation strategy with these ETFs can provide measurable outperformance.
International Sector ETFs	State Street, iShares	For whatever reason, these ETFs have not gotten much volume, but this is a great way to manage exposure to international stocks and tactically navigate the underlying trends—as opposed to simply owning a broad-based developed international ETF like the MSCI EAFE.
Global Sector ETFs	iShares	For those looking for global exposure, this is the way to go. While these ETFs remain significantly overweight in U.S. equities, geographic diversification is broadly increased.
Emerging-Market Sector ETFs	iShares	Emerging markets remain one of the most volatile sectors of the market; this can be especially true when broken down to the individual sector level. With the proper safeguards in place, these ETFs could provide for a very compelling asset rotation strategy.
Fundamentally Weighted Sector ETFs	First Trust	These alternately weighted sector ETFs rank the companies within a given sector based not on their size but their relative valuation. More attractive valuations are given a higher weighting in the ETF.
Subsector ETFs	State Street, iShares, Powershares, VanEck	By subsector we are simply referring to any sector exposure beyond the traditional nine sectors of the market. Categorically, this offers exposure to what can be some very dynamic trends such as biotech, alternative energy, semiconductors, agriculture, miners, gaming, water, etc. Trends in these sectors can be very powerful, but also quite volatile.

Therefore, you can still achieve the primary aim of reducing downside risk, but potentially capture greater returns in a rising stock market.

Earlier in this book, we mentioned the cost of ownership and how lower expense ratios have historically yielded higher returns. It is important that this is not taken out of context. With respect to alternatively weighted sector ETFs, there is often a higher internal cost; this is largely because the ETF provider has to pay more to use the index itself. In no way do we view these slightly higher internal costs as a deterrent to ownership—this is merely the cost of doing business.

If a respective sector-based ETF provides us with the appropriate risk return metrics we are looking for, in our targeted segment of the market, the cost is irrelevant. Of course, if the costs are too high, the ETF will not be able to provide us with the appropriate risk–adjusted returns in the first place. In short, if there is value added by focused exposure or alternatively weighted sectors ETFs, then a slightly higher cost should not be an issue.

Regardless of what type of sector-based ETF an investor might prefer, it should also be known that sectors are not the only areas of the equity markets where we see a relatively low correlation to each other. We also see this divergence in geographically based equity ETFs. While certainly one could focus on regionally based ETFs that include multiple countries (such as the Vanguard Europe ETF or the iShares MSCI Pacific Ex-Japan ETF), we prefer exposure focused on individual countries.

In order to illustrate this point, we have provided a correlation matrix of the 10 largest countries that comprise the MSCI EAFE Index (Europe, Australia, and the Far East), the most commonly used benchmark for international investing. The following 10 countries make up nearly 90 percent of the MSCI EAFE Index: Australia, Sweden, Germany, Hong Kong, Japan, Switzerland, the Netherlands, Spain, France, and the United Kingdom. Each of these country-specific ETFs are available through the ETF provider, iShares (see Table 8.2).

These individual country-based ETFs range in correlation from 77 to 96 percent to the iShares MSCI EAFE ETF. However, more important, their ranges versus each other are even lower, anywhere from 63 to 87 percent. Just as we pointed out in the last chapter when dissecting the correlation matrix of sector-based ETFs versus long-term government bonds, the iShares Barclays 20+ Year Treasury Bond ETF

TABLE 8.2 Correlation and Performance Attributes, Countries, and Treasury Bonds (2003–2012)

Correlation Matrix

Time Period: 1/1/2003 to 12/31/2012

		1	2	3	4	5	6	7	8	9	10	11	12
1	iShares MSCI Australia	1.00											
2	iShares MSCI Sweden	0.83	1.00										
3	iShares MSCI Germany	0.82	0.87	1.00									
4	iShares MSCI Hong Kong	0.75	0.74	0.68	1.00								
5	iShares MSCI Japan	0.63	0.61	0.61	0.57	1.00							
6	iShares MSCI Switzerland Capped Index	0.81	0.84	0.88	0.67	0.62	1.00						
7	iShares MSCI Netherlands	0.83	0.89	0.91	0.72	0.63	0.88	1.00					
8	iShares MSCI Spain Capped	0.75	0.77	0.82	0.61	0.57	0.78	0.84	1.00				
9	iShares MSCI France	0.85	0.88	0.95	0.70	0.62	0.89	0.94	0.89	1.00			
10	iShares MSCI United Kingdom	0.87	0.87	0.87	0.75	0.65	0.86	0.90	0.82	0.90	1.00		
11	iShares 20+ Year Treasury Bond	−0.20	−0.28	−0.28	−0.25	−0.13	−0.21	−0.27	−0.19	−0.27	−0.32	1.00	
12	iShares MSCI EAFE	0.90	0.91	0.93	0.77	0.77	0.91	0.94	0.86	0.96	0.95	−0.26	1.00

(Continued)

TABLE 8.2 Correlation and Performance Attributes, Countries, and Treasury Bonds (2003–2012) (Continued)

Performance

Time Period: 1/1/2003 to 12/31/2012

	Return	Cumulative Return	Std Dev	Beta	Alpha	Sharpe Ratio	Up Capture Ratio	Down Capture Ratio	Max Drawdown
iShares MSCI Australia	15.35	317.19	23.49	1.16	6.46	0.66	128.37	106.33	−62.71
iShares MSCI Sweden	14.88	300.33	25.91	1.28	5.64	0.60	128.45	106.38	−62.68
iShares MSCI Germany	11.56	198.48	25.21	1.28	2.48	0.49	131.92	126.70	−60.52
iShares MSCI Hong Kong	12.91	236.76	21.78	0.92	5.70	0.59	98.17	76.69	−55.21
iShares MSCI Japan	4.36	53.21	16.60	0.70	−1.50	0.24	70.79	77.69	−47.57
iShares MSCI Switzerland Capped Index	10.57	173.17	16.74	0.83	3.32	0.58	89.13	74.63	−46.43
iShares MSCI Netherlands	6.98	96.26	22.60	1.16	−1.34	0.34	111.07	119.35	−60.20
iShares MSCI Spain Capped	9.26	142.51	25.92	1.22	1.08	0.41	122.06	123.69	−58.84
iShares MSCI France	7.05	97.68	22.62	1.18	−1.46	0.34	116.25	125.75	−57.40
iShares MSCI United Kingdom	7.34	103.15	18.02	0.94	−0.27	0.39	90.47	90.58	−59.17
iShares 20+ Year Treasury Bond	7.75	111.03	13.80	−0.19	8.21	0.48	−3.04	−41.80	−21.53
iShares MSCI EAFE	8.07	117.37	18.34	1.00	0.00	0.42	100.00	100.00	−56.55

has a negative correlation to them all. In order to highlight this ongoing inverse relationship, we have included this ETF in our correlation matrix as well.

As far as the availability of additional country-specific ETFs, iShares provides investors with the most expansive lineup in the industry by a large margin, with more than 100 individual countries to choose from. Their suite of international ETFs offer investors exposure to major developed economies as well as the emerging markets, and even some obscure frontier markets.

Beyond either a sector-based or country-centric rotational approach, perhaps the most commonly used method is to construct a rather broad global asset rotation portfolio using some of the most highly liquid equity ETFs trading in the markets today. This can very easily be done just by creating an eligibility list comprised of the following ETFs: the Russell 1000 Growth, Russell 1000 Value, Russell Midcap Growth, Russell Midcap Value, Russell 2000 Growth, Russell 2000 Value, MSCI EAFE Growth, MSCI EAFE Value, MSCI EAFE Small Cap, and the MSCI Emerging Markets. In this manner, one could participate in underlying trends in the equity markets by size, style, and geographic location.

Just as we have for both the underlying sectors of the equity markets, as well as with individual countries, we have illustrated a correlation matrix for this global approach to asset rotation, as shown in Table 8.3. While certainly there can be distinct performance differences among these eligible equity ETFs, and most investors will recognize there are trends of historical outperformance exhibited by either U.S. equities, developed international, or emerging markets—it should be noted that this does not necessarily imply a low correlation among these securities; rather, with relatively high correlations one can deduce that directionally they likely move in a much similar fashion to each other, what often differs is the amplitude of the move.

In order to present a handful of different ways in which the equity portion of a tactical asset rotation portfolio can be constructed, we have illustrated how this might be done with sectors, countries, or even broad-based global equities. This is not to imply in any way that this is how it should necessarily be done; we are simply making reference to a handful of approaches that have been used with varying degrees of success. Beyond these general categorical approaches, one

TABLE 8.3 Correlation and Performance Attributes, Global Equities, and Treasury Bonds (2008–2012)

Correlation Matrix

Time Period: 1/1/2008 to 12/31/2012

	1	2	3	4	5	6	7	8	9	10	11	12
1 iShares Russell 1000 Growth	1.00											
2 iShares Russell 1000 Value	0.94	1.00										
3 iShares Russell Midcap Growth	0.98	0.92	1.00									
4 iShares Russell Midcap Value	0.95	0.97	0.96	1.00								
5 iShares Russell 2000 Growth	0.95	0.92	0.97	0.96	1.00							
6 iShares Russell 2000 Value	0.90	0.95	0.90	0.97	0.95	1.00						
7 iShares MSCI EAFE Growth	0.92	0.89	0.90	0.88	0.85	0.81	1.00					
8 iShares MSCI EAFE Value	0.89	0.91	0.88	0.90	0.84	0.83	0.96	1.00				
9 iShares MSCI EAFE Small-Cap	0.89	0.87	0.89	0.88	0.84	0.80	0.97	0.96	1.00			
10 iShares MSCI Emerging Markets	0.89	0.85	0.90	0.86	0.86	0.80	0.94	0.90	0.92	1.00		
11 iShares 20+ Year Treasury Bond	−0.37	−0.28	−0.39	−0.30	−0.38	−0.30	−0.31	−0.29	−0.29	−0.31	1.00	
12 MSCI World NR USD	0.97	0.96	0.95	0.95	0.92	0.89	0.97	0.97	0.95	0.93	−0.32	1.00

Performance

Time Period: 1/1/2008 to 12/31/2012

	Return	Cumulative Return	Std Dev	Beta	Alpha	Sharpe Ratio	Up Capture Ratio	Down Capture Ratio	Max Drawdown
iShares Russell 1000 Growth	2.95	15.66	19.28	0.89	3.83	0.23	97.53	83.83	−45.85
iShares Russell 1000 Value	0.48	2.41	20.13	0.93	1.55	0.11	96.26	90.94	−51.52
iShares Russell Midcap Growth	3.04	16.15	23.08	1.05	4.66	0.23	114.87	99.42	−51.16
iShares Russell Midcap Value	3.67	19.72	23.13	1.05	5.27	0.26	115.25	97.72	−51.73
iShares Russell 2000 Growth	3.55	19.04	24.80	1.09	5.51	0.25	119.62	102.08	−49.00
iShares Russell 2000 Value	3.48	18.67	24.74	1.06	5.46	0.25	117.57	100.43	−47.35
iShares MSCI EAFE Growth	−3.18	−14.92	22.45	1.05	−1.71	−0.05	99.53	106.46	−52.26
iShares MSCI EAFE Value	−4.40	−20.14	24.74	1.15	−2.53	−0.07	110.30	120.48	−55.77
iShares MSCI EAFE Small-Cap	−0.98	−4.78	25.37	1.16	1.21	0.08	110.07	108.48	−56.14
iShares MSCI Emerging Markets	−1.07	−5.22	28.58	1.27	1.87	0.09	124.22	121.53	−56.56
iShares 20+ Year Treasury Bond	9.60	58.17	16.73	−0.26	10.33	0.61	−16.56	−49.88	−21.53
MSCI World NR USD	−1.18	−5.76	20.89	1.00	0.00	0.03	100.00	100.00	−51.44

could also utilize some of the following eligible securities to distinguish the portfolio:

- *Leveraged ETFs.* Leveraged ETFs can either be used for enhanced long or short exposure in a portfolio. However, it should be noted that when adding leveraged ETFs to a two-asset-class rotation portfolio (composed of both risk assets and those that will provide a margin of safety), when trends become unstable losses can be significantly amplified.
- *Niche ETFs.* The term niche ETF can mean a lot of things to a lot of different people, in this case we are referring ETFs with a process-driven approach. For example, an investor could find value in adding a lower-beta, lower-correlated broad-based U.S. equity ETF such as the Powershares S&P Low Volatility ETF. This ETF holds the 100 least volatile stocks over the trailing 12-month period in the S&P 500; the portfolio is rebalanced and reconstituted on a quarterly basis. While this ETF only came out in 2011, during increased periods of market duress, it has held up far better. Other examples of notable process-driven ETFs include the Guggenheim Pure Value and Pure Growth ETFs, the First Trust AlphaDEX ETFs, the Powershares Buyback Achievers ETF, the Guggenheim Spin-Off ETF, or the popular Market Vectors Wide Moat ETF (based on the historically strong performing Morningstar Wide Moat Focus Index).
- *Additional risk asset classes.* Beyond general equities, there are a number of additional risk-oriented asset classes that could be considered for inclusion as eligible securities in an asset rotation portfolio. For example, investors could elect to include asset classes such as real estate investment trusts (REITs), master limited partnerships (MLPs), or even commodities. With that said, it should be noted that trends in many of these underlying less conventional asset classes have a tendency to move with much greater volatility than, say, for example the underlying sectors of the U.S. equity markets. The volatility inherent in individual commodities in particular may make them a more difficult asset class to utilize with any level of efficiency; rather, if used incorrectly, they could dramatically impair the performance of the overall portfolio.

Whether ultimately constructing the eligible risk assets to be used in a tactical asset rotation portfolio based on sectors, countries, broad global equities, or any other worthwhile approach, the key for increased long-term efficacy is that collectively these ETFs need to have a relatively low correlation to one another. If the goal is to participate in prolonged trends, all of these securities should not be expected to move the same at all times; there needs to be the potential for a streak of ongoing outperformance, like emerging markets in the mid-2000s.

With that said, an argument can certainly be made for maintaining a relatively short list of eligible securities. Not only will a larger list certainly lead you to a higher degree of portfolio turnover, which can create a significant increase in trading costs, our research has proven that more often than not having a longer list can actually prevent you from entering or staying in trends for the optimal time period, as short-term price momentum taking place in another security can cause you to sell out too early, or miss getting in at the right time. From our experience, it is likely best to keep the list of eligible equity ETFs to as little as 10 to 15 securities.

The overall risk and exposure of an asset rotation–based tactical portfolio is generally defined by the focus of the eligible equity ETFs. For example, historically, individual countries can bear greater risks than the cap-weighted traditional sector ETFs; this is generally due to the fact that many other countries have significantly weaker and more turbulent stock markets than the United States. If properly managed, this can create opportunities; if not, this can lead to greater losses.

ADDITIONAL FACTORS TO CONSIDER: ELIGIBLE FLIGHT TO SAFETY/FIXED-INCOME ASSETS

The flight to safety side of an asset rotation portfolio's eligibility list can also take on a myriad of different looks. For simplicity, in our illustrations we used only the long-term Treasury bond. One may or may not agree with this approach. Surely, the long-term Treasury bond faces greater duration risk as interest rates increase; therefore, one might expect at times that the longer-maturity Treasury bond ETFs will face greater downward pressure on price, and accordingly this could present an increased chance for loss out of the what is intended to be the flight-to-safety portion of your overall tactical asset rotation portfolio.

Generally, we believe this to be true, but we also know that historically it is the longer-dated maturities that often move with the strongest inverse relationship to equity prices. Whenever stocks have experienced extended declines, it has generally been longer-dated Treasury bonds that have benefited the most.

With that being said, investors expressing the greatest concerns regarding our potentially dramatic rising interest rate environment may choose to omit longer-dated fixed-income ETFs altogether. Instead, they may choose to keep their focus on Treasuries, but simply use a short- to intermediate-dated Treasury in its place.

Diversifying the flight-to-safety portion of your eligibility list can make a lot of sense, whether that means adding multiple maturities of Treasuries, mortgage-backed securities, municipal bonds, the aggregate bond index, corporate bonds, high-yield international Treasuries, emerging market bonds, or the like. In doing so, one should consider the correlation these underlying classes of fixed income have to one another, as well as their overall correlation to the stock market (with which you would ideally like to see a low to negative correlation). As we have done previously with equities, we have illustrated the relationship among a number of available fixed-income ETFs in Table 8.4.

In looking at this correlation matrix, a handful of items readily stand out to us. As we have now highlighted ad nauseum, each of the three Treasury ETFs listed demonstrate a negative correlation to the S&P 500. What may come as more of a surprise is that the iShares Mortgage Backed Securities ETF has also demonstrated this rare feat. The aggregate bond index also offers a low correlation. On the opposite side of the equation, investors would be wise to pay attention to the relatively high correlation high-yield bonds have had to the S&P 500; with a correlation over this measurement period of 80 percent, it is easy to see why many in our industry have considered high yield bonds as more of an equity supplement, rather than a true diversifier for a portfolio.

Seeing how correlated these fixed-income ETFs are to each other and to the broad-based equity markets should provide investors with keen insights as to how to construct an appropriate risk-adjusted,

TABLE 8.4 Correlation and Performance Attributes, Fixed Income (2008–2012)

Correlation Matrix

Time Period: 1/1/2008 to 12/31/2012

	1	2	3	4	5	6	7	8	9	10	11	12
1 SPDR Barclays International Treasury Bd	1.00											
2 iShares JPMorgan USD Emerg Markets Bond	0.67	1.00										
3 iShares 1–3 Year Credit Bond	0.48	0.71	1.00									
4 iShares iBoxx $ Invst Grade Crp Bond	0.60	0.78	0.78	1.00								
5 SPDR Barclays High Yield Bond	0.45	0.81	0.65	0.59	1.00							
6 iShares MBS	0.36	0.34	0.27	0.42	−0.07	1.00						
7 iShares National AMT-Free Muni Bond	0.15	0.39	0.42	0.46	0.34	0.19	1.00					
8 iShares 3–7 Year Treasury Bond	0.35	0.02	0.07	0.25	−0.38	0.74	0.09	1.00				
9 iShares 7–10 Year Treasury Bond	0.34	0.15	0.10	0.41	−0.28	0.77	0.22	0.92	1.00			
10 iShares 20+ Year Treasury Bond	0.19	0.05	−0.07	0.37	−0.31	0.59	0.21	0.70	0.89	1.00		
11 iShares Core S&P 500	0.52	0.67	0.41	0.39	0.80	−0.10	0.13	−0.33	−0.29	−0.32	1.00	
12 iShares Core Total U.S. Bond Market ETF	0.55	0.56	0.54	0.79	0.18	0.82	0.39	0.71	0.84	0.73	0.07	1.00

(*Continued*)

TABLE 8.4 Correlation and Performance Attributes, Fixed Income (2008–2012) (Continued)

Performance

Time Period: 1/1/2008 to 12/31/2012

	Return	Cumulative Return	Std Dev	Beta	Alpha	Sharpe Ratio	Up Capture Ratio	Down Capture Ratio	Max Drawdown
SPDR Barclays International Treasury Bd	4.89	26.99	10.00	1.52	-3.17	0.49	144.60	294.03	-13.95
iShares JPMorgan USD Emerg Markets Bond	9.54	57.71	11.23	1.76	0.07	0.83	173.01	198.20	-21.72
iShares 1–3 Year Credit Bond	3.73	20.10	2.99	0.45	0.94	1.10	59.24	44.52	-5.50
iShares iBoxx $ Invst Grade Crp Bond	8.20	48.32	8.85	1.94	-2.40	0.89	168.75	238.63	-15.64
SPDR Barclays High Yield Bond	7.50	43.57	15.83	0.87	3.52	0.51	148.10	196.03	-35.86
iShares MBS	5.23	29.02	2.75	0.63	1.44	1.72	71.60	23.25	-1.50
iShares National AMT-Free Muni Bond	5.49	30.64	5.87	0.65	1.71	0.87	82.76	51.53	-5.95
iShares 3–7 Year Treasury Bond	5.47	30.52	4.24	0.82	0.67	1.20	94.24	92.97	-3.42
iShares 7–10 Year Treasury Bond	7.73	45.11	7.58	1.73	-1.84	0.97	152.43	201.49	-6.51
iShares 20+ Year Treasury Bond	9.60	58.17	16.73	3.34	-7.59	0.61	230.70	394.74	-21.53
iShares Core S&P 500	1.62	8.37	19.00	0.44	0.70	0.16	76.40	198.28	-48.39
iShares Core Total U.S. Bond Market ETF	5.78	32.45	3.62	1.00	0.00	1.45	100.00	100.00	-3.81

tactical asset rotation portfolio, as far as which securities might actually demonstrate the requisite attributes of a true flight-to-safety asset class.

Additionally, we should note, beyond the construction of a two-asset-class rotation portfolio, one could also choose to construct a multiasset, income-based approach. Specifically, as concerns mount regarding how fixed-income investors are going to navigate the bond markets in a rising interest rate environment, these needs might very well be addressed by constructing an income-based rotational portfolio, composed of various classes and maturities of fixed income and hybrid securities (e.g., preferred stocks, bank loan ETFs), each of which can be expected to behave very differently at various stages in our interest rate cycle.

ADDITIONAL FACTORS TO CONSIDER: CRITERIA FOR INVESTMENT SELECTION

In the illustrations we have provided in this book and the documented performance thereof, we focused our attention on portfolios that utilized only a single metric to determine what we were going to hold in a given month—simply, what was up the most during the prior month. This may seem like an extremely elementary approach, but ironically, the effectiveness of this single-factor method has clearly been demonstrated.

Having said that, value can certainly be increased by adding some additional vetting criteria for investment selection. Some of the following factors provide investors with critical points to consider:

- *Trading frequency.* How often should an asset rotation portfolio be rebalanced or reconstituted? In our illustrations, we have demonstrated tactical asset rotation portfolios predicated on a monthly timing system. Depending on the nature of the eligible ETFs, performance may be enhanced by either increasing or decreasing the frequency of trades. For example, one may further consider a weekly, biweekly, or even quarterly rebalance.
- *Number of holdings.* For the sake of simplicity and added diversification, in our two-asset-class sector rotation illustration we modeled a portfolio composed of as many as five equity ETFs.

The optimal number of holdings should be determined by the inherent risk/reward objectives of the portfolio. Reducing the amount of holdings provides investors with a more concentrated portfolio; while this may over time prove to increase returns, it also likely increases the degree of risk exhibited in the process. Conversely, while increasing the number of holdings in the portfolio may provide further diversification, it may also dilute an investor's ability to participate in significant trends. Ultimately, what is most important is having a discipline in place to stay out of those sectors of the market under extended pressure.

- *Weighting of the portfolio.* In our two-asset-class sector rotation model we presented a rudimentary system that when fully invested in the equity markets, equally weighted our five holdings. Dependent on what other factors are used in conjunction with this attribute, overweighting the highest-ranking securities may potentially enhance performance.

- *Number of time periods measured.* In the sector rotation model highlighted in this text, we focused solely on one-month price momentum as the determinant for our portfolio holdings. As one might imagine, utilizing only a single month may be misleading as far as identifying and gaining more information regarding trends. In this respect, an investor might wish to consider utilizing multiple time periods, including both short- and intermediate-term trends.

- *Technical indicators.* An investor may benefit further from learning more about the trend currently in place, in an attempt to determine how likely it may be to continue or to gain further insight into what stage the trend is most likely to be in. Fortunately, there are a number of technical indicators available that can provide investors with greater clarity. Examples of some of the more commonly used technical indicators include: volume trends in the security traded, volatility, the relative strength (as measured by the relative strength index), whether the security is currently under distribution or being accumulated, where the current price is in relation to Bollinger Bands, or even with consideration given to MACD readings (the moving average convergence-divergence indicator).

CREATING A SCORING SYSTEM

Once an investor has determined their eligibility list and the factors to be used in their investment selection process, the next step is to create a scoring system to determine portfolio holdings. Specifically, one needs to define a percentage weighting for each selected factor, rank their eligibility list and calculate a weighted score for each ETF assigned to each factor, and then formulate an aggregate score for each security and a final ranking.

The easiest way to illustrate this process is by providing an example. In Table 8.5 we have provided an illustration of a three-factor model for determining portfolio holdings using only the three following metrics: three-month price return, one-month price return, and the current RSI readings. We have assigned a weighting to each of these three factors: dedicating a 40 percent weighting to the three-month price return, a 30 percent weighting to one-month price return, and finally a 30 percent weighting to the current RSI number.

For each factor we have ranked a hypothetical tactical asset rotation portfolio comprised of the nine equal weighted sectors of the S&P 500 (using the Guggenheim equally weighted sector ETFs) and three laddered maturities of U.S. Treasury bond ETFs. Once each of these securities is ranked for a given factor, a weighted score can be assigned. These three weighted scores are then added up to determine the aggregate score for each ETF on our list. We ranked the one- and three-month price return factors from best performing down to the worst; we ranked our third factor, current RSI number, from 1 to 12, assigning the highest rank to those with the lowest RSI reading. In this illustration, our objective was to identify the three ETFs with the lowest aggregate score; these three securities would then represent our current holdings at the time of our portfolio reconstitution.

For those not familiar with the RSI, this is a commonly used indicator that attempts to identify whether a given security is either overbought, oversold, or somewhere in between. Readings below 30 are generally considered oversold, and readings above 70 may be considered overbought. In a price momentum–based strategy, buying an oversold security never really comes into consideration; however, one may wish

TABLE 8.5 A Three-Factor Tactical Asset Rotation Scoring System

Hold the three ETFs with the lowest aggregate score

Eligible Securities	Ticker	Factor 1: Three-Month Price Return 40% Weighting			Factor 2: One-Month Price Return 30% Weighting			Factor 3: Current RSI Number 30% Weighting			Aggregate Score
		3 Month	Rank	Weighted Score	1 Month	Rank	Weighted Score	Current RSI	Rank	Weighted Score	
Guggenheim Equal Weight Technology	RYT	4.43%	2	0.80	−2.47%	6	1.80	27.19	3	0.90	3.50
Guggenheim Equal Weight Health Care	RYH	5.12%	1	0.40	0.26%	5	1.50	37.62	8	2.40	4.30
iShares 20+ Year Treasury Bond	TLT	2.72%	3	1.20	5.22%	1	0.30	64.42	10	3.00	4.50
iShares 7-10 Year Treasury Bond	IEF	0.72%	4	1.60	2.64%	2	0.60	67.11	11	3.30	5.50
Guggenheim Equal Weight Industrials	RGI	0.63%	5	2.00	−4.94%	10	3.00	28.00	4	1.20	6.20
Guggenheim Equal Weight Financials	RYF	0.50%	6	2.40	−4.53%	9	2.70	29.47	5	1.50	6.60
Guggenheim Equal Weight Consumer Staples	RHS	−3.50%	11	4.40	−4.02%	7	2.10	24.27	2	0.60	7.10
Guggenheim Equal Weight Utilities	RYU	−2.03%	8	3.20	0.79%	4	1.20	49.12	9	2.70	7.10
Guggenheim Equal Weight Materials	RTM	−2.07%	9	3.60	−6.02%	11	3.30	19.77	1	0.30	7.20
iShares 3-7 Year Treasury Bond	IEI	0.30%	7	2.80	1.23%	3	0.90	68.68	12	3.60	7.30
Guggenheim Equal Weight Energy	RYE	−4.78%	12	4.40	−4.40%	8	2.40	36.38	7	2.10	8.90
Guggenheim Equal Weight Consumer Discretionary	RCD	−3.18%	10	4.00	−6.98%	12	3.60	30.63	6	1.80	9.40

to avoid those that have experienced both a high degree of relative outperformance and currently possess an overbought RSI reading.

By no means are we suggesting this sample scoring system is the optimal one to be used by investors; nor are we suggesting these to be optimal factors, securities, or number of holdings. The purpose of this illustration is to demonstrate how an investor can apply their chosen factors to their eligibility list and determine their current holdings. This is simply an extension of how an investor can go beyond using our previously illustrated single-factor approach, based solely on one-month price momentum.

REQUIRED DUE DILIGENCE

Once an investor has determined the eligibility list for their portfolio, and the metrics by which holdings will be determined, the final step is to create an unbiased historical illustration of how this process would have performed in the past. We firmly believe that in order for any investor to begin following a tactical asset rotation process with live investable dollars, the efficacy and merits of the exact process must be examined over the longest time periods possible, across multiple market cycles and economic environments.

We are not referring to black box, algorithmic, sophisticated quantitative manipulation. When price momentum is your overarching defining factor, the investment landscape becomes a whole lot quieter and less cluttered. Regardless of what news may come across the table, sticking to a simple rules-based process devoid of outside influence and personal emotion is a mandate for success in the investment markets.

As we have stated previously, in order for investors to be successful, they need to have an integral understanding of their investment process, and more importantly be able to formulate reasonable expectations regarding performance. Otherwise, they may lack the confidence and intestinal fortitude to maintain their discipline when their performance is lagging versus a given benchmark. In response to this, which we should point out, the reality is there really is *no* appropriate benchmark for a tactical asset rotation portfolio. A portfolio managed in this manner is dynamic in its very nature; holdings are not static—they are fluid and susceptible to change with great frequency. This inherent flexibility enables the portfolio to adapt to current market conditions, and over time to present low correlations to both the equity and bond markets.

THE BOTTOM LINE

Just as René Descartes suggested nearly 400 years ago, we have arrived at our conclusions by first rejecting that which is so commonly held to be true. Rather than try and build upon existing notions regarding efficient portfolios and broadly accepted investment philosophies, when we objectively examined their long-term results and the high probability for human error, we felt it best to start from scratch. Not to dispel their merits altogether, but with what we perceived to be an unnecessary level of complexity, we believed a simpler solution could exist.

Starting from scratch enabled us to build a foundation based on only a handful of uncomplicated deductions:

- If stock prices are going up, then investors must feel optimistic about the future.
- The longer stock prices go up, the more investor confidence increases.
- The higher investor confidence, the higher stocks will go.
- If stock prices are going down, investors must feel pessimistic about the future.
- The longer stock prices go down, the more pessimistic investors become.
- The lower investor confidence, the lower stocks will go.

We recognize we are doing nothing more than state the obvious, but when broken down to a very rudimentary level, it becomes abundantly clear that more than anything else, it is the psychological underpinnings of market participants that truly move the markets. These psychological underpinnings generate price momentum, and this momentum is generally sustained until acted upon by an external force (event) that alters the confidence of the underlying investors. This momentum ultimately creates opportunities to generate positive returns, whether by riding the gains made in the equity markets by increasing levels of investor confidence, or by rotating into inversely related assets when this confidence is broken and pessimism begins to set in.

Certainly, there are inflection points where the general direction of markets will whipsaw for a relatively short period of time. This again is due to the underlying condition of the psyche of the investment community, as they are trying to ascertain which way things are going to go. Therefore, at times, the markets can act frenetically and inconsistently, just like the emotional mood swings of the actual human beings acting behind the curtain.

There are a number of different and unique methodologies that can be used to employ a tactical asset rotation approach to portfolio management, and we are not here to tell you that one is any more right than another. Throughout the context of this book, we have presented a pure price momentum–based approach—no charts, no trend lines, no fancy technical analysis. With that said, we recognize that there are other ways to manage a tactical asset rotation portfolio that do utilize some of these common indicators.

One such book that may provide additional insights for investors seeking to increase their understanding of how the markets can be tactically navigated with ETFs is *The Ivy Portfolio: How to Invest Like the Top Endowments and Avoid Bear Markets*. This book was written by an acquaintance of ours by the name of Mebane Faber. In the book, Meb does an excellent job of laying out how to employ a simple multiasset approach based solely on the 200-day moving average, requiring that investors review their portfolio only once per month. The time-tested results documented in this book are intriguing and anyone looking to further understand asset rotation would be well served to read it.

Throughout the scope of this chapter, we have certainly opened up a lot of possibilities; many of which we recognize likely go beyond the scope of the average retail investor. With that said, we remind investors to heed the advice of a fourteenth-century Franciscan monk and *not* overcomplicate things. After all, even a simple single-factor approach based purely on the performance of eligible securities over a prior month provides investors with significant risk-adjusted returns.

While, of course, we will not divulge the specific processes we use in our own current portfolios, we implore others to keep it simple. The more variables you add, the more it can complicate the process and actually take away from the one key metric that should be the driver behind any asset rotation–based portfolio: price momentum. More important than anything else, price momentum, and maintaining a list of two distinct asset classes with low correlations to each other will lead to the long-term success of an asset rotation portfolio.

CHAPTER 9

———

THE ANATOMY OF CHANGE

Setting Appropriate Expectations

Andreas Vesalius was a sixteenth-century Belgian anatomist and physician. While perhaps not as well known as many of the other central figures of the Renaissance period, Vesalius's groundbreaking work in the field of anatomy provided the foundation for our modern-day understanding of the human body.

Vesalius believed that the only reliable resource for developing an in-depth understanding of the human anatomy was through direct hands-on participation in the dissection of a human corpse. At the time, this was a significant break from widely held conventions believing that studying the anatomical structure of animals could provide us with a thorough understanding of our own personal architecture.

In 1543, at the formative age of 28, Andreas Vesalius published his seminal work in what would become one of the most influential books on human anatomy ever written, *De Humani Corporis Fabrica* (On the Fabric of the Human Body). With elaborately detailed pictures, Vesalius highlighted what has come to be known as the "anatomical" view of the human body, for the first time recognizing the interconnectivity and form and function of the human anatomical structure.

For years, Vesalius dealt with the mockery of other physicians regarding him as a barber. In 1551, Charles V even went so far as to commission an inquiry into the religious implications of his methods. While the claims against Vesalius's works were ultimately dismissed, he endured a lifetime of intense scrutiny.

With everything we have discussed up to this point, it is our hope that our much appreciated readers now possess a more enlightened view of the anatomy of the investment markets, and more specifically of the fallacies currently espoused as truth; that one may now, perhaps for the first time ever, recognize the gamesmanship taking place in our surroundings and the emotional pitfalls that so often lead us to buy the wrong thing at the wrong time.

Whether falling for shooting stars, well-articulated economic forecasts, or succumbing to personal sentiments of fear or greed, the investment markets have long proven to be hazardous for investors. In order to navigate the course, one must remove all emotion and follow a time-tested, rules-based, systematic approach to investing, even when it may not seem to be working.

BENCHMARKING SUCCESS

Formulating an anatomical understanding of how an asset rotation portfolio should be expected to behave throughout all market cycles and in any given environment is absolutely critical to achieving long-term success. Otherwise, when investors are not intimately familiar with the process, they may have unrealistic expectations and therefore lack the discipline to stay the course; rather, they may again fall back into the age-old trap of chasing returns.

Every investor should be interested in reducing downside risk and employing a discipline that will not behave like the market during prolonged equity market declines. But it is ironic how quickly the vast majority of these same investors will panic when such a strategy does not rise in a given month with the markets, as they may wrongfully believe it should. If an investment strategy is not expected to look like the markets when things are bad, it should not always be expected to look like the markets when things are good.

When employing a process with historically low long-term correlations to either stocks or bonds, investors should readily expect that the performance of an asset rotation based portfolio will not always behave like a pure risk-oriented benchmark (such as the S&P 500). As we first mentioned in our previous chapter, due to the dynamic nature of this portfolio construct, many of the widely recognized benchmarks really do not apply. Certainly, they can be used to illustrate how the returns of an asset rotation portfolio are superior over the course of a full market cycle or to illustrate how these portfolios exhibit lower risk attributes, but to make assumptions that this is an apples-to-apples comparison would not be fair. Perhaps the closest benchmark by which to more appropriately compare the performance of an asset rotation portfolio would be to use a hedge fund index.

For those readers who may not be familiar with what a hedge fund is, a hedge fund is kind of like a mutual fund, but with even less transparency and significantly higher costs. These portfolios generally utilize a number of advanced investment strategies and often employ high degrees of leverage and complex derivatives to generate outsized returns, or hedge investment risk. They are also regarded as highly illiquid, forcing investors to keep their money in the fund for at least a year. It should also be noted that hedge funds typically have a relatively high barrier for entry; investors generally must have a net worth of more than $1 million, in addition to an extensive personal investment history.

All things considered, the hedge fund structure, more than any other, has the potential to generate a high rate of return, and in some cases, with significantly reduced risks. A great many talented investment managers gravitate to managing these funds, not only because they can be highly lucrative to run, but also because of their inherent flexibility.

While we do not consider a simple price momentum–based asset rotation portfolio to be "advanced," or really to even utilize any sophisticated instruments in the investment process, because hedge funds generally have a history of providing strong risk-adjusted returns, a hedge fund index may be our best bet to benchmark performance.

One of the most common hedge fund indices by which to benchmark performance is the Credit Suisse Hedge Fund Index. This index provides a broad sampling of returns across the entire hedge fund

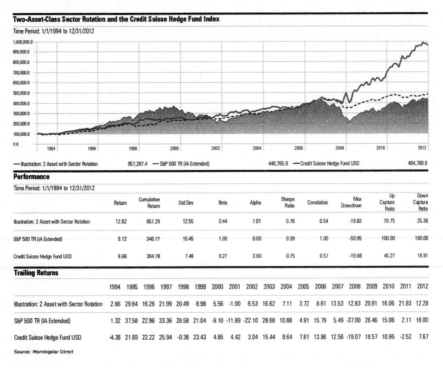

Two-Asset-Class Sector Rotation and the Credit Suisse Hedge Fund Index

Time Period: 1/1/1994 to 12/31/2012

— Illustration: 2 Asset with Sector Rotation   957,287.4   — S&P 500 TR (IA Extended)   440,765.9   — Credit Suisse Hedge Fund USD   484,780.0

Performance

Time Period: 1/1/1994 to 12/31/2012

	Return	Cumulative Return	Std Dev	Beta	Alpha	Sharpe Ratio	Correlation	Max Drawdown	Up Capture Ratio	Down Capture Ratio
Illustration: 2 Asset with Sector Rotation	12.62	857.29	12.55	0.44	7.01	0.76	0.54	-19.83	70.75	35.36
S&P 500 TR (IA Extended)	8.12	340.77	15.45	1.00	0.00	0.39	1.00	-50.95	100.00	100.00
Credit Suisse Hedge Fund USD	8.66	384.78	7.46	0.27	3.90	0.75	0.57	-19.68	45.27	18.91

Trailing Returns

	1994	1995	1996	1997	1998	1999	2000	2001	2002	2003	2004	2005	2006	2007	2008	2009	2010	2011	2012
Illustration: 2 Asset with Sector Rotation	2.86	29.64	16.26	21.99	20.49	8.98	5.56	-1.00	6.53	16.62	7.11	3.72	8.61	13.53	12.83	20.91	16.06	21.93	12.28
S&P 500 TR (IA Extended)	1.32	37.58	22.96	33.36	28.58	21.04	-9.10	-11.89	-22.10	28.68	10.88	4.91	15.79	5.49	-37.00	26.46	15.06	2.11	16.00
Credit Suisse Hedge Fund USD	-4.36	21.69	22.22	25.94	-0.36	23.43	4.85	4.42	3.04	15.44	9.64	7.61	13.86	12.56	-19.07	18.57	10.95	-2.52	7.67

Source: Morningstar Direct

FIGURE 9.1   Two-Asset-Class Sector Rotation and the Credit Suisse Hedge Fund Index (1994–2012)

Source: © 2014 Morningstar, Inc. All Rights Reserved. Reproduced with permission.

industry, incorporating a myriad of different investment styles and approaches. It is an asset-weighted hedge fund index that tracks the composite return of approximately 9,000 funds.

In Figure 9.1 we have illustrated the performance attributes of an asset rotation portfolio versus both the S&P 500 and the Credit Suisse Hedge Fund Index. This illustration depicts performance data going back to January 1, 1994. We would have preferred to have gone back even further, but the Credit Suisse Hedge Fund Index data goes back only to December 1993.

After taking a look at this illustration, there are a handful of noteworthy observations that should be made. First and foremost, it is easy to see that our simple, one-factor, two-asset-class sector rotation portfolio handily outperforms both indices over this 19-year time period, with an average annual return of about 4 percent more than either the S&P 500 or the hedge fund index. It is also readily apparent that the average annual return of the S&P 500 and the Credit Suisse Hedge Fund Index were remarkably similar, with both posting average annual returns of around 8 percent. However, impressively, the Credit Suisse Hedge Fund Index was able to accomplish this feat with about half of the standard deviation of the S&P 500, and with a beta of only 0.27.

Our two-asset-class sector rotation portfolio, on the other hand, demonstrated both a higher standard deviation and a higher beta than the hedge fund index, but still considerably less than the S&P 500. The max drawdown for both the sector rotation portfolio and the hedge fund index were remarkably similar, each posting losses during the period of just shy of 20 percent. They also both generated correlations of around 50 percent to our pure risk-oriented benchmark.

It is easy to see the similarities between the performance of our asset rotation portfolio and the hedge fund index; both registered very strong risk-adjusted returns versus the S&P 500. However, while statistically the Credit Suisse Hedge Fund Index achieved these returns at a reduced level of risk, the overall performance of the two-asset-class sector rotation portfolio was considerably stronger. Even though both the standard deviation and beta were higher for the sector rotation portfolio, the alpha was almost twice as high as it was for the hedge fund index.

THE FOUR SEASONS

In our humble opinion, there are really only four types of market environments possible: up, down, sideways, and sideways with a lot of volatility. While this may seem a bit overly simplistic, believe it or not, given the price momentum–based, trend-following nature of an asset rotation portfolio, it is actually reasonable to presume to know how an asset rotation portfolio will perform in each of these different market environments. What is largely unknown continues to be the magnitude of the returns, and, of course, this is largely predicated on the specific construct of an asset rotation portfolio and the actual exchange-traded funds (ETFs) used in the process.

Throughout the remainder of this chapter, we will provide an overview of how an asset rotation portfolio should be expected to perform in each of the market's four seasons. In doing so, we remind our readers that we are referring to these descriptions as they relate to portfolios previously highlighted in this book, and specifically our two-asset-class sector rotation illustration. Once an investor has formulated their own version of an asset rotation portfolio, depending on the factors selected, this could obviously impact our depictions.

WHEN EQUITY MARKETS RISE

During any prolonged run-up in the equity markets, any asset rotation–based portfolio based on price momentum and trend following should be expected to provide investors with a relatively high degree of participation. While in some years investors may achieve returns that are higher than a risk-oriented benchmark (i.e., the S&P 500), this should not be expected.

In a sector rotation–based portfolio, for example, years of outperformance are typically attributable to the presence of strong trends in the underlying sectors of the market and owning focused exposure to these sectors for prolonged periods of time. With that said, even good calendar years in the equity markets typically don't go straight up. Therefore, this outcome can be less likely, either because at some point in time weakness in equities triggers a reduction in the percentage of your holdings in stocks, and then the equity markets continued to rise while you are not 100 percent invested, or simply because chances are that some of the rotational trends during the year will work in your favor, while obviously others will not. These inflection points are natural, as again this often reflects short-term periods of uncertainty by market participants, and this has a significant impact on the performance of the various asset classes that make up our investable universe.

Like any trend-following process, investors taking an asset rotation–based approach will likely not be invested at the onset of a trend. Once the trend is in place, they will typically ride the trend until it ends. *The trend is your friend until the end.* Depending on the relative performance of the other eligible securities, you may end up owning the trend as it begins to reverse course. This often happens when trends change dramatically. However, in a sector rotation–based portfolio, when trends unwind in favor of others it does not necessarily mean they turn negative. It just means that the relative strength of another sector has surpassed that of your current holdings.

WHEN EQUITY MARKETS FALL

During prolonged equity market declines, one can expect that a two-asset-class sector rotation portfolio will hold up exponentially better than the markets. This is largely due to the ability to rotate out of equities entirely, but is also attributable to the portfolio's ability to participate in positive price momentum that may be present in more defensive sectors (as in the year 2000 when four sectors were up more than 20 percent).

When equity markets begin their decline, investors in an asset rotation portfolio are likely to be exposed to the initial downward move. Should the decline continue and/or increase in magnitude, the portfolio will rotate into positions demonstrating relative safety. This is not to say that the securities it will rotate into will necessarily register a positive return. There are times in the equity markets when all asset classes can move together with a high degree of correlation for a short period. We have certainly seen this before and should expect to see it again.

In order to demonstrate further how an investor might expect an asset rotation portfolio to perform when equity markets are under extended pressure, in Figure 9.2 we have provided an illustration of our two-asset-class sector rotation portfolio versus the S&P 500 during 2008.

As we all know, in 2008 the S&P 500 was down 37 percent. During this same time period, our two-asset-class sector rotation illustration would have been up nearly 13 percent, seemingly avoiding the decline altogether. However, as one may clearly see by looking at the growth of $100,000 graph in Figure 9.2, for a large portion of the year, even our sector rotation portfolio was down. While throughout the entire period our asset rotation portfolio held up far better than the S&P 500, it wasn't until the end of year when capitulation began to set into the equity markets that our portfolio turned positive.

The year 2008 was the perfect storm for an asset rotation–based portfolio, since long-dated Treasuries were up more 30 percent for the year. We have elected this time period simply because it was our most recent calendar year with a negative return in the equity markets. However, due to the extreme nature of this environment, the disparity in returns between our modeled asset rotation portfolio and the S&P 500 has never been greater.

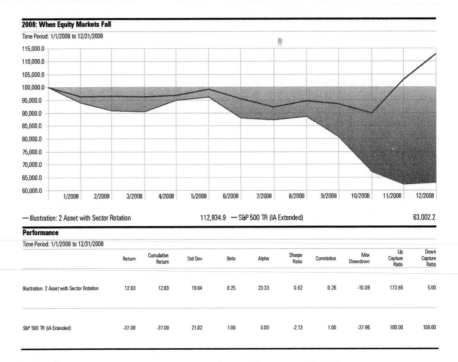

FIGURE 9.2 Two-Asset-Class Sector Rotation vs. the S&P 500 (2008)

Source: © 2014 Morningstar, Inc. All Rights Reserved. Reproduced with permission.

Recall that 2008 was the worst annual decline in the U.S. equity markets since 1931. An annual decline this steep is obviously not common. Typically, when the equity markets are down on the year, it is in the 10 to 20 percent range. With that said, even if we were to illustrate 2000, 2001, and 2002, the same points could be made.

In order to get a closer look at precisely how 2008 would have played out for our two-asset-class sector rotation portfolio, we have provided a monthly breakdown of returns versus the S&P 500, in addition to holdings throughout all periods (see Table 9.1).

By looking at Table 9.1, we can clearly see the tactical nature of the portfolio; during 2008, the portfolio allocation ranged anywhere from 100 percent in equities to 100 percent in Treasuries. There were also many months where the allocation represented a mix between the two, looking more like a balanced fund for the time being.

Additionally, you can see that during the first three months of the year, the equity markets generated a negative rate of return. During

TABLE 9.1 Two-Asset-Class Sector Rotation Monthly Returns and Underlying Holdings (2008)

	Jan 08	Feb 08	Mar 08	Apr 08	May 08	Jun 08	Jul 08	Aug 08	Sep 08	Oct 08	Nov 08	Dec 08
Two-Asset-Class Sector Rotation Allocation	−3.67%	0.18%	−0.22%	0.54%	2.48%	−3.73%	−3.34%	2.54%	−1.24%	−3.83%	14.43%	9.67%
Composition	60/40	0/100	40/60	60/40	100/0	100/0	20/80	100/0	40/60	0/100	0/100	0/100
	20% Utilities	100% Treasuries	20% Energy	20% Utilities	20% Utilities	20% Utilities	20% Energy	20% Cons Staples	20% Cons Staples	100% Treasuries	100% Treasuries	100% Treasuries
	20% Energy		20% Materials	20% Cons Staples	20% Energy	20% Energy	80% Treasuries	20% Health Care	20% Con Disc			
	20% Materials		60% Treasuries	20% Industrials	20% Materials	20% Materials		20% Industrials	60% Treasuries			
	40% Treasuries			40% Treasuries	20% Technology	20% Technology		20% Cons Disc				
					20% Financials	20% Cons Staples		20% Financials				
S&P 500 TR	−6.00%	−3.25%	−0.44%	4.86%	1.29%	−8.40%	−0.84%	1.44%	−8.91%	−16.79%	−7.15%	1.08%

179

each of these monthly measurement periods, our asset rotation portfolio maintained an allocation of less than 100 percent in equities, holding up far better than the equity markets. However, when the equity markets rebounded in April, even though our allocation was 60 percent stocks, we were positioned defensively. When markets quickly rebounded up nearly 5 percent, we only modestly participated. This is typical for an asset rotation portfolio, when after successive months of declines there is a significant one-month rebound in equities; generally, an asset rotation portfolio should be expected to miss the first leg up.

Later on in the year, when trends in the equity markets turned decidedly negative over the final four months, fear dramatically increased and the markets began to capitulate down. During this time, our asset rotation portfolio went from owning 40 percent in stocks to owning 100 percent Treasuries, avoiding this sharp decline altogether.

It should also be noted that in each of the three months where we were 100 percent in stocks—May, June, and August—each time our underlying sector allocation provided a return superior to the S&P 500.

WHEN EQUITY MARKETS MOVE SIDEWAYS

The third type of market environment is when equity markets move sideways. This is not to say there aren't peaks and troughs throughout the year, but generally in this case we are defining sideways as performance that by the end of the calendar year provides little to no gain (nor any significant losses) for investors. The last time we experienced a market environment such as this was in 2011, when by year-end the S&P 500 posted a total return of 2.11 percent; excluding dividends, the return was ~~literally~~ ACTUALLY 0.00 percent.

In a sideways market, a capitalization-based asset rotation portfolio may still achieve relatively strong returns, but a sector rotation–based portfolio has a much greater opportunity to participate in underlying trends. In Figure 9.3 we have illustrated a statistical analysis of how that year would have played out, for both our two-asset-class sector rotation portfolio and the S&P 500. While the return on the U.S. stock market was marginal at best, our sector rotation portfolio managed to generate a return of 21.93 percent.

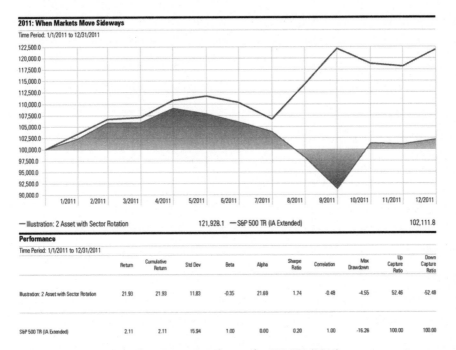

2011: When Markets Move Sideways

Time Period: 1/1/2011 to 12/31/2011

— Illustration: 2 Asset with Sector Rotation   121,928.1   — S&P 500 TR (IA Extended)   102,111.8

Performance

Time Period: 1/1/2011 to 12/31/2011

	Return	Cumulative Return	Std Dev	Beta	Alpha	Sharpe Ratio	Correlation	Max Drawdown	Up Capture Ratio	Down Capture Ratio
Illustration: 2 Asset with Sector Rotation	21.93	21.93	11.83	-0.35	21.69	1.74	-0.48	-4.55	52.46	-52.48
S&P 500 TR (IA Extended)	2.11	2.11	15.94	1.00	0.00	0.20	1.00	-16.26	100.00	100.00

FIGURE 9.3   Two-Asset-Class Sector Rotation vs. the S&P 500 (2011)

Source: © 2014 Morningstar, Inc. All Rights Reserved. Reproduced with permission.

Taking a closer look at the underlying holdings throughout all monthly measurement periods, it is evident that our sector rotation portfolio benefitted from both sector selection and the ability to rotate entirely out of stocks (see Table 9.2). During the first five months of the year, we maintained a 100 percent allocation to equities; in four out of the five months, our returns were superior to the S&P 500. Over this five-month time period, our cumulative return was 11.74 percent, versus a return of 7.83 percent for the S&P 500.

In May 2011, uncertainty began to creep back into the markets; 2009 and 2010 had already provided investors with strong returns, and 2011 had gotten off to a strong start as well. Then we began to hear whispers regarding a Greek default and a potential breakup of the euro. Month after month, these whispers grew louder, until shortly after the market close on Friday, August 5, when Standard & Poor's came out and did the unthinkable, for the first time in history downgrading the credit rating of long-term U.S. debt. The markets opened up with significant losses on the following Monday, and the selling

TABLE 9.2 Two-Asset-Class Sector Rotation Monthly Returns and Underlying Holdings (2011)

	Jan 11	Feb 11	Mar 11	Apr 11	May 11	Jun 11	Jul 11	Aug 11	Sep 11	Oct 11	Nov 11	Dec 11
Two-Asset-Class Sector Rotation	3.44%	3.13%	0.37%	3.51%	0.82%	−1.27%	−3.32%	7.20%	6.84%	−2.74%	−0.51%	3.15%
Allocation	100/0	100/0	100/0	100/0	100/0	0/100	100/0	0/100	0/100	0/100	100/0	20/80
Composition	20% Energy 20% Industrials 20% Materials 20% Technology 20% Financials	20% Energy 20% Industrials 20% Utilities 20% Technology 20% Financials	20% Energy 20% Cons Staples 20% Health Care 20% Cons Disc 20% Financials	20% Energy 20% Cons Staples 20% Health Care 20% Industrials 20% Materials	20% Utilities 20% Cons Staples 20% Health Care 20% Industrials 20% Cons Disc	100% Treasuries	20% Industrials 20% Utilities 20% Health Care 20% Materials 20% Cons Disc	100% Treasuries	100% Treasuries	100% Treasuries	20% Industrials 20% Energy 20% Cons Disc 20% Materials 20% Financials	20% Cons Staples 80% Treasuries
S&P 500 TR	2.37%	3.43%	0.04%	2.96%	−1.13%	−1.67%	−2.03%	−5.43%	−7.03%	10.93%	−0.22%	1.02%

pressure continued on for two more months. Strangely, the very security that was downgraded performed the best over this period.

In August and September 2011, the S&P 500 lost more than 12 percent; September marked the fifth straight month of declines. While this environment may have proven perilous for long-only stock investors, this proved to be a fantastic trend for our two-asset-class sector rotation portfolio. From May through September, the S&P 500 declined more than 16 percent; conversely, our two-asset-class sector rotation illustration was up more than 10 percent!

In October 2011, the S&P 500 posted the strongest one-month return since December 1991, up nearly 11 percent! With no discernible positive price momentum coming into October, our asset rotation portfolio maintained its defensive posture and actually posted a negative return on the month of nearly 3 percent. Therefore, after six months of market instability, the S&P 500 for this period (May through October) was still down 7 percent, while our two-asset-class sector rotation portfolio was up just over 7 percent (despite missing out on the strong equity gains registered in October).

The remainder of the year muddled along, with the S&P 500 posting a 0.2 percent decline in November and a modest 1 percent gain in December. In November, our allocation rotated 100 percent back into equities and generated a monthly return of −0.51 percent. It should come as no surprise then that our December allocation then rotated largely back out of equities, as we reduced the equity exposure to only 20 percent; our return to a focused exposure in U.S. Treasuries provided us with a respectful return of 3.15 percent in the final month of the year.

WHEN EQUITY MARKETS MOVE SIDEWAYS WITH VOLATILITY

Every investment approach has its kryptonite, and a sideways market with significant volatility is just that for a trend-following asset rotation portfolio (particularly if one employs the use of leverage in their process). When there are no discernible trends to latch on to, an asset rotation portfolio can be whipsawed, rotating into the very asset class that ends up going down, then rotating out of it only for it to go up, and have what you buy go down.

This type of up–down–up–down environment is not uncommon to see during the course of a calendar year for a short stretch, but the persistence of this extreme market environment is rare. This volatile environment is so rare in fact that during the course of our entire 23-year illustration on our two–asset-class sector rotation portfolio, it did not happen once.

To be clear, this is not to say it didn't happen at all; it's just that when it did, our ability to participate in some of the stronger underlying trends in the equity markets enabled us to avoid the full effect. Without the ability to participate in underlying trends, surely our portfolio would have had greater difficulties. This provides further support for our contention that among the eligible list of risk assets, it is imperative that there is a variance in correlations.

While the presence of a mildly whipsawing environment did not appear to have an impact on our sector rotation model, it did have an effect on our basic two–asset-class illustration. During 2005, for example, there were a number of times when our hypothetical portfolio rotated into the very asset class that ended up lagging on the month (as shown in Table 9.3).

As you may recall from Chapter 6, the eligibility list of our basic two–asset-class portfolio can only assume two allocations: either 100 percent in stocks or 100 percent in long-dated U.S. government bonds. The only factor determining which one is owned in a given month is simply which of the two was up the most the prior month.

In 2005, in almost every measurement period, it seemed like the asset class our single-factor approach lead us to hold did worse than the opposite asset class. For example, because the S&P 500 was up more than the government bond index in December of 2004, this made up 100 percent of our portfolio allocation for January 2005, during which the S&P 500 was down 2.44 percent and the government bond index was up 3 percent. Because of the outperformance demonstrated by the government bond index in January, our allocation rotated into 100 percent fixed income for February, during which the government bond index was down 1.28 percent, while the S&P 500 rebounded up 2.10 percent. This zigzagging change of leadership continued on for much of the year. By year-end, this whipsawing environment between the two asset classes created a loss of 3.95 percent for our simple two–asset-class rotation portfolio; while the S&P 500 managed a modest gain of 4.91 percent.

TABLE 9.3 Simple Two-Asset-Class Rotation (2005)

2005	Dec	Jan	Feb	Mar	Apr	May	Jun	Jul	Aug	Sep	Oct	Nov	Dec
IA SBBI US LT Gov TR USD	2.50%	3.00%	−1.28%	−0.72%	3.73%	2.97%	1.67%	−2.88%	3.33%	−3.38%	−1.96%	0.76%	2.67%
S&P 500 TR	3.40%	−2.44%	2.10%	−1.77%	−1.90%	3.18%	0.14%	3.72%	−0.91%	0.81%	−1.67%	3.78%	0.03%
Two-Asset-Class Rotation		**−2.44%**	**−1.28%**	**−1.77%**	**3.73%**	**2.97%**	**0.14%**	**−2.88%**	**−0.91%**	**−3.38%**	**−1.67%**	**3.78%**	**0.03%**

While this may not exactly be a very dramatic example, this should give investors a basic understanding of how choppy markets can impact an asset rotation–based portfolio. An environment such as this is the rarest of the four market environments we have outlined, but in theory should we ever see a whipsawing environment with significantly larger moves in either direction (like investors experienced during the Great Depression), this is where an asset rotation portfolio can bear increased levels of risk.

As we have previously stated, and we hope we are clear in stating this, *no one* should ever use just the basic two-asset-class illustration as an actual investment portfolio. The purpose of this rudimentary model is simply to demonstrate the efficacy of isolating price momentum between two asset classes with extremely low, if not negative, correlations to each other (depending on the time period). Once an investor understands that there is merit to even this elementary approach, taking it one step further by increasing the size of the eligibility list and therefore being able to participate in underlying trends only makes sense.

THE BOTTOM LINE

Adopting an asset rotation–based approach to investing represents a significant change for the majority of investors. Because this approach is something they may not be familiar with, they may be more likely to fall prey to unrealistic expectations. When they do not have a good understanding of how an asset rotation portfolio should be expected to perform in a given environment, they may be less apt to commit to the discipline long term.

Granted, the returns depicted in this book for a two-asset-class sector rotation portfolio seem on the surface to be almost too good to be true. That is why we elected to lay out the entire process behind this rudimentary approach, to prove it unequivocally, so that investors could truly understand that not only is this possible, it is already being done by a handful of leading tactical ETF portfolio managers.

While their specific processes for determining their investment selection is assuredly quite different and likely to have far more factors involved, the general premise remains the same: developing a rotational discipline using ETFs to participate in rising markets but, more important, reduce participation in prolonged declines. Even when using only one vetting factor, this works! Of course, adding more, when done appropriately, has the potential to increase efficacy even further.

However, when investors look solely at the incredulous long-term risk-adjusted returns, they often formulate false expectations like the portfolio will never be down, or that when the stock market is down the portfolio should necessarily be up. Of course, this is not true. The performance of an asset rotation portfolio is highly dependent on which of the four seasons of the investment markets we find ourselves in. But once you have a good understanding of what to expect in each of these different market environments, you can begin to formulate reasonable expectations for performance.

The reality is that the dramatic outperformance achieved by an asset rotation portfolio over time is due largely to avoiding the big dips, or as we so commonly refer to them, "prolonged declines." In other words, there must be a downward *trend* in place and a relative flight to safety, whether in historically safe asset classes like U.S. Treasury bonds or simply in more defensive sectors of the market demonstrating a higher degree of relative strength. Should we see a cataclysmic decline out of nowhere, unless prior to that point momentum in equities had been waning, we will likely participate just like any other investor.

Tactical, asset rotation-based portfolios will at times look like the stock markets and at others look like the bond market. Over longer periods, the flexible nature of this portfolio construct will cause it to look like neither of these underlying asset classes. This is to be expected and therefore makes this dynamic portfolio more difficult to benchmark. When illustrating the propensity of the portfolio to outperform a pure risk-oriented benchmark over the course of a full market cycle and with considerably less risk, the S&P 500 can make sense as a benchmark. But from a month-by-month standpoint, this does not make sense at all. As discussed in this chapter, this is where comparing performance to a common hedge fund index, like the Credit Suisse Hedge Fund Index, can make a lot more sense over both shorter- and longer-term measurement periods.

In order to truly understand the anatomical construct of an asset rotation–based portfolio—the form, function, and interconnectivity of all of the moving parts, just as Andreas Vesalius opined nearly 500 years ago—you need to first dissect the entire body of work, beginning with the most basic organs and progressing on to those that sustain life. Once an investor can understand the inner workings of the vessel itself, they can develop a measurable standard of care and dedicate themselves to a plan of action.

CHAPTER 10

―――――――――

LETTING GO OF YOUR CRUTCH

Integrating Asset Rotation into Your Overall Approach

Sixteenth-century French Army surgeon Ambroise Paré is widely considered to be the Father of Amputation and Modern Day Prosthetics. In 1529 he introduced amputation as a life saving measure in medicine. Soon after, Paré began to develop prosthetic limbs in a scientific manner, engineering revolutionary prosthetic advances for both upper and lower extremities.

Until this time, prostheses were heavy, crude devices that provided their wearer with little functionality; moreover, they were used as little more than a crutch. For the first time ever, Paré introduced practical movement to the prosthetic limb, inventing a hinged mechanical hand as well as prosthetic legs that featured advances such as locking knees and specialized attachment harnesses.

The mechanical hand designed by Ambroise Paré was made by Lorrain, a French locksmith and one of the most famous makers of artificial limbs during the Renaissance period. For the first time ever, a prosthetic hand operated using springs and catches. The utility of the prosthesis was so great that it was even worn into battle by a French Army captain. The hand later came to be known as "Le Petit Lorrain" ("the Lorrain Baby").

In 1996, for the first time in history, a disabled athlete was allowed to compete on an NCAA, Division I track team. Her name was Aimee Mullins. She was a student at Georgetown University, a sprinter with aspirations of competing in the 1996 Paralympic Games.

Aimee Mullins was born with fibular hemimelia, a congenital absence of the fibula in both legs. When she was only one year old, both of her legs were taken from her; amputated halfway between her knees and ankles. Unlike most infants at this age, Aimee had never even had a chance to stand, and doctors told her parents she might never learn to walk.

With the use of prosthetic legs, Aimee not only learned to walk, she learned to run. From an early age, Mullins set out to defy the limits of what others might perceive as a disability, excelling in nearly every endeavor she pursued. As a high school student she was one of three, out of 39,000 applicants, to receive a full academic college scholarship awarded by the United States Department of Defense. After spending her first two years focused solely on academics and working in the intelligence department at the Pentagon, Aimee decided to relinquish her scholarship so that she could pursue her athletic dreams. In the 1996 Paralympic Games, after spending a year participating on the Georgetown University track and field team, Aimee Mullins went on to establish new world records in both the 100- and 200-meter dash, as well as in the long jump.

In the years that followed the 1996 Paralympic Games, Aimee continued her lifelong ambition of defying others' limited expectations. Not only was Aimee to be recognized for her achievements as a world-class athlete, she went on to become a successful actress, model, and motivational speaker as well. Just recently, she was selected as a global ambassador for the cosmetic brand L'Oreal Paris, and in both the 2012 Olympic and Paralympic Games she was appointed the role of leader of the U.S. delegation, widely considered the highest honor bestowed upon an athlete by the United States Olympic Committee.

"CITIUS, ALTIUS, FORTIUS"

"*Citius, Altius, Fortius*" has been the Olympic creed for more than 2,500 years. Translated from Latin, it means simply "Faster, Higher, Stronger."

Not necessarily faster, higher, or stronger than our competitors, but more importantly, more than one has ever accomplished in their own right. The perseverance modeled by our Olympic athletes is deserving of our exaltation. Their daily commitment to continued improvement, to overcoming obstacles and setbacks, refining their approach, and remaining focused on accomplishing the ultimate goal establishes not only a framework for success in the athletic arena, but for life itself, and even for how one might approach the investment markets.

The story of Aimee Mullins's lifelong battle to overcome a personal handicap in order to achieve her dreams is an embodiment of the Olympic spirit and a reminder of what can be achieved when an individual no longer sees themselves as having a disability. Aimee Mullins did not let her disability define her, she used it as a springboard for success with humility, understanding full well the commitment required to achieve her goals and establishing a model for success and personal accountability.

After reading about asset rotation and learning about both the potency and efficacy of this process, the first question we are often asked is, "Now what am I supposed to do?" Or more specifically, "How am I supposed to integrate asset rotation into my overall portfolio approach?"

Before Aimee Mullins could ever learn to run, she first had to learn to walk, to learn how to overcome the overwhelming obstacles life had so cruelly placed before her at such a young age. And so our response to this question is really very simple, just like Aimee Mullins, "Before you can run, you first need to learn how to walk."

More important, you need to let go of your crutch. No longer should you see yourself as handicapped in the investment markets. Just as Ambroise Paré's contributions to the field of prosthetics nearly 500 years earlier ultimately paved the way for Aimee Mullins to achieve her dream of competing in the Paralympic Games, you are now equipped for battle.

ASSET ROTATION AS A CORE APPROACH

There are a number of ways to integrate an asset rotation–based process into your overall investment approach. To a large degree, of course, this depends on what it is you are trying to accomplish, and what your views on the current state of the markets happen to be.

With what we regard as the increasing risk premiums present in both the current equity and fixed-income markets, we do not wish to dedicate ourselves to either of these two asset classes long term. In doing so, we believe we would be exposing ourselves to undue risk. As is likely clearly evident by now, we would strongly prefer to play the trends between the two. Therefore, it should come as no surprise that we firmly believe a well-constructed asset rotation portfolio provides investors with a strong, risk-adjusted core approach to investing, far superior to conventional approaches used by investors today.

When one considers the risk/reward dynamic of current investment approaches regarded as "core" philosophies—whether a "buy and hold stocks for the long run" approach, or a traditionally allocated Modern Portfolio Theory (MPT) portfolio, we believe there is something clearly missing. In following these widely accepted core strategies, how does one account for downside risk? Bonds used to provide that cushion for an MPT portfolio and mitigate downside risk, but now they present risks as well. While investors with a dedicated exposure to bonds will surely incur losses at some point, those employing a tactical discipline predicated on owning them only when the trends are favorable stand to benefit.

Because of an asset rotation portfolio's inherent ability to avoid prolonged declines, and our belief that investors are less likely to follow a discipline that does at times provide sharp losses for investors, we believe this approach provides investors with a more reasonable and sustainable blueprint for success in the investment markets. As we have suggested previously, an approach predicated first and foremost on winning by losing less provides the engine for the sustainable growth of an investment portfolio. When you are significantly less likely to participate in big investment losses, you don't have to capture all of the upside, and you certainly don't have to look like the markets on a month-by-month basis. Additionally, your financial planning objectives are more likely to be met and not consistently altered by the volatility of wins and losses in the markets.

When a prospective client first sits down with an adviser, it is a requirement in our industry that a complete and thorough client profile is completed. In addition to getting a clear understanding of an individual's net worth, their assets, liabilities, investable assets, and so on, this assessment also provides documentation of a client's risk profile—how comfortable they are with volatility and accepting losses in order to achieve higher long-term returns. Age is also a consideration, assuming the older a client is, the less they should have invested in stocks and the more they should have in bonds; conversely, the younger the individual, the more they should have in stocks and less in bonds. Really?

We understand the premise, and surely this is intended to be for the benefit of the client, but here, too, we see an extension of MPT and capital market assumptions that, to the attentive observer, are changing right before our very eyes. What about timing? We are in the midst of a very powerful bull market move, off of the bottoms carved out in the equity markets in March 2009. Just because we are just shy of 40 years old, does that mean it is more appropriate for us to be subject to a 40 percent decline in stocks than someone older than us? After all, recall that we are now the first generation of homeowners to lose nearly half of the value in our initial homes. We have already incurred significant losses, wage growth is anemic, and good job opportunities are harder to come by. Couple this with the untenable amounts of student debt we incurred just to get into the job market, and our generation is also faced with decades of personal deleveraging. And yet we can afford to accept greater losses?

Of course, this does not make sense. Nor does it make sense that my mother in her late 60s should have 70 percent of her investable assets in bonds, where she would be increasingly likely to lose money throughout the remainder of her lifetime. Simply put, we are not a big believer in risk profiling individual investors. Ask anyone in the late 1990s, and they were an aggressive investor regardless of their age; no one wanted to miss out on the party. Ask someone in 2010, and suddenly they weren't so aggressive anymore; they were shell shocked, having incurred the trauma of being bombed twice in the equity markets over the course of the prior decade.

Therefore, it can be said that we ascribe to a risk-adjusted approach for all investors, irrespective of their age or net worth. Shouldn't all investors be provided with an opportunity to achieve sustainable success in the markets, regardless of what stage of the market cycle they are investing in, whether buying into a market top or bottom (which surely no one ever knows)? Asset rotation gives investors unknowingly buying into a market top a discipline to reduce losses, rather than incur a permanent impairment of capital; buying into a market bottom, they stand to participate handsomely in the rise. It only makes sense.

Asset rotation, more than any other currently widely accepted conventional approach, provides investors with an all-weather investment process that will grant them the ability to achieve long-term success. Better yet, it should ease their mind, as no longer do they need to subject themselves to the angst of incessantly second-guessing when to buy or when to sell, let alone what. No longer do the headlines or sensationalistic economic forecasts of doom and gloom matter. One need only step outside of the game, out of the minutia, and onto the path of least resistance.

Beyond simply employing asset rotation as a core approach, we are also advocates of providing investors with additional layers of diversification. More specifically, we don't believe investors should only own one singular asset rotation portfolio, but rather apply asset rotation to other conventional asset classes and own them all. For example, if one were to only adhere to an extension of the two-asset-class sector rotation portfolio outlined in this book, they would be limiting their risk exposure only to the U.S. equity markets and not participating whatsoever in what may very well be prevailing trends present in the international markets, or in other asset classes. Therefore, in order to increase the diversification of an overarching portfolio, an investor should employ multiple asset rotation portfolios.

In addition to owning a U.S.-centric asset rotation portfolio, they could complement this discipline with another asset rotation portfolio with concentrated exposure to either global or international equities. One could also build out a global income asset rotation portfolio, including a myriad of different fixed-income exchange-traded funds (ETFs) that can be expected to behave very differently at various points in the interest rate cycle. For example, an ETF like the Powershares Senior Loan Portfolio (ticker: BKLN) may provide investors with the ability to adapt more quickly to a rising interest rate environment, as the underlying loans reset at prevailing rates. A global income–based portfolio could then be used to supplement the conventional bond portion of a traditional asset allocation, giving investors a modicum of flexibility and defense to navigate a more difficult fixed-income market going forward. One could also provide further diversification by taking a multiasset approach to asset rotation, including real estate investment trusts (REITs), master limited partnerships (MLPs), or commodity-based ETFs.

Ultimately, it's the eligible risk assets that will define an asset rotation portfolio. Combining multiple asset rotation portfolios with a complementary focus in risk assets can give investors a more highly diversified and sophisticated approach to weather the oncoming storm—whenever it may arise.

BABY STEPS

We wholeheartedly recognize that imploring investors to adopt the virtues of asset rotation throughout their entire portfolio and turn their backs on what they have always done may very well be like asking an infant to run before they have ever walked. Our son crawled for 18 months. As parents, we were very frustrated and we were growing increasingly concerned, and then one day it happened. He stood himself up, took a couple of steps, and then proceeded to run down the hallway from our family room and into his bedroom. We thought to ourselves, "It's about time!"

In most cases, for those less familiar with asset rotation or first learning about it by reading this book, it may be prudent to begin by adopting asset rotation as a diversifier to what they may already be doing. After all, our son did not have the benefit of walking before he decided to run, and as a result he did end up bouncing off of walls on more than a few occasions. We'd rather not see investors run until they have a full grasp of the true power of asset rotation, and understand full well how best to assemble multiple asset rotation portfolios together into a comprehensive risk-adjusted approach.

The question then becomes: if not adopting asset rotation as a core, how precisely should an investor begin to integrate asset rotation into their overall approach? As we intimated at the beginning of this chapter, there are a number of different ways this can be done.

SUPPLEMENTING EITHER EQUITIES OR FIXED INCOME

One way in which investors can begin to integrate an asset rotation–based portfolio into their overall investment approach is by using it as a supplement to an asset class they have growing concerns about. In this regard, an asset rotation portfolio can be used to supplement either equities or fixed income, depending on one's outlook.

For those investors wishing to reduce their long-only exposure to equities, fearful that we may soon experience a measurable pullback, an asset rotation portfolio can be used to supplement a portion or all of their equity allocation. In this manner, investors would still stand to gain should a rise in equity markets continue, but, more important, they would have a discipline to provide a measure of capital preservation should they decline.

For those investors more concerned with the impact a rising interest rate environment may have on the fixed-income portion of their investments, an asset rotation portfolio may be used to supplement a portion or all of their traditional allocation to fixed income. In this case, when the trends in the underlying fixed-income securities demonstrate a favorable opportunity to achieve positive returns, an investor would own them, but they would have a discipline in place to avoid the longer-term declines.

In Figure 10.1 we have illustrated a very basic example of both of these scenarios, demonstrating the long-term performance attributes of two portfolios: one composed of the S&P 500 for 50 percent of the portfolio and the other 50 percent in our two-asset-class sector rotation portfolio, and the other made up of Barclays Aggregate Bond Index for 50 percent of the portfolio and the other 50 percent in our two-asset-class sector rotation portfolio. As a measure of risk, we compared these two portfolios to both the S&P 500 and the Barclays Aggregate Bond Index.

The first portfolio illustrated in Figure 10.1, composed of an asset mix of 50 percent the S&P 500/50 percent our two-asset-class sector rotation portfolio, is intended to be compared against the S&P 500 itself. In doing so, we are highlighting the benefit of reducing a portion of one's previously fully dedicated allocation to equities. As you can see, by integrating 50 percent of an all equity portfolio into our tactical, sector rotation portfolio, the overall rate of return increased and the standard deviation decreased throughout this 23-year time period, up from an annual return of 8.55 percent, to 11.15 percent, and with a standard deviation of 12 versus 15. A number of other metrics also reflect this positive impact, including a lower beta, higher alpha, higher Sharpe ratio, lower correlation, and lower max drawdown. Therefore,

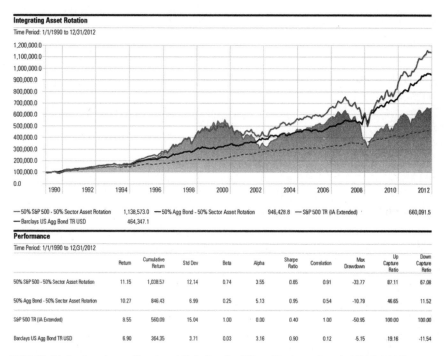

Integrating Asset Rotation

Time Period: 1/1/1990 to 12/31/2012

—50% S&P 500 - 50% Sector Asset Rotation	1,138,573.0 —50% Agg Bond - 50% Sector Asset Rotation	946,428.8 —S&P 500 TR (IA Extended)
—Barclays US Agg Bond TR USD	464,347.1	

With the fourth legend entry: S&P 500 TR (IA Extended) 660,091.5

Performance

Time Period: 1/1/1990 to 12/31/2012

	Return	Cumulative Return	Std Dev	Beta	Alpha	Sharpe Ratio	Correlation	Max Drawdown	Up Capture Ratio	Down Capture Ratio
50% S&P 500 - 50% Sector Asset Rotation	11.15	1,038.57	12.14	0.74	3.55	0.65	0.91	-33.77	87.11	87.08
50% Agg Bond - 50% Sector Asset Rotation	10.27	846.43	6.99	0.25	5.13	0.95	0.54	-10.79	46.65	11.52
S&P 500 TR (IA Extended)	8.55	560.09	15.04	1.00	0.00	0.40	1.00	-50.95	100.00	100.00
Barclays US Agg Bond TR USD	6.90	364.35	3.71	0.03	3.16	0.90	0.12	-5.15	19.16	-11.54

FIGURE 10.1   Supplementing Asset Rotation for Either Stocks or Bonds (1990–2012)

clearly for the investor concerned with reducing the risk of an allocation that is currently 100 percent dedicated to equities, integrating an asset rotation portfolio into the mix makes a whole lot of sense.

The second portfolio illustrated in Figure 10.1, composed of an asset mix of 50 percent the Barclays Aggregate Bond Index/50 percent our two-asset-class sector rotation portfolio, should in this case be compared to the Barclays Aggregate Bond Index. In all fairness, by adding an asset rotation portfolio that will at times be fully invested in equities together with the broad aggregate bond index, one should expect a slight increase in both the relative volatility and the potential max drawdown, versus the bond index. The question is whether historically this has been worth it. Based on a review of the overall performance of this combination portfolio versus a broad-based bond index, clearly it has. The overall returns were significantly higher, with the combination portfolio achieving an average annual rate of return of 10.27 percent versus only 6.9 percent for the aggregate bond index.

The slightly higher standard deviation and beta are to be expected, but based on our Sharpe ratio of 0.95 versus 0.90, and the significant level of outperformance achieved, integrating an asset rotation portfolio provided a significant benefit, as opposed to maintaining a 100 percent allocation to bonds. Should the climate of the bond market going forward prove to be anything like we fear it may, this impact will be even more pronounced in the future.

ADOPTING A CORE/SATELLITE APPROACH

Another common approach often utilized in the financial industry is to construct a core/satellite model; employing a traditional core investment discipline with a complementary investment strategy that, in a perfect world, should possess a low correlation. If executed properly, this complementary approach will reduce the overall volatility of the overarching portfolio and increase the returns.

While many practitioners in our industry may attempt to do this, the reality is that more often than not the two portfolios selected do not provide complementary returns; rather, it is more likely they end up with a strong correlation to each other when investors need this complimentary relationship the most. Consider that in 2008, when the S&P 500 was down 37 percent, the Credit Suisse Hedge Fund Index was down 19 percent, while our two-asset-class sector rotation portfolio was up nearly 13 percent.

In Figure 10.2 we have illustrated how complementing a traditional 80/20 MPT allocation with our two-asset-class sector rotation portfolio would impact performance, as compared to a benchmark composed of 80 percent S&P 500 and 20 percent Barclays Aggregate Bond Index. In this illustration, our modeled core/satellite strategy is very simply a 70 percent allocation to an 80/20 MPT portfolio, and a 30 percent allocation to our sector rotation portfolio. As suggested, by complementing the traditional portfolio approach with our less conventional and lower correlated asset rotation portfolio, our performance improved.

Over this 23-year measurement period, our core/satellite approach generated an average annual return of around 10 percent, while our benchmark 80/20 portfolio averaged about 8.5 percent. It should also

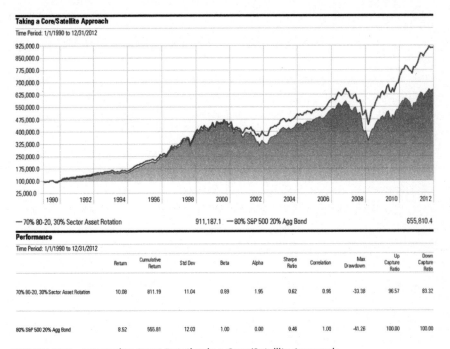

Taking a Core/Satellite Approach

Time Period: 1/1/1990 to 12/31/2012

— 70% 80-20, 30% Sector Asset Rotation	911,187.1
— 80% S&P 500 20% Agg Bond	655,810.4

Performance

Time Period: 1/1/1990 to 12/31/2012

	Return	Cumulative Return	Std Dev	Beta	Alpha	Sharpe Ratio	Correlation	Max Drawdown	Up Capture Ratio	Down Capture Ratio
70% 80-20, 30% Sector Asset Rotation	10.08	811.19	11.04	0.89	1.95	0.62	0.96	-33.38	96.57	83.32
80% S&P 500 20% Agg Bond	8.52	555.81	12.03	1.00	0.00	0.46	1.00	-41.26	100.00	100.00

FIGURE 10.2   Integrating Asset Rotation in a Core/Satellite Approach

Source: © 2014 Morningstar, Inc. All Rights Reserved. Reproduced with permission.

be noted that our standard deviation and beta decreased, as did our max drawdown. Furthermore, our alpha and Sharpe ratio increased.

This illustration clearly demonstrates the impact of integrating an asset rotation portfolio together with a more traditional investment approach. With that said, in this case, we only highlighted a 30 percent dedicated weighting into our tactical asset rotation portfolio, and in most cases we would recommend a much higher percentage be allocated to this less conventional approach. Allocating an even higher percentage will provide an even higher rate of return and with lower risk attributes. However, in most core/satellite approaches, no more than 30 percent is typically allocated to the satellite.

It should also be noted that, while in this case we demonstrated the impact of adding an asset rotation portfolio to a traditional growth allocation (80/20), the same increase in returns and reduction of risk would result when applying asset rotation as a satellite approach to either a moderate (i.e., 60/40) or conservative (i.e., 40/60) allocation.

THE BOTTOM LINE

It has often been said that our failures define us more than our successes. For it is in these moments that we learn to rise, to overcome whatever obstacles might present themselves. For those cognizant of the humility, commitment, and perseverance required to succeed, there is no handicap that cannot be overcome.

When Ambroise Paré looked down at wounded soldiers lying on the battlefield, rendered helpless by their brothers in arms, he did not see the frail or the weak; he saw a passion to live and a will to stand back up and fight. He made it his life's work to ensure that they could.

The investment markets have a history of scarring their participants. Along the way, some have endured greater sacrifices than others. But now, with the vehicles available in today's investment landscape, investors no longer need to bow down in passive resignation in a fight they have long since given up on winning—they, too, can rise.

No longer must we continue on with the mentality that we have a disability, or a handicap that prevents us from achieving success. On an individual level, as investors, we must take accountability for our actions and look to take advantage of the tools and resources that are now available for us to more appropriately navigate the markets.

Whether integrating an asset rotation portfolio into your overall portfolio as a core strategy, supplementing it for either stocks or bonds, or creating a core/satellite portfolio allocation, the time-tested efficacy and long-term returns of this less-than-conventional approach to asset management commands a presence in everyone's investable assets, for both the individual investor and institutions alike. To elect not to incorporate asset rotation into an overall portfolio would be like turning a blind eye to that which is so clearly evident.

With headwinds increasing in the investment markets, investors need to employ a strategy that will enable them to both preserve capital and grow it with an acceptable level of risk, with the ability to adapt to current market conditions. Taking an asset rotation–based approach to investing provides a practical solution to addressing today's real-world problems.

While his time may have come long after the end of the Renaissance period, we find meaning in the words written by French author

Alexandre Dumas, in his 1844 novel, *The Count of Monte Cristo*, and we consider them to be a fitting end to this chapter:

> Life is a storm, my young friend. You will bask in the sunlight one moment, be shattered on the rocks the next. What makes you a man is what you do when that storm comes.

When next our storm arises, investors would be well served to be prepared.

CHAPTER 11

THE ROAD AHEAD

Real-World Solutions for a Changing Landscape

Perhaps one of the most overlooked discoveries of the Renaissance period was the advent of the printing press. Without it, the reformation of knowledge for which the Renaissance period is so profoundly remembered, may very well have been lost in time.

The printing press was invented in 1440 by a German blacksmith by the name of Johannes Gutenberg. Up until this time, books had to be copied by hand, and that could often take more than a year for each book, not to mention the people copying these texts very often made mistakes. As one might imagine, without a means by which to provide the masses with widespread distribution of educational content and literary works, illiteracy rates during this period were extremely high.

The printing press enabled scholars and playwrights to spread the word, for the first time to share with the world their new discoveries or creative ambitions. No longer were students reliant on sitting at the feet of their master to acquire knowledge; they could achieve mastery of their own accord.

It was this deeply profound innovation that provided the foundation for all of the great discoveries that took place during the Renaissance period, altering widespread conventions, and leading us to an educational, philosophical, and cultural rebirth.

Even the tiniest of seeds, when provided with the appropriate sustenance and planted in fertile ground, has the potential to grow from a sapling into the tallest of trees, providing shelter from the oncoming storm. Creating a legacy, one that will endure and sustain oneself throughout their lifetime and even potentially grant a multigenerational benefit, requires discipline—a discipline to plan with prudent measures and to manage limited resources with the appropriate degree of risk mitigation, mindful of the challenges at hand, but steadfast in the commitment required to succeed.

The challenge of creating, sustaining, and ultimately distributing wealth has never been greater. Never before has any generation of investors had to endure the cataclysm of events that surely lie in front of us, while at the same time still cleaning up from all of the damage that has been wrought in recent years. Our path is clear, and one need only look out onto the horizon to see the storm clouds brewing.

The paradigm has shifted, and what has worked in the past likely will no longer continue to work in the future. In order to provide a solution, as first suggested by René Descartes, the Father of Modern Philosophy, back in the seventeenth century, one must first take a step back and clear their mind of all that they currently hold to be true, to begin with a blank slate, and through deduction arrive at a logical conclusion.

As a wise old fourteenth-century Franciscan monk once clearly taught us, the best solution is often the simplest one and provides us with the smallest margin for error. As we make our way into the "new normal," our prior blueprint for success may very well become our largest impediment.

As a trend follower, we are excited to see markets making higher highs, but we are also reassured to know that at the core of our investment process is a discipline to reduce participation in prolonged declines. Whether we are standing on the precipice of the next great bull market or once again find ourselves staring into the abyss, we will continue to take action indiscriminate of personal opinions, market headlines, or economic forecasts, forgoing the very intuitions that far too often lead investors astray. Rather, we will continue to ignore the noise and follow wherever it is that positive price momentum will lead us; whether in risk assets, or in those that provide a modicum of capital preservation.

While we are unsure as to precisely when one should own equities or rotate into a relative flight to safety, we are confident that there will always be trends; there always have been. These trends serve as a testament to the underlying psychological condition of market participants and enable us to gain from arbitraging their emotions.

In the future, asset rotation will serve as the vessel that will guide us into safe harbors, with the opportunity to explore and ultimately discover brave new worlds, and with the power to change the face of our industry, and by what pretenses investors can expect to achieve long-term success.

No one can say for sure when it is most appropriate to "buy, buy, buy" or "sell, sell, sell." There is no such button. The epiphany that by now should be clearly evident is that we don't need to have all the answers, and it is an exercise in futility to pretend to.

We are standing at a crossroads, and investors will once again soon be forced to choose a path. Should they choose the wrong path, they may once again find themselves with their head in their hands and their brokerage statements unopened, sitting in a pile in some obscure corner of a room that they dare not enter. There is a better way.

THE BOTTOM LINE

Wiley & Sons is one of the largest publishers in the world and a preeminent fixture in the investment community at large. Much like Johannes Gutenberg, nearly 600 years ago, they are charged with the responsibility of providing educational content to the masses and spreading a wealth of knowledge.

It is this inherent ability to disseminate information in large quantities out to the greater investment community that will lead us into our rebirth, to provide the educational sustenance necessary for the tiniest of seeds to grow from a sapling into the tallest of trees and provide investors with shelter from the oncoming storm.

This book should not be viewed as a means to an end, but instead as a foundation upon which further discoveries can now be made, ultimately leading us all into the next generation of intelligent investors.

ABOUT THE AUTHOR

Matthew P. Erickson is the CEO and chief investment officer for Renaissance Capital Management, LLC, a boutique investment management firm located in metropolitan Detroit, Michigan. Concurrently, Matt also serves as the CIO for Legacy Planning & Associates, Inc., an affiliated financial planning firm based out of Grand Rapids, Michigan. Among Matt's primary functions is the day to day oversight and portfolio management of the firms' proprietary investment portfolios.

Each of the Renaissance Portfolios are managed in accordance to Matt's proprietary systematic and tactical methods of asset management; blending together three stylistically different approaches to investment management, including tactical managed ETF portfolios, opportunistic individual stock portfolios, and traditional Modern Portfolio Theory based allocations with a "beta rotation" overlay. By combining these three unique approaches into one overarching portfolio, investors are provided with a higher degree of diversification.

Prior to starting his own asset management firm, Matt was a partner in a successful wealth management advisory practice at UBS Financial Services, overseeing more than $350 million in private client assets.

Matt and his wife, Jill, currently reside in Canton, Michigan, with their daughter, Mackenzie, and son, Jacob.

INDEX